T0192301

Polished Game Development

From First Steps to Final Release

Steven Goodwin

Apress®

Polished Game Development: From First Steps to Final Release

Steven Goodwin
London, England, United Kingdom

ISBN-13 (pbk): 978-1-4842-1878-5   ISBN-13 (electronic): 978-1-4842-2122-8
DOI 10.1007/978-1-4842-2122-8

Library of Congress Control Number: 2016946625

Managing Director: Welmoed Spahr
Acquisitions Editor: Ben Renow-Clarke
Development Editor: Matthew Moodie
Technical Reviewer: Jodessiah Sumpter
Editorial Board: Steve Anglin, Pramila Balen, Aaron Black, Louise Corrigan,
    Jonathan Gennick, Robert Hutchinson, Celestin Suresh John, Nikhil Karkal,
    James Markham, Susan McDermott, Matthew Moodie, Natalie Pao,
    Ben Renow-Clarke, Gwenan Spearing
Coordinating Editor: Nancy Chen
Copy Editor: Kim Burton-Weisman
Compositor: SPi Global
Indexer: SPi Global
Artist: SPi Global
Cover Image: Freepik

Distributed to the book trade worldwide by Springer Science+Business Media New York, 233 Spring Street, 6th Floor, New York, NY 10013. Phone 1-800-SPRINGER, fax (201) 348-4505, e-mail orders-ny@springer-sbm.com, or visit www.springer.com. Apress Media, LLC is a California LLC and the sole member (owner) is Springer Science + Business Media Finance Inc (SSBM Finance Inc). SSBM Finance Inc is a **Delaware** corporation.

For information on translations, please e-mail rights@apress.com, or visit www.apress.com.

Apress and friends of ED books may be purchased in bulk for academic, corporate, or promotional use. eBook versions and licenses are also available for most titles. For more information, reference our Special Bulk Sales–eBook Licensing web page at www.apress.com/bulk-sales.

Any source code or other supplementary materials referenced by the author in this text are available to readers at www.apress.com. For detailed information about how to locate your book's source code, go to www.apress.com/source-code/.

Printed on acid-free paper

For Holly. Whose world is nothing but toys and games.
Like all of ours should be.

Contents at a Glance

Contents

About the Author

Steven Goodwin (London, England) is a veteran developer in the games industry with over 20 years of experience in both development and management roles in companies as diverse and prominent as EA, Playfish, Microprose, Fox Interactive, Sierra, Glu Mobile, and Criterion. In addition to five published boxed games for PC and consoles, he has released many online and mobile products. This includes *Grand Prix Manager*, the #1 selling game *Die Hard: Vendetta*, *Project Gotham Racing* on mobile, education titles such as *Quizly Bears* and *Spell It Right*, and Facebook games such as *Pet Society* and *Restaurant City*.

As an international speaker and author, Goodwin has written two games industry-standard textbooks, *Cross-Platform Game Programming* (Charles River Media, 2005) and *The Game Developers Open Source Handbook* (Charles River Media, 2006), as well as two editions of the IoT-focused *Smart Home Automation with Linux* (Apress, 2013), which included a breakdown of his Minerva home platform. He has also written more than 60 articles covering programming, management, or open source.

In addition to his work as a CTO, developer, and mentor, he regularly lectures at universities to encourage students into the industry, explaining the real-life situations they will face and how to solve them.

His interests outside of computers also involve computers. He is the lead developer and chief architect of the SGX game engine.

You can reach him on @MarquisdeGeek and MarquisdeGeek.com or give him a job at FindSteveJobs.com.

About the Technical Reviewer

Jodessiah Sumpter is currently the chief technology officer for numerous start-up companies, including Perfomatix Innovations and Food Cowboy. He has over 10 years of software development experience at Fortune 500 companies and has 20+ years experience developing websites and Internet marketing materials for individuals, non-profits, start-ups, and small businesses.

Joe has also developed and deployed numerous mobile and TV applications for Android, iOS, Blackberry, Windows, and Samsung Smart TV. His company Blue Crystal Web Design has won numerous awards, with the most recent being the AT&T U-Verse Hackathon and the Extreme Reality Android Challenge. Joe has a strong passion for gaming and cross platform game development.

You can reach Joe on Twitter @bcwdesign or view his blog at http://bluecrystalwebdesign.com/.

Preface

Learning to write a computer game is only the start of the journey. You next have to make it good. For every game that is started, few are finished. And even fewer finished to a standard that might be termed "professional." This book is aimed at helping developers graduate to the latter category.

There is no doubt that there are many reasons why games are never finished to a good standard. Everyone has, at some point, bought a game, played it, and thought, "That's awful," "Why didn't they fix that bug?" or "They missed a bit." If the professionals can't polish a game, is there hope for the rest of us? Of course there is!

> *The first 90 percent of the code accounts for the first 90 percent of the development time... The remaining 10 percent of the code accounts for the other 90 percent of the development time.*
>
> —Tom Cargill

The lack of polish can be the result of many things. There might have been a release deadline that needed to be hit. While Indie developers might nonchalantly use the phrase "We'll release it when it's ready," they do so without the benefit of commercial understandings that come from a professional business. In essence, scheduling is at fault here since the maxim of the "the last 10% of the code takes 90% of the time" has not be truly considered. Furthermore, if there is a marketing department waiting to push promotional material into the hands of grubby journalists in time for Christmas, then a delay of even one week will prevent those materials from being send to those journalists in time, and therefore missing the deadlines further down the chain.

Sometimes there are financial reasons to release a game before it's ready. Or rather, before it's *really* ready. As a game developer, it isn't hard to build and deploy a feature in a day. However, business works at a more glacial pace, often taking 30 to 60 days before they will pay you for your work. Hitting those deadlines ensures the money coming in exceeds the money going out, without needing to wait 29 or 59 days until it can. Even if you're writing the game from the comfort of your bedroom and don't think that such money isn't pivotal—just think how much it costs to run your bedroom (in rent, heating, water, electricity, and food.)

Sometimes a game will look unpolished because of a lack of good quality assurance (QA.) There might be a number of small items which are inconsistent with the game world, in either terms of design or style. While one such irregularity might not be explicitly noticed, when combined with several others there could be more inconsistent items and consistent ones, lead to an unsatisfying experience.

In some cases, the game could look unfinished simply because the developers haven't realized it isn't finished! This is the difference between a product that's functionally complete (e.g., the score goes up when you collect an object) and a product that's polished (e.g., in the same scenario, the score goes up, the score bar grows slightly in size to catch your eye, it flashes a different color, a small sound plays, and it all happens smoothly with pleasant animations that fit the style and mood of the game). It's difficult to know how to fill a gap, when you can't see that the gap even exists.

Maybe this is the best game they can do. Not all developers are created equally. Sometimes a team will have all the willpower in the world, but lack that spark of X-factor talent to make a truly wonderful game.

For many developers, feature creep is the thing that kills any attempt at total polish. Think for a second of how many ideas you alone had for your last game. Now imagine that everyone on the team has a similar number of ideas. And everyone wants to see their idea in the final game. The larger the team, the larger the problem as with every new feature brings a new round of new ideas and required polish. Maybe there are too many features to polish them all in the given time, or budget. Maybe you saw one (of the few) items left unpolished due to those constraints.

And finally, some games are not polished because the developers can't be bothered! It could be for any combination of the reasons given previously, or just the simple fact that they know it's another piece of shovel-ware, with a broken design, poor graphics, being published by a third-rate publisher without an audience, and no amount of polishing will make their turd shine!

While this book can't teach you to fix budgets or deadlines, it does teach you how to realize when there are gaps in the work, and give concrete examples of the sort of things you can change in your game to increase its perceived quality. (Even if it is a turd!)

This book attempts to cover all games, in all genres, on all platforms. It does this by covering the methods of *what* you need to do and *why* you need to it, rather than how each programming language works to facilitate that goal. Of course, we will cover the implementation specifics for all the examples where possible to assure you, dear reader, that all approaches are practical. For the sake of clarity, all general-purpose code samples shall be in JavaScript, since it's accessible to everyone and not just those living with console NDAs!

To this end, this book includes a full walk-through of a brand-new game, "Space Bounce." It is a simple game about a spaceman trying to collect trilythium halite from the bottom of a cave to power his broken spaceship. It's a simple game, for sure, but as a tutoring example, it features all the necessary elements in a professional game and gives us a common reference point that we can both share. What's more, it shows how each of those elements came into existence, starting with the basic ideas and gameplay, and building up to the final version available to play online for free. By covering each step, you will see the questions I asked along the way and a progression of the route that I took, so that you can apply those learnings to your own work.

You can play it at `MarquisdeGeek.com/spacebounce`.

The source is available at `github.com/MarquisdeGeek/SpaceBounce`.

Maybe you'll take my "finished" game and polish it further. I hope you do! I'd love to see what you build next!

—Steven Goodwin
London 2016

Acknowledgments

This is the section of the book where the author is meant to make whimsical or profound statements about the art of writing, the art of computer games, or both. They're meant to include pithy quotes from someone more famous and talented to levitate their work. They're also meant to say how much of a pleasure it is to be able to write games for a living, how enjoyable it is that publishers value your wisdom that they'll commission a book, and how nice it is being able to pass those experiences on to a new generation in the form of books.

They're meant to.

But I'm not. I'm here to write the truth.

Developing games is hard. Even the simplest game, which might take a week to write, isn't the result of an intense period of furious work. It's the culmination of many years experience in writing games, reading articles and books, sharing experiences with co-workers, colleagues, and members of the game-buying public.

Writing books is hard. Determining what stories, advice, and commentary to include, leave out, and expand upon takes considerable effort and requires sound editorial judgment from others in the field.

With both of those thoughts in mind I wish to formally acknowledge the efforts of game developers, writers, helpers, groupies, and hanger-ons who have help contribute to this volume!

To the stalwarts of my development career, I thank you. Jerome Muffat-Meridol, Dave Wall, Mal Lansell, Alan Troth, Ben Crossman, Steve Shipton, and Ed and Margaret Grabowski.

For those that read my work and ensure it's "written and not wrotten," and who've helped on the journey, I dedicate that joke to you! Todd Chaffee, Mark Hinchcliffe, Julian Freeman, and Dean Butcher. And never forgetting John Southern and Anne Mullane.

I would like to thank the team at Apress for this book, my third book with them, for continuing to make me appear competent.

Finally, I would like to thank the close network of friends that allow me to combine both disciplines and suffer the multiple-personality affects that come with it! All the members of TULS, the Mystic Ring, FAB, Chaos Chaps, Randomness, The Chaos Engine, and the individual support of Lily Madar (muse and creator of the wonderful spaceman graphics in the book), David Eade, Andy Leigh and Betsy Weber, Tracey Spencer, Jason Polis, Phil Lunt, Janey Barnett, Rob Manton and the students at Bedfordshire University, Raffaella Garavini, Lucas Grange, Justine Griffith, Phillip Hart, Phil Downer, Shane O'Neil, Bruno Baillorge and Josiane Baillorge Valverde. All without whom…

And, of course, and as always, to the family. Grandma, Shirley and Ken, Juliette and Dean, George and Matilda, Melanie and Dan, Grace and Rose, Mum and Dad, Angela and Colin, and Holly.

CHAPTER 1

■ ■ ■

Introduction to Game Polish

Development is a black art; games development even more so. There seems to be no correlation between the quality of a game and the technical ability of the programmers, the artistic brilliance (or otherwise) of the artists, the purity of melody of the composer, or the innovation present within a game design. A good game just seems to sparkle with magic. It has that special "something" that can't be defined or taught.

But a polished game is always distinguishable from an unpolished one.

In fact, it is probably easiest to talk about a polished game by virtue of there being nothing to talk about! If you look at a game and find yourself saying, *That animation is a bit jerky*, or *Why didn't the sound fade out at the end of the level?*, or *Is the loading bar stuck—or has it crashed?*, then those are examples of something unpolished. Something incomplete. Something unloved.

When the only complaint you can level against a game is *I didn't like it, but someone will*, then you are looking at a polished product.

Yet despite this, if you don't know what you're looking for, it can be very difficult to spot these elements of imperfection, and therefore impossible to improve upon them. This is doubly true when it's your own game, as you become blind to the minor imperfections through either constant exposure or because of parental pride.

To quantify what is necessary in terms of polish, let's consider a released product by looking at *Angry Birds* for a moment. No, seriously, look at it. Put the book down, search for a video on YouTube, and watch it for a while. Ignore whatever personal feelings you have about the game, its creators, or its style, and just watch.

That game is polished.

I'm sure that when you watched it, and especially when you first saw it, several thoughts went through your mind; some of which may have been the following:

- Those graphics are cutesy and trite

- The music is annoying

- The fonts are childish

- The UI is basic/incomplete

- It's a rip-off of *Crush the Castle*

Electronic supplementary material The online version of this chapter (doi:10.1007/978-1-4842-2122-8_1) contains supplementary material, which is available to authorized users.

It'd be difficult to argue with any of those points, to be fair. However, while *Angry Birds*[1] is a major success that needs no introduction, *Crush the Castle*[2] is a game that you might need to look up. If you do, you'll notice the complete opposite. None of the points raised against *Angry Birds* can be leveled at *Crush the Castle*. *CtC* has nice graphics, bombastic music, and a UI that gives you a complete breakdown of the castle under attack. So why did it fail to reach the dizzy heights of *Angry Birds*? It's like *CtC* is a first draft of the "projectiles knock stuff down" game design, and *Angry Birds* is the polished sequel.

One argument is that *CtC* is too serious—by going for a semi-realistic portrayal of a castle and medieval slingshots, it alienated part of its potential audience. While it's true that the silliness of *Angry Birds* (and the cute design of the characters) helps sell the game into a wide demographic, that would only help the *initial* sales. It's easier to make someone buy or download a game than it is to make them play it. And if they don't want to play it repeatedly, then you, as a games developer, have failed.

A second argument is that *CtC* is too difficult. Again, an argument that is true but misses the point. *Flappy Bird* was difficult, but that became a success despite (or maybe because of?) its difficulty.

Thirdly, the purely negative actions of *CtC* lead you (as a player) into a line of thinking that is rarely fun. In *CtC*, you are crushing the castles for the sole reason you've been ordered to by the king. Compare this to the more positive conceit in *Angry Birds* where you are rescuing your stolen eggs. When comparing the respective game's color palette (dark vs. bright), graphic style (cartoon violence vs. realism and blood), and the operant conditioning[3] (reinforce good play vs. punish bad play), you can see that it is likely to only appeal to a niche crowd—which, for a mechanic firmly rooted in casual gameplay, isn't going to be the easiest sell.

Now, that's not to say that *CtC* is a bad game. Far from it. *CtC* is a very good game, but it could have been so much better by polishing these aspects until they shone, in the same way that Rovio polished their game.

So knowing that, watch a video of *CtC* in action. What would you change?

In the first case, *CtC* could have added characters to fire the slingshots, giving the player a character with which to empathize. Introducing a backstory, no matter how minor, would give the player a reason to care about the game and those characters within it. The graphics could also have been improved by adding variety, without affecting the basic aesthetic, as giving the player something new to look at along the way would help stickiness and prevent the eye being satiated.

Secondly, they could negate the difficulty by having more on-screen hints, including special bombs to destroy twice as much real estate as usual, or even just allowing a "win" if the player cleared 80% of the level on the earlier stages. Neither would have detracted from the environment or its realism. The hints would ease the players into the game, so they're not alienated by the difficulty curve too early on in the game. The special bombs could be played like a "joker"; a special item that you can use once per level. They might be twice the size of a normal missile and you earn one every 1000 points as a reward from the king; this wouldn't break the suspension of disbelief, but it would give the game longevity because it would limit the opportunities the player would have for playing themselves into a corner that they couldn't back out of.

---

[1]See https://en.wikipedia.org/wiki/Angry_Birds
[2]See https://en.wikipedia.org/wiki/Crush_the_Castle
[3]A full breakdown of this is beyond the scope of the book, but the précis is good enough for now.

In the third case, *CtC* could have been less matter-of-fact with your successes as a player. Sure, you're a soldier attacking on behalf of a king, so you wouldn't expect a cup of tea and a slice of cake for completing each mission; but a little variety, extra animations, an occasional bonus level, and some positive reinforcement of why you're attacking these buildings (instead of the negative impact of seeing dead bodies at the end of each level) would have improved things.

None of these changes would affect the fundamental game. But all are elements of polish that encourage the player to attempt "just one more level." If you had seen *Crush the Castle* before *Angry Birds*, would you have honestly considered there to be any way of improving the game? Could you have seen the issues outlined earlier? The difference between a good game and great game is in those differences. And the difference between a good developer and a great developer is being able to foresee the need to make those changes.

Planning to Polish

Applying polish isn't just a task for the end of the schedule, nor is it a single person's job. Polish is quality. And, like quality, this isn't something you do. If it were, no one would have ever needed to invent the phrase "You can't polish a turd," since no one would build a turd in the first place! Quality is something engrained into the product at every step, by every developer. It's the attention to detail that a crafts(wo)man applies to their work. Throughout the book, we'll cover various checklists to ensure that the obvious (and not so obvious) quality metrics are being attained. For example, an animator would need to ensure that every animation does the following:

- Runs smoothly from one frame to the next.

- Loops correctly.

- Flows from whatever animation is to be played before and after it. (There may be a lot of combinations here.)

- Uses colors that don't vary between frames.

- Has correct metadata; for example, "when to play the footstep sound" synchronized to the correct frame of a walk animation.

And this is just a basic list.
To add a second layer of polish you could do this:

- Create multiple animations for the same event, to introduce variety. (Watch someone walk; their limbs are never in exactly the same positions at each step.)

- Add new animation sequences to reflect the character state. If the character is injured, for example, create a walk animation that introduces a limp. Add more (and specific) transitions between crouch and jump, for example, to make it more naturalistic.

- Draw part of the character in a set of "magic colors" that are replaced by the game engine to customizable colors. This could be used to affect the skin tone of the player, for example.

- Provide an alternate set of animations so that the player could be left- or right-handed. This might be possible with code, depending on your graphical style and engine technology. Be warned, however, as seemingly simple changes can have indirect consequences. (We'll see more of this later.) For example, if the shadows on the characters are baked into the graphic, you might need to redraw them all because a mirrored image would produce incorrect the shadows.

None of these changes are difficult. Even the most basic of game engines, running on the most limited hardware, are capable of everything mentioned. The amount of polish your game has is directly proportional to the amount of effort you are prepared to put in.

■ **Note**   Polish is not complexity. Polish is effort.

At this point, you must take off your game developer hat and wear your project manager hat to consider the relative benefits and trade-offs in determining what work gives the best return on investment.

- Is it worth two programmer days to write a routine that mirrors a half-drawn character into a full one, compared to one day for an artist to do it manually in Photoshop?

- Can we afford to pay the senior animator to create ten (mundane) variations? Or is it better to hire a junior?

- Should we spend the memory on a new walk animation or on a new monster?

- Can we afford the processing power to recolor the player's spacesuit on the fly? Or should we use those CPU cycles on a particle system?

So, as you see, there is a blend of responsibilities here with no one person being more prominent that any other. Indeed, some things often seen as art tasks can be better handled by the programmers—and vice versa.

Developer Roles

When working on a small team, especially in the indie scene, the blend of responsibilities is often confusing, as the artist might also be the designer, or the programmer might also be composer. So deciding whether to spend time on code or music is an impossible choice, since one person is on the critical path for both tasks. This is where the small team is both a benefit and a curse.

From one perspective, having a few multitalented individuals means a more cohesive product, because less artistic intent is lost when communicating between the various team members. On the other hand, it's more likely to lead to bottlenecks and split focus when there are two equally important problems that need solving, and only one person capable of solving them. (Or, occasionally, there's only one person who is *allowed* to work on the problem—through their own bullishness, or social or corporate standing.)

All game development roles are split into the same six categories. At the outset of a game project, you should highlight these categories and indicate the team members within each group. This creates a clear division between the logical roles and the physical people fulfilling them. The list might start like this:

- Programming: SG (lead), AT

- Art: LM (lead), JM

- Design: AT

- Audio: SG (lead), DW

- Testing: AT (lead), DW, SG

- Production: SG

Although people may also help in most, if not all, areas (especially testing), it ensures that there are some basic ground rules from the start. It also provides ownership to the leads, as well as a person who is ultimately responsible for ensuring the quality of any specific section of the product. This might appear too corporate or hierarchical for a small indie project, but it encourages an air of professionalism. It is possible for the team to run themselves through a collectivist anarchism, but doing so will only work when there are implicit leaders (because of previous work history) or with a lot of effort. Game development already requires a lot of effort—do you really want to work any harder than necessary?

Additionally, by thinking in the manner of *logical* roles (rather than *physical* people) it makes it easier to upscale when/if your team grows. Then, instead of thinking, *To whom do I send this new art asset for testing—is AT or DW the lead at the moment?*, you instead think, *I shall send this to the lead tester.* I recommend setting-up email groups for each discipline so that *programmers@yourprojectname* goes to everyone in the programming team, because that is easier and less error-prone than having to remember to include each person in that part of the team. (It also ensures that no arguments break out if someone is accidentally forgotten.)

No Golden Rules

While it's true that there is no single checklist to create a professional-looking game, it is possible to create a list that stops you making a game akin to something from amateur hour! With that in mind, we can detail the elements that comprise a good game to ensure that the player enjoys a rounded experience. That is to say, we can describe the direction of travel, rather than the means of transport that should be used. Along the road, you should see signposts for each of the following areas, and consider them at every junction. These are the questions to consider:

- What is the smallest amount of work that I need to do to make this work?

- How can I make incremental changes to improve my work?

- What are the ramifications of making this change? To myself? To others? To the project as a whole?

- Is this consistent within the game world?

- Does this in-game action have a reaction?

Notice that none of these points includes a discipline. This is intentional. They apply to all disciplines to a greater or lesser extent. And all will affect the overall quality of the game. We shall cover each point briefly, with examples, but we'll return to them all throughout the book in the context of each discipline to give specific examples.

The MVP

An MVP, or *minimum viable product*, is a term used within the start-up community to mean "the smallest thing you can possibly release that will be used." A similar approach applies to games development: the smallest thing you can code, draw, compose, or design that you need to. In the first instance, this often means creating "coder art" of a black square that represents the player moving across the screen, which is necessary artwork for the programmer to start building a control system. But once the real illustrations are available, its meaning changes to *Is this art usable? Could we ship the game now, with those assets?* If not, iterate on those assets until it can be. Then stop and move on to the next item that is not ready for release.

Imagine a simple platform game. In the beginning, the programmer creates an object to hold the player data, such as their x and y coordinates. They then draw the black square on the screen at those coordinates and allow the player to move it around. This is often considered the first pass.

But it isn't.

Once the real art is created, the programmer has to return to this code to include an animation frame and a reference to which animation it is. Traditionally, all games start with the programmer making a basic framework while the artist generates the first set of assets; so it is certainly recommended that the programmer build animation into the system in the first instance to give immediate feedback to the artist on how their graphics look in situ. This means the programmer's MVP for the player code is as follows:

- The ability to use the controls to move the player in all directions (up, down, left, right, jump, squat)

- Store the current animation and the current frame within it

- Draw the current animation

At this stage, there is no need to load replacement animations from disc or memory. No requirement to recolor them. Or flip or mirror them. Just the ability to move the character around the screen in a realistic fashion.

■ **Tip** Start all games of this type by designing the lead character and its movements. Get this perfect in the first instance and sign off on it. In this way, you can build the world around the character and prevent problems like having to tweak the jump height (for example) on specific levels to make the puzzles work. Build the levels around the characters—not the other way around.

Naturally, the programmer might be unaware as to how many animation frames any specific animation will be, or the sequence in which they will be triggered, so it's perfectly normal to create a working animation set, as shown in Figure 1-1, without any real graphics, and consider "walk" to be "8 through 12," for example.

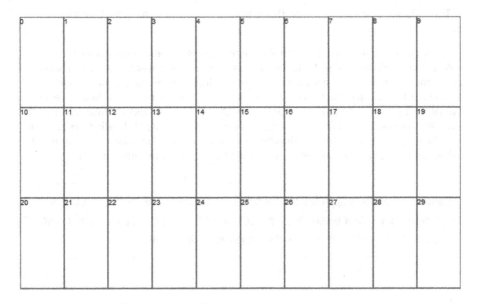

Figure 1-1. *Placeholder art for a walk animation*

Once this code is built, it can be archived or marked in source control, so that the artist can trial their assets at any time without bothering the programmer. Creating an artist-only internal release is also handy in the early stages of a project, when the code is constantly in flux. The programmer might not be able to show the art assets working at a given time, because they've just started a refactoring, for example.

Incremental Changes

In development, there is a rule to "change only one thing at a time." The same applies to most, if not all, disciplines. After all, if two things are changed at the same time, how can you be sure which of the two was most instrumental in the change? Is one a red herring and has no effect on the game? Did nothing appear to happen, but in actuality item A canceled out item B?

So once any part of the project has a working MVP, you can ask yourself, *What one thing can I add, or change, to improve this?*

You will have hundreds of ideas and hundreds of changes that you want to make. But I urge you to make only one at a time and to consider each carefully. (See the next section for the reasons why.) After each change, you should test it and commit back to version control.

■ **Tip**   Do one thing and do it well. That is always preferable to doing ten things badly.

Although deadlines seem very far away at the start of the project, they creep up quicker than you'd like. Getting into this habit at the start makes it easier at the end, when pragmatism and logic leave from the nearest open window. A task might only be scheduled for an hour, for example; but if you have 100 tasks, then be prepared for 100 hours of effort. Even if you're crunching like crazy (a process I dislike immensely and recommend against), it is still two weeks of solid work. It's better to release a game with only five features properly added and tested, than to miss the deadline with the promise of "just one more feature," or to have all 100 features added, but 95 of them are broken or poorly implemented.

■ **Caution**   Deadlines approach like the bottom of a hill when you're freewheeling down it on a bicycle. They appear progressively closer, you can't do anything about it, and you know the disaster that awaits at the bottom if you can't apply the brakes!

Planning Ramifications

The word *planning* is used intentionally to scare you! Planning is hard. More often or not, this section gets interpreted as "think about the ramifications" or "play through the game, and see if you can spot any ramifications."

In essence, any change you make affects something else in the game. That something else requires extra effort to build, fix, or bring up to the same level of quality as everything else in the game. In a tank warfare game, for example, you might allow the turret to rotate to one of eight different positions. Now, imagine you have a lot of memory left, and the artist decides that they have time to make the animations smoother by having 16 positions. What are the ramifications of this?

- Do you have to change the control system so that the player can position the turret in all 16 positions? Or do you need to write extra code that quantizes the final position to one of the original eight?

- If the tank is destroyed, do you need to draw new destroyed versions showing these positions?

- Have you redrawn all the missile graphics to look correct when fired at 22.5 degrees, instead of 45 degrees? Do you have to write code to rotate the missiles to an arbitrary angle?

- If a missile hits a target graphic at 22.5 degrees, such as in Figure 1-2, do you need to upgrade the collision code knowing that the missile would (technically) miss the target?

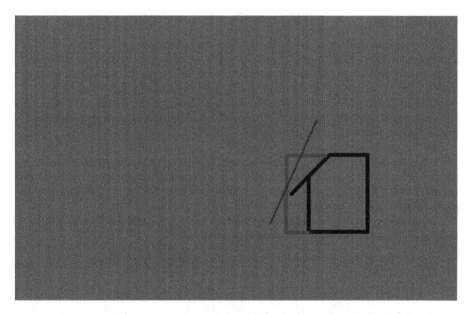

Figure 1-2. *This missile trajectory intersects with the object's bounding box, but misses the object*

- If a missile hits a target graphic at 22.5 degrees, and it just clips the edge of a graphic, what do you do? If you consider it a miss, will you redraw that image so that it misses entirely? Will you enlarge the graphic to make it a more obvious, and therefore satisfying, hit? Will you add a new animation set showing the building being partially destroyed?

All of these changes might have further ramifications themselves. In the last example, where you might decide to partially destroy a building, does this add any complications? After all, if the building is only partially destroyed, then any incumbents inside the building would not have been killed (as they would have previously), so now can they now fire out the hole in the roof! It's logical from the perspective of a character within the game and it is something the game players would hope to see—and would definitely coo about online. But is it worth the time and effort to make it so?

As with our discussion on trade-offs, you need to be able to take a step back and consider the merits of making these changes. It is so tempting for a developer to see a list of changes like this and think, *I could do that in an evening*,[4] but there are usually gotchas. For example, in one game I worked on, I was asked to increase the jump height to make the levels slightly easier. Against my better judgment, I did as I was told! The next day, I was asked to change it back because the producer had discovered[5] it made a jumping puzzle in level 6 impossible. Again, another fine reason for designing the world around the character— not the other way around. Also, as a justification for considering the ramifications of any change.

Consistency

In the film *Jurassic Park*, there is a highly memorable scene where Lex Murphy says, "It's a Unix system. I know this." At that point, every geek in the audience is destroyed! We're happy to believe in dinosaur cloning and all the other dodgy science because we accept that as a part of the fictional world the storyteller has created for us. But when, for no reason and without warning, something as incongruent as the representation of that Unix system appears, we know it's not part of that world and it sticks out like a proverbial sore thumb. Games are identical in this respect.

In fact, games are identical and harder.

It is quite difficult to convey a uniform world in a game. Most of the time, we're concerned about the interactivity and guiding the players through a story or level to worry too much about backstory or consistency. However, we need conventions and we need to stick to them to avoid angering our players.

Unfortunately, most games fail here. Why? Because it's easier than doing it right. Just think of all the standard first-person shooter tropes to see why.

- Why is there a medkit inside that crate? And only one medkit at that?

- Why can I shoot that wooden door to bits, but not that one?

- Why do I need one shot to kill that human, but three to kill their boss?

Alas, the answer in all cases is because the game needs it that way so that it is balanced and fun, and to direct the player accordingly. To be realistic, the game would probably be no fun, too easy, or too hard. As a designer, the number of tropes that you permit within your game is up to you; but be aware of pushing them too far.

When considering non-trope examples, think back to the *Crush the Castle* examples. Having a special bomb that causes double damage would solve many issues around complexity. However, does it fit the medieval game world? Is it anachronistic? Does it look out of place? If this special bomb is so readily available, why doesn't the king give you more of them?

---

[4]This is the natural hubris of the developer, thinking in terms of building something rather than building, testing, and maintaining that thing.

[5]It wasn't a real discovery—everyone said that increasing the jump height would, in turn, increase the jump distance

The Foley/Newton Method

This section is named for Jack Donovan Foley, a post-production artiste who started working at Universal Studios back in 1914, and for physicist Sir Isaac Newton.[6] Foley was part of a team that added sound effects, like footsteps, to film soundtracks. He realized that when something appears on-screen (or occurs off-screen, but is important to the plot), the audience expects to hear it. Every action needs an auditory reaction. Additionally, some sounds (such as walking on snow) do not sound the same on a film set as you'd expect them to sound in real life, so these are rerecorded, too. The same is true in games. You often hear footsteps when walking around in a first-person shooter, even though in reality, the sound of your feet is probably too quiet to be noticed, or your ears are more attuned to something else in the scene, such as a car horn or a non-player character talking.

How does this affect us? Well, every time we introduce a character or an event, there is a set of associated sounds. These are sounds that your audio designer has to create or purchase. Every action and interaction needs to be considered. This can be a fairly large list, as you imagine!

When taken together with the preceding ideas, what other sounds will be necessary if you change another part of the system? Changing a floor texture from light brown to gray might appear like an innocuous change, but to the player's eyes, it could change the material from appearing as wood to looking like concrete. And that would imply a different footstep sound. If that texture is applied to a wall, it would require a different sound for the bullet ricochet effect.

To maintain consistency with the world, you might need to create a version of the footstep sound for when the player is in a tunnel (by adding echo and reverb) or a more muted sound if they're in a padded cell!

Outside of the sounds themselves, there's the metadata. As mentioned earlier, the footstep sound would need to trigger on a specific animation frame. So, if the animator decides to add a couple more frames to make it look smoother, are they also able to change the frame on which the sound is triggered? Is there a separate data file for this information? Can only the programmer change it? How easy is it to compile that information back into the game for testing?

Pragmatism vs. Perfectionism

Just as every job interview I've conducted includes the candidate telling me that they are both a perfectionist and a pragmatist, so every game developer needs to understand both sides of this conflicting coin and find a way to resolve it.

Unfortunately, it is more conflicting in the real world than it is in a job interview. Worse still, if you're developing a game for yourself as an indie, then you feel inclined to push yourself harder to achieve perfection—at the expense of pragmatism. When you are employed or being taught, there is an outside influence forcing the pragmatism upon you. Maybe the boss is telling you to release the code (in whatever state) so that the game can hit the Christmas market. Or maybe it's your university lecturer giving a deadline in which all work is to be submitted for grade marking. Either way, there is a hard limit on the resources that you can apply. This means that you must be pragmatic about things like.

---

[6]I hope I need not explain who Newton is—or why his third law of motion is relevant here!

- Which bugs get fixed

- Which features are essential and which are nice to have

- Whether more frames are added to the animations

- Whether three variant screams are to be added to the death sequence

And so on.

The perfectionist would answer *Yes, all of them* to these questions, and push the team into implementing them, with whatever expense is incurred. As a pragmatist, you need to be very specific about which bugs get fixed, along with how much time should be spent fixing the bug before a work-around is sought, and so on.

Pragmatism is not a case for wondering if the game is hard enough or too easy, or whether you should change the title font, or if the player jumps high enough. These sorts of decisions should have been made a long time ago—preferably before the alpha release.

No, pragmatism is the Art (with a capital A) in determining which of the annoyances that you (as a developer) can spot, will offend more of your audience, and will offend them greater. It's also the ability to tell the difference!

Perfectionism, on the other hand, is a justifiable evil—perhaps even more so. In the film industry, it is very rare for directors to put their own money into their films, even when they are multimillionaires themselves. Why? Because there's a strong emotional bond to their work that can blindside them against the pragmatic use of their cash. Having someone else stand over them forces them to be pragmatic in their art. If you find yourself working on personal projects into the early hours of the morning, adversely affecting your day job, then it's truly likely that you have a perfectionist mindset and you would benefit from another member of the team being in charge of the final builds.

This duel between the dual disciplines of pragmatism and perfectionism leads to the idea of (sometimes) being forced to "kill your babies." This is true in any area of the game, but it mostly occurs within game design. Sometimes a feature or puzzle just doesn't "work." Not in the mechanical sense of the word, but the intention. Maybe it doesn't connect with the player enough, or it's not in keeping with the rest of the game. It's tempting to polish it repeatedly, despite knowing (in your heart of hearts) that you're polishing a turd and it'll never be *that* good. Consider moving it to a different part of the game, placing it as a bonus level or mini-game (thereby not disrupting the main game flow); but, ultimately, be prepared to kill it.

▪ **Tip**   Keep everything you make. It will always be useful… just not necessarily in the game you think it will be.

First Impressions

Somewhere between truism and cliché is the phrase "You never get a second chance to make a first impression." Game polish is all about improving that first impression. So consider all the cases in your game where a first impression is made.

Title Screen

An obvious starter for ten. Having a good title screen, detailing the name of the game, establishing mood, and preparing the player for the journey is an easy thing to get right. It's probably one of the first things you create as part of the pitch document. However, often during development you'll get bored with it and be tempted to tinker with it, just to keep it fresh for yourself. Don't bother! Unless the screen is totally awful, the player is more keen on getting to the game itself. Therefore, ensure there's a quick and easy path from the title screen to the game itself. One rule of thumb is no more than two button clicks, preferably the same button, and without needing to move the joystick or mouse in between clicks. We'll cover this fully in Chapter 5.

Level 1

In most cases, this is a training level, whether it's explicitly stated or not. The player must be led by the hand through the level, with easy or lenient AI (artificial intelligence) and a gentle learning curve. This doesn't mean that it needs to be boring, however. In fact, the first level must be the most polished, interesting, and fun of them all!

Consider a case where you have two problems—one is an uninteresting first level and the other is the final cut-scene of the game, which includes an old art asset. Maybe the character changed from having a goatee beard to a Van Dyke beard mid-development, and you forgot to change it here. You will spot the error. And your audience will spot the error. It's a bad bug to have.

If you only have time to fix one of these problems, you have to ignore the cut-scene problem in lieu of fixing the uninteresting first level.

Why? Because the number of gamers who'll actually reach the end of the game will be very few, and the number reaching the first level will be... well... everyone! After all, any players that reach the end will be so contented that they did so, that a minor graphic glitch will be inconsequential in comparison to most of the other things on your to-do list.

■ **Tip** Start polishing the game at level 1 because this is the part seen by the most players.

Unfortunately, it's also true to say that the more vocal players are generally the minority, and you're likely to receive various off-color comments on Internet forums and message boards. If you have the time to fix it, then go ahead, but you have to accept that you'll never please everyone.

■ **Tip** Only polish level 1 once you have done a cursory polish of several other levels. This will ensure that you have a firm idea of the sort of things that need to be improved and the best ways to do so. If this isn't possible, schedule time to repolish levels 1 and 2 at the end of the project.

The First Minute

With the first level bursting with perfection, the next element to improve is the first minute of all subsequent levels. That's not to say the rest of the level should be allowed to rot, but consider this: When watching a box-set marathon, when do you stop watching? Is it at the end of one episode? Or at the beginning of the next? In most cases, people watch the pre-title sequence of a TV show, or play the first part of a level, to see if it's something worth staying awake for. And it's for this reason that I suggest polishing the levels in this manner.

Unique Selling Points

The *unique selling points*, or USP, of your game is something that you're aware of when writing the pitch and the game design documents. It's also something that will encourage observers to become players, and players to become fans. Therefore, start work on those gameplay features that you know will receive the most attention, and neglect the others, even though it might run contrary to other "rules" or "advice."

Consider the original game of *Doom*, for example. It had little in the way of story—you are a space marine (without a name), on Mars, whose job it is to kill the enemies before they kill you. The developers, id Software, realized that while they *could* spend effort on improving this narrative, they didn't need to because they knew that people would be more interested in the USPs presented by the game's 3D graphics and network capabilities.

Thinking back even further to the computer game collapse in the 1980s, there was a dearth of licensed products, few of which were any good. Why? One reason was because the game wasn't built around the license. The developer would use the engine for an existing platform game (for example), replace the graphics, and ship it out. At no time did they consider the unique traits of their lead character. Imagine playing a Spiderman game, but being unable to spin webs. What if you're controlling Superman, but there isn't enough graphics memory to store all the animation frames of a nicely flowing cape? Or being James Bond, and not have the title sequence play *that* music. Whether or not you have a license, there will always be something very obviously different about your game, so you should make that stand out.

Of Old Age

There is a common misconception that new is better. *Call of Duty 3* must be better than *Call of Duty 2*, right? Or the latest version of Windows must be better than the previous version? Similarly, it is often said that you can't repackage an old game and make it sell. Both viewpoints are wrong. You've already seen how the gameplay mechanics of *Crush the Castle* were transformed into *Angry Birds*. Did anyone think that the match-3 game *Bejeweled* could ever be toppled from its spherical perch until *Candy Crush Saga* came along?

What this shows us is that old formats and mechanics are ripe for the picking. There are so many advantages in creating your own clone, but primarily, it's because it gives you an understanding as to what polish really is, how to balance your pragmatism and perfectionism, and encourage you to get the game published. The fact that the traditional gameplay elements have been honed is just a bonus.

The only problem (if it can be called that) with cloning traditional games is that you need to add a lot of new features and extras to the game to make it appear polished, and to lift it up from being "yet another clone." And you still need to polish all the traditional features to the same, or better, level of all the preceding versions.

As an example of this, let's consider the most famous game developed for the Electronika 60—*Tetris*. Now, consider the number of variations that have been made since 1984. Each new version added one or more features to the original game, making it easier, harder, more visual, and so on. In most cases, the new feature that made each iteration of *Tetris* different would have been polished to perfection because that's the one feature everyone would be curious about. If you are re-creating an old game and looking for inspiration, then you could do worse than consider some of the embellishments that have been applied to *Tetris* over the years, such as:

- More colorful graphics.

- More texturing of the tiles.

- Changing square tiles to cylinders and dropping them down a spiral.

- Switch from 2D to 3D, both as a visual representation and as a playfield. (There was even *Frac4D*, which used tesseracts.)

- Temporarily increase the speed of a pieces descent while holding down a button.

- Changing gravity to be heavier, or direct the pieces to the left or right.

- Extra special effects and animations when lines are cleared.

- Adding bomb blocks to destroy surrounding tiles.

- The pieces form the image of a face or other picture.

- The pieces include letters for you to make words.

- Periodically raising the playfield.

- Adding blocks into the middle of the playfield, either randomly or at game start.

- Earthquakes to randomly shake the playfield and move blocks around.

- Applying real physics to the blocks when they fall.

- Adding achievements.

- Add multiplayer, on either a single machine, taking it in turns, or across a network. *Tetris Friends* on Facebook had ten different game modes, allowing the permutations to multiply.

Naturally, the older or more popular a game is, the more you need to add, both visually and game-wise, to appear different.

The Pragmatic Approach

The pragmatic game developer also needs to consider *How much polish is needed?* This is a question that cannot be answered directly because it's an interactive question. You cannot assign ten days to polish at the end of the schedule, nor can you assign one hour every day to the task. Instead, you need to polish as you go, looking at each feature, graphic, and sound individually and ask yourself the following:

- Can I improve this?
- How can I improve it?
- How long will it take?
- What ramifications are there?
- What benefits will it bring?
- What players (if any) will notice?
- To what extent do I need to pander to these players?

Those who build freemium products or games with downloadable content need to pay attention to the final point. While it's true that only a handful of people may finish your game, it's also true that only a handful bought the "super-deluxe fluffy unicorn," and they might be the ones that spend $1,000/month on other in-game purchases. A broken animation on the fluffy unicorn would raise ire against the "whales" who spend the most money, and so it might be worth placating them before considering the 1,000 freeloaders who've never spent a penny on the game, but all demanding that you add a race track for their "non-super non-deluxe non-fluffy unicorns"!

And while you contemplate that, ask yourself how you'd know which users are spending the money? Do you have an in-game dashboard that shows the total spend of your users and their purchases? Is it connected to the online forum, or users' email or Twitter accounts, so when you get a support query asking for a better animation, you can easily tie the user who made the request to their in-game bank balance? Without it, how would you know how to prioritize bigjoe47's request for fluffy unicorn animations?

Everything Is Possible

It might seem, at first glance, that there is a lot of work to making a polished game. There's a reason for that. There *is* a lot of work to making a polished game! But, with rare exceptions, everything you might need to do to make a fully polished game is possible. It's only a matter of effort.

As I've said, even if you can improve an element of the game in an hour, there's still a couple of weeks work if the number of improvements total 100. And if you improve one element, which other elements need to be improved so that everything is of a consistent standard? All of this requires planning and scheduling. By adopting an MVP approach, you can build the smallest possible amount of game before shipping it, and then work iteratively to add small features until the day of the deadline. This is essentially the "ship any day" metaphor, where you create a release-ready build after each feature/bug/change so that (if the worst happens), you can always release *something*.

Developers of online games have a distinct advantage here because new game clients can be pushed out as soon as they become ready, and the player automatically downloads them the next time they start the game. For everyone else, it's a guideline worth following regardless. There's always the opportunity to make a version 2.0 if the first version was released with suitable polish. After all, people might complain about a short game, but they'll still recommend it if the experience was worth it. And if duration is the only issue with it, you've succeeded.

Summary

We started the chapter looking at *Angry Birds* and *Crush the Castle*. Two very similar games, but with different outcomes and degrees of polish. From here we considered how this polish can be achieved, first through the team structure and then with a solid process working from the MVP, through incremental changes, to a pragmatic finished product that displays consistency throughout.

With those thoughts firmly in mind, we considered how your game should make a good first impression through the title screen and first level, and playing up to its unique selling points.

The chapter finished with another case study—*Tetris*. Here we looked at a breakdown of possible improvements made to this gaming classic over the years. It shows that even an old product can be improved if there is the desire to do so. It is this essence of games that we'll look at next, discovering what is fundamental to the gameplay experience to know what to polish first.

CHAPTER 2

■ ■ ■

The Essentials

Even those that play a lot of games, or go through university courses, miss the fact that games comprise of a set of standard elements: title screens, training levels, an off button for the music, and so on. We expect them to exist, and barely notice them as we click Next, Next, Next in our effort to get into the game. So while the presence of such items is taken for granted, their *omission* is enough to cause quizzical and distracting thoughts for the player. In this chapter, we create a checklist of every element that needs to exist and what it should contain. The precise methods by which this can be achieved are covered in the later chapters, categorized by discipline.

Before You Start

It is wise to consider a few procedures to put in place prior to writing or designing the game. I shall cover these as quickly as possible, since I suspect that you will pay them only cursory mind as you act in haste to build the game. So let's begin.

Know the Device Conventions

When working with any device, be it an iPhone or a console, there are a set of terms with which you need to be familiar, called the *nomenclature*. They are specified by the manufacturer and include words to describe the buttons on the controller or the facilities of the machine. These conventions ensure that every user has the same positive experience, since every game uses the same words to describe the same thing. With the exception of PC and Android games, all other devices belong to a walled garden where the device manufacturer has final say on whether your game is released or not. Apple, Nintendo, Microsoft, and Sony are all at liberty to reject your game if you refer to the *A button* as *The a button*, or *a button* if the official nomenclature states it must be *A Button*. (And yes, I've been caught out on that specific case because the *b* wasn't correctly capitalized!)

In addition to spelling, the nomenclature also indicates what letters should be capitalized (or not) and when and where the TM (trademark) and © (copyright) symbols should appear. This extends to all companies, not just those belonging to the manufacturer. Even within this book, you will notice the adoption of specific rules. Flash, for example, is referred to as Flash throughout the book, even though in real life, some people will call it Adobe's Flash, Adobe Flash, Macromedia Flash, or Shockwave

S. Goodwin, *Polished Game Development*, DOI 10.1007/978-1-4842-2122-8_2

Flash, depending on their age. Those lucky enough to be working on a new generation of consoles may experience a change of naming conventions partway through the project. (The Nintendo 64 used to be called the Ultra 64, for example.)

Know Your Own Conventions

In addition to those conventions laid down by someone else, you need to get your own house in order. So, if you are writing a missile attack game, for example, determine ahead of time whether the projectiles you fire toward your opponent are to be known as missiles, bullets, bombs, round shots, or balls. This will keep your intra-team conversation on-point, but the discipline it instills will ensure that the instructions page uses the same vocabulary throughout and that it will match any in-game text your write. And that will match the filenames of the graphics and audio assets. And in turn, they will match the variables you write in code. You can always change it later, but fixing the words in place ensures consistency at the start, at least.

Design Guide

We'll explore conventions more fully in Chapters 5 and 6, but the sooner you can create a style guide, the better. This guide should cover items such as the placement and styling of buttons (e.g., is *Return to previous screen* to be placed on the left, right, or center? What if this is the only button on the screen?); the set of typefaces to be used and in what context; and the sizes and styles of the buttons used.

It should also include visual and auditory guides for the dynamic elements of the user interface (UI). Is there a common wipe effect to transition from one screen to the next? Is there a specific sound effect for this?

When working on the web, you also need to know the minimum browser window size that you're prepared to support and the position of "the fold" to ensure that no vital content or buttons are lost beneath it.

Technical Requirements

As with conventions, there are a set of manufacturer-supplied guidelines that *must* be followed, else the release of your game will be refused. The technical requirements include the naming conventions covered previously, but extend far beyond that. These requirements extend to encompass everything about the device and the code itself. It usually includes stipulations about using undocumented APIs, how to handle the case if the phone rings during play, expected battery life (if you use the camera, for example, but forget to call the correct API to close it down properly, you will drain the battery and fail), and so on.

Depending on the manufacturer, the technical requirements may be named one of many things (including TCR, TRC, and Lot check), but they all serve the same purpose and have the same tested foibles, meaning one product might pass the requirement checks but another (identical product) might fail because the human checking it was more (or sometimes less) zealous. Consequently, it is worth spending the time to check (and recheck) your game against the requirements before submitting it because the turnaround time from submission to return can be in the order of weeks. (In the case of console games, it can be months.)

■ **Note**   Manufacturers of purely software-based products—such as Facebook—also have requirements that your game must fulfill to be included on their service. One typical example is that the OK and Cancel buttons must be of similar size, style, and color. This was introduced in response to game developers using anti-patterns in their design. It was (is?) not uncommon for games to display a big bright-green button labeled *Sign up* and a smaller gray button labeled *Skip*. Many users considered the gray button to be disabled and so were coerced into signing up.

Furthermore, because Facebook is a software-based service, it is more likely to update the requirements on a regular basis. Therefore, you need to keep a maintenance staff ready to fix and conform to any new changes to prevent your game from going offline for any extended period of time.

To make matters worse, if you get popular, you'll get haters. Not just from the players, but from rival companies. If they spot anything in your game that doesn't conform precisely to the requirements, they may have no hesitation in alerting the service provider or manufacturer that your game contravenes the guidelines. Your game will then be removed from the service until you fix it. All of which wastes valuable time, while the competitor publishes their game and steals your market share.

And yes, I've had this done to me!

Legal and Licensing

Unless you are creating a specifically licensed game, you should assume that not every product you've ever seen in a store will be used within your game. If you want to include some red and white tin cans that hold a soft drink made from sugared water, then go ahead... but if you add any words that might be construed as reading Coca-Cola or Coke, you are likely to have issues. The same is true for people's names and likenesses. And company logos. And car body shapes. And sound effects. And music. And almost anything else, since there's usually a copyright or trademark involved somewhere. If in doubt—leave it out!

■ **Caution**   Games can infringe on copyrights and trademarks even if they are made available for free.

If you are making a licensed game, then you will be provided with a list of guidelines on what you may and may not do with the license. Everyone on the team should read it thoroughly before agreeing to make the game. A driving game using licensed cars often has rules about not being able to destroy the cars or to damage them in any spectacular way. While this limits the art assets needed, it also limits the scope of the gameplay. While it's tempting to think of clever ways around the letter of the law included in the license agreement, you will also find a clause that states the licensor has final say over anything in the game. Therefore, get everything signed off (on paper or in an email) before expending resources on it.

Another licensing case to remember is that the field of intellectual property (IP) law contains more unwitting hurdles "than are dreamt of your philosophy." Imagine you have been handed or you bought a license for a *Terminator* game. (It is very likely that, in your haste, you didn't read the legal documents as closely as you should.) It contains exactly what you are licensing, since there are so many different forms of IP involved in a film like *Terminator*. If you think of all the elements that make up the film, each has its own IP and (generally) requires its own license. This list is not exhaustive:

- The name *Terminator*, to reflect a game set in the universe of the John Connor and the T-800.

- The typeface and styling of the word *Terminator*

- The story (and stories) present in the film and the franchise

- The likeness of Arnold Schwarzenegger

- The likeness of the mechanical elements of the T-800

- Voice recordings and sound bites ("I'll be back" would probably be a separate license because it's an actor trait.)

- The name and/or likeness of any other character in the film

- The music

- And probably a few others...

As you can see, clarify everything before spending time on a design that will have to be rejected because the license doesn't include a key feature of your game.

For any living franchise—that is, one that is still in production, you may also need to get other legal approval documents for your game to ensure that your story lines do not conflict with any planned future developments.

If you try to sidestep these issues by hiring an actor to provide a voice that sounds like another actor, you will probably still fall into problems. When writing a *Die Hard* game, my team had permission to use the voice actor normally used for dubbing Bruce Willis's work, but on the condition that Bruce's agent was in the recording session to ensure that our actor didn't sound too much like Bruce!

■ **Tip**   If you're ever in this scenario, be in the recording session yourself. Look sad and ask for a retake when the actor performs a really good impression, because the agent will probably believe it *doesn't* sound good and let you use that take!

Third-Party Material

As another potential complication in the legal department, every time you use an external piece of material as reference to build the game, you should make a formal note of it. I term this the "externals" or "external reference" file. It contains a list of every source asset that the team didn't create, but which your own assets are based upon. In this way, should one of your assets be considered so good it's worthy of a copyright infringement case, then you are able to go back to the source material and say, "No—we took the basic image from here. This is the version we traced. Here's our colored version and here's the final version." Having any form of version control that keeps every instance of the work is a good tool to have here since you can show the various iterations that took place, proving it's your own work.

As a matter of course, the programmers are expected to note algorithms, web sites, and similar resources in the source code next to the place where they're used. Art assets don't lend themselves as directly to the storage of such metadata, which is why a secondary file is often needed.

The Game Flow

■ **Note**   The easiest way to ensure that you fulfill expectations is to create a checklist of each component that needs to exist by taking a basic user journey through the game.

Behind the simple journey of "start the game, play for a while, and exit the game" are a number of elements. Even though some of these won't apply because of the type of game you're building, or the platform for which it's built, you are encouraged the read them all because there might be some ideas that you can incorporate into other areas of the game.

Loading Screen

Sometimes the loading screen is called a *pre-loader*. Even in cases where a loading screen is not required, it is advisable to have one because it provides a nice starting bookend to the game and can help mask any issues such as slow loading times.

The screen should contain the game name and logo, at a minimum, along with some images that convey the awaiting experience. Naturally, all of these elements should be "on-brand" and conform to the style guide. This helps build an element of anticipation.

For native, Flash, and web-based products, it is recommended that the loading screen contains two dynamic elements: a progress loading bar showing which resources have been loaded thus far and a spinner to indicate that the game code is still running (and hasn't crashed). The loading bar can appear in many forms; it's up to you how much (or little) you show. Although most games adopt a visual feature of either a linear bar or a circular clock face, the meta information shown might be the following:

- A percentage indicator

- Details of the current resource being loaded, such as its file name

- Accumulative file size and the current size loaded

- Approximate time left

- Nothing—an absence of all data markings

During development, you might opt for the resource list and switch out to a simpler percentage indicator for release. Although implementing a progress bar is quite simple in most cases, there are a couple of instances where it becomes problematic and it provides a less-polished experience.

First, if the loading sequence and associated game resources are not fixed, weird things appear to happen. This can occur if you first load the player's current state, and then load only the level data and assets relating to that state. Consequently, when the game starts to load, it is impossible to know the amount of data that is required or its expected temporal duration. In this case, you need to consider the worst-case scenario (i.e., the largest level, with all inventory assets being loaded) so that the percentage indicator is never seen to move backward.

Second, if any assets need to be loaded from a network, the time remaining will be difficult or impossible to correctly estimate. Also, in many cases, you will not know that a file on the network called X will be Y bytes, until it has fully downloaded. In this case, you need to create a manifest to store this information, build it into the game-loading routines, and remember to keep it up to date when assets change.

Luckily, these are minor problems. And while the player really isn't focusing on the game at this point, any quirks (such as progress bars going backward, or the estimated time jumping between "about a minute" and "8–9 hours") are going to unsettle the new player slightly.

Of course, you do not need to rely on a perfunctory loading screen. On those platforms that support it, you could include a mini-game on the loading screen, or a cut-scene indicating the backstory. While the latter might appear counterintuitive, since the streaming cut-scene takes up bandwidth and CPU power that could be (better?) spent loading the game, the player experience 60 seconds of watching (or playing) something fun, than 30 seconds of a blank screen or progress bar.

For those without animated loading screens, you can be more creative and include instructions, a breakdown of the enemies, or the point scoring system. If you have the ability to dynamically affect the loading screen by using the player's current state, you could give them a brief rundown of what their next objective is on this screen.

■ **Tip**   Break the game code into small pieces so that it loads as quickly as possible, even if it means writing a separate pre-loader. The same is true for the assets; load only what you need.

Licensing Screens

Depending on the software and hardware that you use, it may be legally necessary to include one or more screens that indicate the other parties involved in producing the game. The specifics of each legal requirement vary, but usually revolve the following basic points:

- The size of the logo and/or company name on-screen

- The size of the logo and/or company name relative to other logos on the same screen

- The amount of time that it must be present on-screen

- Whether the screen can be skipped or not

- If the screen can be skipped, for what amount of time must it appear before it *can* be skipped

- Whether the logo can be transitioned in any way, other than a fade-in and a fade-out

- The position of the license, within the order of all the others

As always with legal compliance, there may need to be some leeway, as it won't be possible to put every licensee's details on the first screen. In most console games, the first slot is reserved for the console manufacturer, to be followed by the publisher, the third-party software libraries and engines used, and finally ending with the developer's logo.

Also note that there are often two timing numbers involved: one indicating the amount of time that the screen appears in a non-skippable state and the amount of time that it remains after that, before fading out naturally.

Title Screen

Once the game has finished loading, you should display a single screen, preferably animated, to welcome the player into the game. This need not contain anything special, but serves only to indicate that the loading sequence (and any licensing screens) is now over and the game is about to begin.

You can easily omit this and use the main menu to serve the same purpose. Indeed, many do. If you decide to keep a separate title screen, then it only need be present for a couple of seconds before transitioning directly in the main menu. Of all the pregame "bumf" that often appears, this is the least important.

Main Menu

This is where your game is able to display its personality. Everything that has gone before has been restricted by legalese or platform limitations. Here your creativity can flourish. That said, there are some essentials that convention dictates you should include.

- Play game button

- Instructions

- Credits

- Quit button

It's up to the design and logistics whether credits appear as part of the main menu itself or on a separate screen accessed by a button on this screen. We'll cover the thorns of the credits issue later.

Likewise, the instructions might be so simple that a single line on the main menu (or even the loading screen) is enough to teach the player the rules. Or it might be that you choose to educate the player via the first game level. Additionally, there might be many instructions, nuances, and hints you'd like to convey and so need a separate screen. Or you might require the player to read the basic instructions before they are allowed to continue into the game; in which case, the Play Game button takes you to the instructions screen and a Start button on *that* screen takes you into the game.

Casual and social games often do away with the menu altogether, placing you directly into the game after loading and instructing your play through in-game helper bubbles. As I said in the introduction, there are no golden rules, so this is also fine if it suits your game.

The final option, a Quit button, is generally only necessary on native PC games and Android devices. On Apple iOS devices, the current requirements are that you press the device's physical button to leave an app and return to the main screen; you're denied a release if you add a quit button. On the Web, the player generally just closes the window.

Instructions

Writing the rules for a game is usually fairly low on most developer's checklist, and for obvious reasons. It's a pain to do. And most developers are not cunning linguists—nor do they want to be. So the task is usually left late in the process to whoever has time to create a few hastily written lines covering the basic interactions and the win condition.

It would be very easy for me to say, "This is one of the most important features of the day," but I know that plays to my perfectionist side and not the pragmatist, as *every* feature in the game is one of the most important features. However, consider the touch points between the player and the game. In the first instance, it's the control system: How do the controller buttons, mouse, keyboard or touch screen give an expressive element of control to the player such that they feel part of the game? In the second instance, there are the instructions that teach the player how to gain that control. Whether the tuition is via a page of text, diagrams, or tutorial level, there must be an element of quality instruction so that the player feels comfortable when the game starts for real. This is another reason why level 1 should earn more developer hours while being polished.

■ **Tip**   If you put the instructions on a separate screen, having a button that takes the player directly to the game means that the player isn't required to head back to the main menu before play can begin.

For those games with written instructions, we'll cover a number of the finer points in Chapter 8. In the interim, consider what information you might need to convey to the player for them to fully appreciate the game.

They need to know their player character. This always applies, even it's a one-player puzzle game and the character is described simply as "you." For any other character, include as many traits that you can, such as age, gender, location, family, and history.

From here, you can cover the goal that they must achieve as the player, along with the reasons for wanting to attain that goal and the obstacles that they will face in achieving it.

The control system is the most important part of the instructions. It can be presented at any point, but I prefer it at the end so that it's the last thing the player sees before the game starts, making it more likely to be remembered. When discussing the controls, be sure to use the correct nomenclature for the buttons, and, if possible, include visual reminders. If you're developing for console, the manufacturer will have preapproved graphics that you need to use to comply with their guidelines. Otherwise, you have to generate your own.

■ **Caution**   If you download graphics from the Internet, be sure to check the legal standing of the assets before adding them to the "externals" file. The image might appear to be a freely usable keyboard image, for example, but all human-created content has a copyright attached and it's not worth the risk to use it within your own game without checking the license.

For games that use a touch screen, it's beneficial to have short animations demonstrating the various moves, like swipe. These should indicate the motion itself and the position on the screen where the action can occur. If the action can only occur next to the icon to which it's attached, then make this explicit in the instructions. Games that create a virtual joystick on touch-screen devices have an overriding issue, which is that the finger obscures the object that you're trying to manipulate, so you can't see whether there's any feedback. Instead, some games allow you to use the joystick when your finger touches the screen.[1] Again, if you support this, then let the player know.

For PC-based games using the traditional mouse and keyboard approach, include a list of all the key shortcuts. If there are options or buttons on-screen that can be clicked, then consider adding key shortcuts to them. Just because you don't ever use them, doesn't mean that an enterprising speed-run player won't!

If your game is likely to need written instructions, then plan the instructions page(s) early on in the development cycle. While you might start the project believing that you only need a scrolling list of text, if you later realize you need to include images alongside the text, then there needs to be some code to determine the correct position for those images, and potentially some code to ensure that the text wraps around the pictures. Those developers with commercial game engines or building web-based products probably have an HTML-like container that handles the layout automatically using some form of markup language. Indeed, many companies have successfully incorporated interfaces designed in, and for, HTML5 and Flash into native applications. Or you could simply build each page as a whole in Photoshop/HTML5/Flash and export a series of image files. This does cause problems with translations and dynamic content, but depending on your needs, it might suffice. We'll cover various options in Chapter 10.

---

[1]This problem isn't restricted to touch-screen joysticks. The touch screen itself is inherently unable to produce any meaningful feedback, which is why the common solutions are to play a short "click" sound (which becomes very annoying, very quickly) or to vibrate the phone slightly.

Credits

If you have ever worked in a corporate games development studio, you will appreciate the wrangling and issues that occur with something as simple as the credits page. In fact, some companies do not allow their developers the moral right to be associated with their work, so in this case, the credits page is nothing more than the standard corporate template.

For everyone else, the design and designations on the credits page can be made within the team. And this is where the problem starts. Let's consider the easy case...

If you're building a game for a university project, it is usual to submit the game alongside a written report detailing how you (as a team) built the game, along with individual statements indicating what you personally did. Your term grade is based on this, so it doesn't matter where on the screen your name appears or what job title you're given. In this case, alphabetical by surname is often the simplest and fairest approach.

When you move into indie development, where your standing in the games community is governed by the importance of your credit in the game, the emotive side becomes more prominent, even within teams as small as two people. Worst still, this is not a situation that can be agreed upon at the start of the development cycle, or written into a contract, as other developers may join (or leave) the game between the point of inception and final delivery. Developers who were previously shy and retiring might suddenly develop a fire in their belly when they don't get the title they believe they deserve. Friendships and companies have been lost over less!

Most game developers consider their craft to consist of two main disciplines: code and art. Design is third; it is often shared (at least in part) between all team members. Testing, audio, and production drop to a distant fourth in most cases. But even between code and art, which should take priority? In the western world, we generally read left-to-right, top-to-bottom. So should the programmers' credits be on the left, or at the top, preceding the artists? Or vice versa? Even if both credits are on the same horizontal line, there is still an implicit preeminence to the name on the left. Should all the programmers appear before all the artists? Or should the leads be listed first, followed by the individual team members?

Consider further what should happen if someone leaves the project. Do they retain their credit, even if they leave before the final release? If it depends on the work that they've done, how do you qualify that? Quantitatively by the number of hours? Days? Percentage of time? Or is it a qualitative assessment of the work?

Consider the same situation if someone new joins and contributes either new work or fixes the work of a previous team member. Do they now have to share a co-credit? What if, as in the Ship of Theseus,[2] there is little-to-no discernible work from the original creator left? Even though the original artist inspired the original art direction and characterization, should they remain on the credits? Or be removed entirely? Or be moved to an "Additional inspiration from..." line?

As you can tell, I've offered no solutions here, as the ultimate solution will be a highly emotive one and very specific to your team and its members. Nor have I commented about whether you should include the credits in a printed manual (if appropriate in this day and age) or online. That again, is a specific team decision.

---

[2]A philosophical thought experiment that asks: If an object has had all its original parts replaced in some form, is it truly the same object? UK readers might know this better as "Trigger's Broom."

Other Main Menu Pages

Polish is about ensuring that everything you create functions as well as it possibly can; it does not ensure that you have created everything you possibly can. Therefore, this section suggests some other game elements that you may wish to include for a more fulsome game experience. Not all will be appropriate for your game, naturally. This section highlights the (seemingly vital) game elements that can be safely omitted without impact to the game itself.

Load Game

Many play sessions begin where the last one ended. So having a load option is usually required. It might not be wise to load the last game session automatically, however, as you can't always tell if the person in front of the computer is the same player from last time. Nor whether they want to continue that game or give it up as a bad lot and try again.

This option might also include consideration as to whether starting a different mission or difficultly level are the same as "loading."

Game Options

This page could collate all the various music on/off and sound on/off features found within the game, and present them on a single page; potentially with a volume slider, too, which would not be practical within the game itself. In practice, you would not want to leave your game just to turn the music off, so this functionality is a duplicate of what's available in-game.

The game options screen might also include settings for gore level, inverting the mouse direction, affecting the mouse speed, specifying network routers, and so on. But its use in casual and online games is fairly limited.

The main use of an options screen in modern gaming is for tweaking graphics performance on a PC game. This might include options for full-screen or windowed modes, the resolution, the level of detail to be rendered, and which graphics filters, effects, or modes are to be used.

Customize

If you've developed your game in a data-driven fashion, then providing customization to the player probably involves smartening up the tools you've already written for yourselves as game developers. This might include options to create your own avatar, affect the colors of existing avatars, or change the names of the in-game characters. This last feature is especially good for sports simulations, so that your players can adapt the game to use next year's team data, should you and your development team not be willing and/or able to do so. Speaking personally, I provided such functionality in *Grand Prix Manager* back in 1995, and its successor, *GPM2* in 1996... and the game is still being updated by fans!

About

For games played offline, an About page detailing the current version and where to go for support is a useful addition. If you have a company web site or an online manual, then this is a good place to include that information. Online games normally load the most recent version anyway.

Difficulty

Incorporating a difficulty level into most puzzle games is an easy addition and gives the game an extra amount of perceived polish. Of course, you don't need to do much to make this feature a reality. Add a screen between Play Game and the game itself, whereby the player can select one of three buttons (Easy, Medium, and Fiendish!). Store it in a game state variable, and then whenever determining a particular game parameter (such as how fast the game reacts), take the difficulty factor into account. These parameters might reflect how quickly the enemies respawn, or how much damage they take themselves compared to what they inflict on you.

In a puzzle or strategy game, the difficulty level does not need to change the game itself, only how you (as a player) are forced to react to it. So, the difficulty level could vary the percentages of getting more useful pieces; or the time (or algorithmic search depth) to which the AI is allowed to compute a comeback response. And again, there are the standard fallbacks of game speed and the regularity of bonuses and hazards.

In many genres (of which puzzles are the most obvious), the gameplay's emergence is based on a few core variables. When playing the game to test it, you can note the values at which the game becomes notably harder and "moves up a gear," so to speak. These values can be written back as part of the difficulty-level code to introduce a very cheap, but effective, element of polish.

High Scores

For games where this is relevant, a stand-alone page with the most recent set of highest scores is invaluable. Many online games provide this as a means to encourage play between friends and to ensure that their games maintain high stickiness or usage. Offline games should also include this, complete with visible game branding, download links, and so on, so should a successfully player decide to publish the high score online for bragging rights, they will also be offering a (small amount) of online promotion.

■ **Tip** Even if a game has no online presence, being able to upload a high score table screenshot to Twitter or Facebook is highly recommended. APIs exist for both platforms and can help the virality of the game.

The Game Itself

Whenever moving to or from a functional piece of UI (such as the main menu) to the game, it's a nice idea to have a transitioning screen. Old arcade games have engrained this screen into our culture with phrases like "Ready Player One" that always preceded the game itself. Or the "Game Over" that appears at the end. Neither is on screen for very long, but each has a definite purpose: to bookend the game and provide a moment of anticipation or reflection for the player. Using this screen to indicate the number lives, the score, the level, or its objective is often worthwhile. And although you can decorate this screen with effects and animations, just remember that it does not need to be complex. It just needs to exist!

Within the game, there are a few elements that should always exist.

Music Controls

You might love the score that your composer has written for the game, but your players, for the most part, will not! This is probably the first option to be turned off, especially with social and casual games. It's probably not even worth adding a volume control, just an Off button. This should be on the game screen and actionable with a single click or touch.

Sound Controls

You might love the sound effects that your audio designer has created for the game, but your players might not. Here I refer to the spot effects that react to on-screen events, such as bonuses being awarded, objects being picked up, and so on. The sound controls should be on the game screen and actionable with a single click or touch.

Sound controls are different from music controls insomuch as these sounds tie directly into the game, and therefore provide a necessary feedback loop as to what is happening, which is why they are turned off less frequently and have their own button.

Voice Volume

If your game includes a lot of prerecorded speech, such as conversations with non-player characters (NPCs), then you might want to consider adding a volume control to the speech playback system. This is different from both sounds and music because the voice operates in a very defined frequency range (around 500 Hz to 2000 Hz) so when music or other audio effects are taking place in the game, people who have trouble picking out the voice among the other sounds in that frequency range can hear it. This is one of the few accessibility points to consider for audio. Visually speaking, we cover the others in Chapter 5.

Usually, it is not useful to provide a "voice off" option, since any conversations in a game are initiated by the player (meaning the player wants to hear them) or they convey important plot points that you don't want the player to turn off, and therefore miss. It is a good idea, however, to have the option of muting the audio component of the voice and allow the subtitles to tell the story.

When the voice is used only as a prompt, such as the *Mortal Kombat* sound bites of "Finish him" or "Fatality," then it can be considered as a mere sound effect (since the content of the speech contains no pertinent information) and muted as normal.

Pause

In almost all games, a pause button is a necessity. It provides two purposes:

- Comfort breaks for the player

- Access to the in-game menu

For many, the act of opening an in-game menu is enough to pause the game as a whole, but it is one of the features most often forgotten, especially in university projects.

Like many features that need polish, the root complexity of the pause feature (and in-game menu) lies within the realm of the programming discipline, so its time needs to be considered when scheduling this work. We'll discuss the low-level details of this functionality in Chapter 9, but until then, please consider what happens when the game is paused: the audio must freeze and then restart at the same point when the menu is canceled. Any vibration effects (for mobile and console games) must also be suspended (otherwise, the batteries will run flat) for the duration of the pause, and automatically restart when the menu is canceled. The game screen should generally be visible behind the menu, but it's a design decision as to whether benign animations, such as flowers swaying, may continue to animate.

In-Game Menu

Every game should have an in-game menu (IGM), if only to offer pause functionality and a way to return to the main menu. Therefore, the following are the only two essential options:

- Resume game (i.e., unpause and continue)

- Exit to the main menu

However, you might also like to consider adding options for the following:

- *Restart level.* The save the pain of exiting to the main menu, and navigating to another restart level option.

- *Save game.* Useful in mobile games, where the device might be switched off at any point, but not always applicable (and sometimes a hindrance) if it encourages the players to save before every difficult part and restore from that save point if they fail— reducing the game to a meaningless loop of "play-restore-play."

- *Instructions.* General help for the player to review a key shortcut they might have missed or to fill in a minor point of gameplay.

- *Level objectives*. Specific help for this level.

- *Audio options*. To provide a one-stop shop for switching off music and sounds.

- *Game options*. If your game has these, such as for affecting the graphics performance, then providing in-game access can be a boon to the player who overestimates the ability of their graphics card!

Naturally, including these options in the IGM might mean doubling up the work to write and design the screens, and creating a sub-menu system. After all, when viewed as a full-page interface from the main menu, the graphic options page is likely to be larger than that present within the IGM, so it would need to be redesigned.

Also, the music on/off controls are likely to appear in three different places within the game: in the game options on the main menu, on the game screen, and on the IGM panel. All need polish.

Summary

In this chapter, we planned our development strategy by quantifying the conventions, design, and technical elements of both the game and the hardware platform. This includes things that we need to do (such as lot check), as well as things that we don't (using elements outside the remit of our license.)

We then followed a user on their journey through the entire game: the loading screen, licensing, titles, main menu, instructions, credits, and the game itself; all supplemented with the necessary options.

Next, we focus on the game itself, looking at how to build up the design so that it is worthy of all the options that we created here.

CHAPTER 3

Gameplay

There are probably as many definitions of the word *gameplay* as there are people trying to define it! For our purposes, it's that illusive element of the game design that allows your game to stand apart from all others. At the AAA end of the market, this is usually down to the graphics and animation quality, as these studios have the mighty dollar on their side. With money on their side, they are able to ensure unique animations for each character and to have each frame mercilessly fussed over. The rest of us have to focus on the maxim "work smarter, not harder."

This chapter is about working smarter by focusing on those features that matter, and the actions (and interactions) they perform, both graphically and aurally. We have to underline the word *focus* when discussing our game designs, as we do not have the luxury of introducing every feature or idea whose neurons crosses our cerebral cranium during the development cycle. Focus occurs in many places, particularly in the design, as a single change at this stage can (and will) have a significant domino effect on every subsequent stage of the process.

> *We are very careful about what features we add because we can't take them away.*
>
> —Steve Jobs

Alas, there is no "right" way in which to design a game, or produce a game design document. The first important element of the process is that there *is* a process, and that there *is* a document. The second important element is that it is kept up to date, so that any change or suggestion can be reviewed by the team to see what other systems or subsystems the new idea will affect.

The Design Approach

Games, like most creative arts, begin in myriad different ways. Sometimes you begin with the big picture vision of the game, often with a USP, and proceed to break it down into pieces. Imagine the case where you have to design a quiz game. At its core you will have a series of questions, and the player must answer them to score points. You will then start thinking about how to enhance the idea: how many points will you award per question? Does it vary? Is there a bonus round? And so on. This is top-down.

S. Goodwin, *Polished Game Development*, DOI 10.1007/978-1-4842-2122-8_3

Alternatively, you may have a core mechanic or idea (like the falling blocks of Tetris) and design a game around it by enhancing the basic idea, expanding on its themes and so on. This is a bottom-up approach.

The reality, most of the time, is that game design is a little bit of top-down, a little bit of bottom-up, and a little bit of middle-out. Even when there is a single designer in charge of the process, your mind drifts and wanders into a thousand corridors of imagination. And at this stage, no idea is a bad one. Each one is written down, expanded upon, and their place in the scheme of things considered. Many ideas will have to be removed because they don't fit the concepts of reality, as defined by the rest of the game. Many will have to be removed because they don't "fit." And many will have to be removed due to time or resource constraints. What remains is a focused design.

■ **Tip**   Develop personal techniques for these brainstorming and idea scoping sessions in which you should expand the game to include everything possible, and then reduce it back so that it distills the ideas into the core components. You can do this with Post-it notes, mind maps, or other online tools such as Text 2 Mind Map (www.text2mindmap.com) or MindMup (www.mindmup.com). The end goal is an elegant design, where the maximum amount of gameplay can be wrought from the fewest number of rules.

It's important to not get attached to any one idea. Be prepared to "kill your babies," as there will always be another game waiting to be developed that could the use the idea you've just discarded.

Worked Examples

In a book of this size it is impossible to work through every game genre, and discuss all the possible design elements within such a game. Indeed, a book of *any* size could not hope to contain everything necessary to reason every design decision possible, in every genre. What we *can* do, however, is provide a breakdown of the type of questions that you should be asking yourself during the design process. These questions will help you either:

- Expand the basic idea, such that it has enough depth and replay value to remain part of the player's regular game rotation.

- Focus the idea to a point, such that you have a suitable unique selling point for your game.

Perfection (in design) is achieved not when there is nothing more to add, but rather when there is nothing more to take away

—Antoine de Saint-Exupery

By giving three concrete examples, you practically see the scope of the thoughts discussed. The first of the three examples will be a theoretical design and discussion concerning the game of Hangman, its options and possibilities. It poses many questions and thoughts you may (or may not) have that relate to how the game plays out.

The second example is of a TV quiz game and how a seemingly simple quiz, with nothing but questions and answers, can have many facets.

Finally, we look at Space Bounce. This is a simple game that we will build and use as an example throughout the rest of the book to explain the evolution of both design and implementation of a polished game.

Let us start...

A Theoretical Example: Hangman

Hangman is a simple children's game that asks the player to guess at letters in order to uncover a secret, hidden, word. At its core it is a very simple game to build, and can be achieved by any novice developer in a very short period of time. The only complication *used to be* the effort involved in sourcing a list of words suitable for the computer to choose from. Now, however, there are many free dictionaries that can be used to provide a good quality word list, there is no excuse for any game developer to not build a Hangman game. Indeed, it is one of the standard projects I ask of my students for them to demonstrate an understanding of game polish, since the game element itself is considered to be so simple it gives them a chance to push the idea as far as possible, improving both the basic game (which we discuss here), and the way in which each element is visually and aurally presented (which is covered in Chapter 6.)

The Letters

The first rule is seemingly simple: at each turn the player has the chance to pick a letter. Even this simple, fundamental, element of the game is open for discussion. In fact, if any element of the game design is *not* discussed it's usually a sure sign that your team is drifting into malaise and cliché since you're not actively looking for better ways of doing things. Nor are you wanting to find a more interesting way of presenting it.

Maybe the first, most obvious, question is *Which letters?* Do you allow the player to pick from any letter of the alphabet at any time? The answer is usually no, since the standard rules do not allow you to guess the same letter twice. Therefore, once a letter has been picked, the interface should adapt itself so it can't be selected again. If you have a point-and-click interface this might mean that the previously selected letters are disabled (eliminating the wasteful need for message boxes that proclaim *You have already used this letter*), or in an interface where you scroll left or right it would automatically skip over the used letters. (This would probably be drawn in gray or a similar color, to indicate that they are disabled and cannot be selected.)

But the questions shouldn't stop there. Are all the letters available at all points in the game? Do you help the player by showing them one, or more, letters at the start of the game? In English, it is fairly easy to predict which letters should appear in a word by looking a chart of letter frequency. Depending on the dictionary you use, this order will probably look like:

e t a o i n s r h l d u c m f p g w y b v k x j q z

With the exception of the *t* in the second position, it wouldn't be unreasonable to prohibit the player from choosing a vowel in the first few turns, lest the game become a simple case of working through the list, in order, to uncover the answer.

If you decide to restrict specific letters from being chosen, then there must be a frame of logic to it. The logic doesn't need to be obvious, but it does need to be consistent. That is to say, you don't need to tie the vowels into a "vowel wheel" or a "vowels are only allowed to be chosen 10 seconds after the game has started" announcement, but the player must know why they're not always available, and when they will be.

Perhaps you can buy the ability to select a vowel. If so, with what currency are you buying them? If the currency is earned via in-game play, then does this get awarded at the end of each level, or during play?

In the case of the former, then the player would start each round knowing how many vowels they could buy, and therefore could create a strategy accordingly. That approach suffers insomuch as it might be impossible to guess the word if you have very little credit left and are unable to but vowels. (This may be truer on the first level of the game.)

In the case of the latter, you would need to correctly guess a letter in order to earn currency... which might be a pure guess (rather than an educated guess) if there are no vowels, thus creating a vicious downward spiral of negative gameplay.

As a final thought in this section, if the game is charging for letters, is there a different cost for guessing an *e*, compared to a *u*? How will you choose these numbers?

How Many Guesses?

When I used to play Hangman using a pencil and paper with my sister, this part of the game was rather fluid. The picture of the hangman looked like it does in Figure 3-1. Sometimes.

Figure 3-1. *Hangman, as played normally*

If one of us were winning by a large margin then the image would look closer to that shown in Figure 3-2. Notice that instead of six struts, there are now only four, since the support struts are missing. This gives the player two fewer guesses before losing the game.

Figure 3-2. Hangman, when played with a handicap

Any game that randomly switches game boards would, quite rightly, be bitch-slapped for cheating the player in such a fashion. Of course, you could have a different board for easy, medium, and hard, but this is the player's decision, and it is the computer's responsibility to fulfill that role fairly.

You also have to decide whether the arms are drawn as two elements, or one. This is one case where our visual design needs to overlap with our game design, as through careful artwork you can communicate this to the player, as shown in Figure 3-3, by having illuminated and non-illuminated sections to indicate the difference.

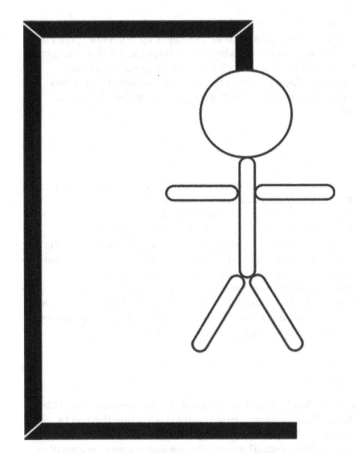

Figure 3-3. Hangman, explicitly clarifying the moves remaining via visual means

As previously noted, in English, 80% of all common words can be written using just 12 letters: e t a o i n s r h l d c, so having 12 guesses before the game ends could mean it's too easy for those with a rigid method of play.

The Word List

Although I opened this section by glibly mentioning that you could use any freely available dictionary, the reality is that you need to be more careful when curating your content. Sure, you could use a standard dictionary, but do you really want the player trying to guess words like syzygy, isthmus, or inchoate? And what about vulgarity? Unless you are writing an 18+ certificate version of hangman, then you need to manually remove the swear words and all their variations. In many cases you need to expand the definition of "swear words" to mean all "bad" words... for whatever definition of *bad* is appropriate to you and your target audience. The definition of what people find offensive is growing every day and you can be sure that, by the time your game is ready, there will be another word that is now considered off-limits in polite conversation.

At least if the game is themed, you will be forced into manually curating a set of words. This comes with its own set of issues, such as spell checking. Someone (preferably two someones) needs to take ownership of verifying the spelling of all words in the game. It might seem like a minor inconvenience when play-testing the game to find Gorilla misspelled as Horrilla,[1] but if the player discovers this, they will consider the machine to have cheated. And they will believe that the rest of the game is similarly lacking in quality—and quit immediately.

Game Length

Hangman has a fixed maximum length; it can never be more than 10 moves long, for example. However, this might not be the only limit you place upon it.

You could add a time limit in choosing each letter. Or, as in competitive chess, have a time limit within which *all* letters must be chosen. While this might seem like a silly idea, there is nothing from stopping a devious player from spending 20 minutes on the game—1 minute to select the first 11 letters and 19 minutes to look up all possible words using those letters in a dictionary (physical or online), thus achieving an unbeatably high score. (In single-player games, this might be a case of "they are only cheating themselves," but any form of multiplayer or online components, such high scores, could turn away prospective players because of impossibility or game imbalance, since the extra unlockable elements and prizes undeservingly go to the cheaters.)

The Scoring System

Although discovering the word should be an intrinsic reward, it is customary to include extrinsic benefits in the form of points. These can amass into high scores that can be posted and shared online as part of the viral marketing strategy. But how many points should you get for correctly guessing a word? It would be possible to create an algorithm that looked at the frequency of each letter in the word, and assign higher scores for the more rare letters. This could then be modified by the word length, since longer words are easier to find. If this is too much effort, or is likely to produce too much uncertainty, you could manually curate a score for each word. Sure, there is probably more work in thinking up a score for each word, but it is work that could be done by a non-programmer or carried out on the train or bus, where a development machine was unavailable.

Or you could assign scores based on which letters have been discovered. The fewer letters you need to guess the whole word, the more you score. Again, this can be adjusted based on the letters visible.

In addition to awarding points, you could subtract points in certain cases. Maybe the fourth[2] letter of the word, for example, is "unlucky," and when you uncover it, you lose 100 points.

---

[1]But would you really notice such a bug when testing? Most testing happens for functional items.
[2]Four is considered unlucky in Chinese culture in the same way that 9 is in Japan, or 17 is in Italy, or 26 is in India, or 13 is in the Western world. The justification on picked the fourth letter is that there are more words with four or more letters, and fewer with nine.

Perhaps each letter guessed causes you to lose points. The number of points could vary according to the letter, or it could be random if that fits within the game logic. The Android game *Wheel of Fun*, for example, has a wheel that you must spin before each turn. This feature not only provides a way to randomize the scores between each game (always a good thing as it increases replay value), but provides a means whereby other game mechanics can be easily introduced since the wheel may also contain options like *uncover any letter*, *lose a turn*, or *reveal whole word*.

■ **Tip**   Introducing a random element into a game provides a simple mechanism that facilitates new ideas that emerge during the development cycle.

Once you have determined all the ways in which the score can change, you can consider the range of the scores. From a practical point of view, there is no difference in scoring 1 point per victory or 100 points. If you win 10 games, then your score is either 10 or 1000. There is no real difference. From a psychological viewpoint, however, there is a massive difference. If the game takes an hour to play through, and you score only 10 points, then it might not feel particularly productive.[3] Also, if the game is targeted toward children, then large numbers makes them feel more special and the game could even be educational.[4]

As discussed, having a random element is always good if it can be justified. Earlier, we used the example of a spinning wheel to govern the score. By having each word worth a random amount, say between 200 and 300 points, then it means you could score more points with two words, than with three. While this might not seem fair, it fits within the rules if the player is aware of it at the start of the game. Also, it means less able players still have a chance to beat the more experienced by getting lucky via the random element. (And I use the word "chance" intentionally!)

Having large multipliers also provides an opportunity to introduce small scores for additional events. Maybe guessing the word in under a minute will award the player a 20-point bonus. It's not much, compared to the 200 they could get for guessing the word, but it provides a point of difference between two (otherwise equal) play-throughs.

Giving Clues

One possible addition to the traditional game is one of introducing clues as to the identity of the final word. But how does it fit into the rest of the game? Does a clue cost you a guess? Does it cost you some points? Or are they a separate entity where you are given a total of three clues that must last the whole game, regardless of how many words you ultimately find? Perhaps it's possible to buy more clues; but if so, for how much? Are there different types of clues available? If the word is *gorilla*, the clues could be:

---

[3]I'm ignoring all questions about whether game playing is "productivity" in the traditional sense of the word.
[4]In 2015, I ran a "How to Code with Bolt" session with 10- to 12-year-old students. One girl only wanted to learn how to change the score increment in a game from 1 to 1,000,000! So do not underestimate the power of larger score multipliers.

- A similar word, like *monkey*

- A rhyming word, such as *Polyfilla*

- Knowledge-based, such a description reading "herbivorous apes from Africa" or "animals with subspecies of Eastern Lowland, mountain, and Cross River"

The style of game may define this for you. An educational game is the obvious example here and it may even mean that the clue should be on-screen the entire time.

Handling the Final Guess

Once the player has realized that the letters g-rilla suggest the word to be *gorilla*, you have to let them prove it. Does the game have any opportunity to be interesting here? Or does the player have any opportunity to cheat?

If you are restricting the vowels during the main game, then you need to remember to relinquish that rule here. If the player can type any letters, then ensure that the usual "cannot select previous chosen letters" rule still applies.

Does your game have a time limit? If so, does it still apply at this stage? A right-thinking developer might reason that once the player clicks Guess Now, they are fully aware of the word, and it'll be a simple matter of typing it in. However, if the time limit isn't applied in this section then nothing stops a player from finding a few letters, and using this screen to search for suitable words in a dictionary without the time pressures normally applied within the main game.

Oh, and do you allow the player to guess the full word only once? That is, does a failed guess automatically hang the player, or does it simply lose one turn?

A Work Example: The Quiz Game

Having seen the range of possibilities when designing a game, let us now consider an existing (worked) example to demonstrate that even a simple quiz has many facets that often go unnoticed. For the sake of variety, we consider the BBC TV show *Mastermind*. Many episodes are available to watch on YouTube and it is recommended you do so before reading on, so that you can make your own notes on the design decisions made.[5]

The Setting

While many may fast forward through the introduction, and skip straight to the questions, it is important that you do not do so. It sets the scene. And the scene is one of foreboding that permeates the show. It begins with a darkened studio with ominous music.[6] A single spotlight isolates the solitary chair in the middle of the room; no one else is in shot which

---

[5]This is also the reason for choosing a passive medium, as making objective notes during active play is more difficult.

[6]Called *Approaching Menace*, composed by Neil Richardson, should you find that fact useful in a quiz sometime!

highlights the fact that you are alone. The contestant sits in the chair to answer the questions, which are delivered in a rapid and unwavering style. If it looks like a gestapo interrogation scene then you are right, since that was the inspiration for the show! Your game should have something that sets the scene, too, and continue with that theme throughout.

The setting—a strict interrogation—is enhanced by the vocabulary used. The participants are always called *contenders*, which are greeted only by asking their name and occupation in a manner that is formal and sparse (akin to the delivery of "name-rank-serial number" from war films). You'll note also that the presenter doesn't enter into a dialogue with the contenders to put them at ease, or deviate from the script.[7]

The Two Rounds

The most obvious design decision revolves about the fact that there are two rounds: one for specialist questions, and one for general knowledge. The topic for the specialist questions are chosen by the contestant themselves, although these can be vetoed by the show's researchers if they find them distasteful or lacking in scope. In doing so, a complexity is introduced behind the scenes that ensure each contenders' subject has questions of a similar difficulty level. It is often said that questions are only difficult if you don't know the answers, so balancing the questions between topics is vital. Consider how you would do this in a game. If two different designers each created a level, then how could you, as an independent third party, judge which is more difficult? By playing them both? Really? How would you be sure that one level wasn't easier *for you*, because it matched your style of play? Or that it used gameplay elements with which you're more au fait? Now imagine the scenario when you're asked to judge two sets of questions, but have no knowledge of either specialist subject. This is the problem of gameplay balancing, which we'll consider in Chapter 4.

Each round has a fixed duration of two minutes during which the questions and answers are given. There is also the phrase "I've started so I'll finish" which (unusually for a quiz) allows the host to finish asking the question, and permit the contender a chance to answer that final question, even though the time has expired.

The order of the two rounds is also important. By starting with a specialist subject, the contestants are given some (minor) comfort, since they should be able to score well on a topic they've researched. (Although it may also introduce complacency.) For the audience it's also better, since most will know nothing of the specialist subjects meaning they can more invest themselves by answering questions in the general knowledge round toward the end of the quiz, as tension builds.

The Questions and Answers

All questions are asked directly with very specific parameters, such as dates and places, with the answers required to have a similar factual specificity. This ensures that there can be no misunderstanding of the question (since the question master wouldn't be able to judge an *almost* right answer.) Some quizzes reverse this approach and ask very long questions that have very short, and often obvious, answers. For example,

---

[7]The celebrity versions break this rule by employing some banter prior to the second round.

Which subatomic particle belongs to the first generation of the lepton particle family, generally thought to be elementary particles because they have no known components or substructure, and have a negative elementary electric charge?[8] This style of question is not really testing facts, it's testing an understanding of what constitutes a subatomic particle and the lepton family. It is also structured such that you might be able to answer from the first part (if you know a lot about the subject) allowing you to preempt the whole question. Or, if you wait to the end, most people could correctly answer upon hearing the phrase "negative charge," but with the risk of being preempted of someone who understand the rest of the question.

■ **Note**   In quiz games, the format and language of the question affects its difficulty, and is more important than the answers, or the topic.

Being fact-based, the Mastermind questions continue with the strict conformance in tone of the interrogation room. Some quizzes take answers from the general public, and ask questions like, *Of the 100 people surveyed, how many knew the actor who played Obi-Wan Kenobi in the original Star Wars trilogy?*[9] In this way, you are being tested on knowledge and meta-knowledge to determine whether you think the answer is common or not.

In Mastermind, the answers are free-form so the presenter must know (or be told) that an answer of Louis XIV, King Louis, Louis the Great, or the Sun King are acceptable answers,[10] ensuring that the difficulty is balanced between all contenders. Other quizzes, especially in games, ease this problem by having multiple-choice answers, which are easier to mark by algorithm.

Since the rounds are timed, it's also important to balance the questions to be of a similar length, when read aloud. The same is true of the answers, since any incorrect answer given is corrected at the time, and not at the end of the two minutes.

The Scoring

The scores are a simple case of one point per correct question. Both specialist and general questions are awarded the same score, even though the general knowledge (being about any topic, and not just the ones revised for) could have been given a higher weighting. The designers, in this case, chose to not do so. In a game it's more likely to introduce an element of interactivity by allowing the player to choose a question type, 1 point for easy, 2 points for hard, for example.

In addition to scores, there is the system of passing. If the contender doesn't know the answer, they may say, "Pass," to move quickly on to the next question. (As noted, a wrong answer requires the quizmaster to read aloud the correct answer, thus consuming time, whereas a "pass" does not.) In the event of a tiebreaker for equal scores, the number of passes is taking into consideration. This leads to a gameplay tactic of answering every

---

[8]The answer is *electron.*
[9]Alec Guinness (born Alec Guinness de Cuffe), and later knighted Sir Alec Guinness.
[10]The question is "Whose reign of 72 years and 110 days is the longest of any monarch in a major European country?"

question, even if it is with a silly and obviously wrong answer, just to avoid the possibility of losing out from passes. (This presupposes that you have the capacity to think of such answers when under pressure, and have no objection to the time wasted when the correct answer is read aloud—especially if the answer is long or there is audience laughter that delays the answering of the next question.)

The "pass" is also the only means of escaping from a question. In a more frivolous quiz game, you might get a joker, which gives you a clue as the answer. Or maybe three lifelines, whereby you can ask the audience or a friend, or reduce the multiple-choice answers from four to two. Again, the ominous tone of the show eliminates these options, but they are questions that should be asked during the design phase of any similar game.

Finally, and perhaps most importantly, it should be noted that the playing order is reversed in the second round; that is, the person with the lowest score in the first round gets to play first in the second round, and the best performer in the first round is last in the second. This helps build tension as each new contender will, most likely, end their second round with the highest score overall.

A Practical Example: Space Bounce

The third case that we study is of the game we're creating within this book, Space Bounce. It's a simple game about a spaceman trying to collect Trilythium Halite from the bottom of a shaft to power his broken spaceship. The original idea was to have a simple one-, or two-, button game where the player was to collect one type of item while avoiding another. Like the other examples we've just seen, there is a hidden complexity to be considered. While I am generally considered a "re-designer" of games (rather than a designer[11]), there are a few principles I try to hold on to:

- There must be a goal—preferably one that is achievable.

- Create the rules of the game at the outset—and stick to them.

- Everything the player needs to know about the internal logic can be discerned by watching.

- Gameplay should be emergent.

- Obey realistic rules whenever possible.

So let's consider our first draft. The player has to rescue some trilythium halite from the bottom of a mine shaft, as shown in Figure 3-4.

---

[11]This means that I take existing an original design, point out its logical flaws and inconsistencies, and turn it into something more stable.

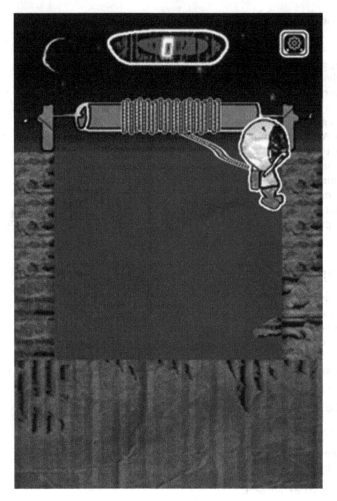

Figure 3-4. *The basic play area*

If this were the entire game area, it'd be fairly small. In fact, it would hardly seem worth our spaceman spending time with a winch, because he could probably lasso it from such a shallow shaft! Therefore, we make our game area larger than the screen and scroll vertically as the character descends. While this seems like an obvious idea, be aware of the differences in design necessary between these two situations. If everything is visible on-screen, then there's a lot more strategy and pre-thought that needs to go into each move for there to be a challenge. If new information comes onto the screen over time, you have to consider questions like these:

- How fast do things appear?

- Are there any clues as to what's next?

- How long does the player have to react to the new elements?

- Can you revisit previous areas?

And so on.

My principle of realism requires me to ask myself, *How would someone recover halite from such a shaft?* A rope is the obvious answer, even if a little non-science fiction! The spaceman can let himself down the shaft gradually from a winch, collect the halite, and on the ascent, the character runs into problems...

...or he might have problems on the way down, instead. Or as well.

■ **Note**   The nomenclature is very important, and a consistency in language at the design stage helps ensure that all developers have a common reference and use effective names while implementing the game, so the team can communicate as efficiently as possible. In this chapter, for example, I purposefully use the term *character* to mean the spaceman on-screen, which you, the human being to whom I always refer as the *player*, control.

The First Approach

Before we start worrying about the minutia, we consider the big picture. Why would the character descend into somewhere dangerous? We've given him a goal (getting the halite), but if there's a problem with the winch, why wouldn't he fix the winch before descending? To me the answer of "because it's a game" is not acceptable, and so the conflict and goals need to come from the game itself. Therefore, the winch needs to break during the descent. This would cause the rope to go slack, so instead of plummeting 100's of meters down, he clings to the walls, jumping from side to side so that the rope is never too taut or too slack. This raises a few more questions.

- Why doesn't his copilot help?

- Why doesn't he cling to one wall, wait until all the rope has unraveled, and then climb down?

- How does he go up again?

We can solve the copilot problem by not having one! This isn't a gameplay problem, but one of communicating the information to the player in such a way that it doesn't break their belief in the situation, and that it pushes the player in the correct direction so that the game makes more sense. Consequently, our instructions mention a "solo mission to planet X" to cover the case.

As the rope unravels, it remains taut as his weight, under gravity, pulls it down. This means he can either descend vertically and centrally between the two sides, or climb down one side, swinging across to the other when there are no more hand holds.

In the first case, the game allows the player to climb up or down the rope, avoiding enemies and moving horizontally across the playfield. Climbing up or down is generally a slow action. The player doesn't have a lot of scope for avoiding enemies because they can only climb up or down and it's obvious which is necessary to survive. It becomes a Twitch game, which isn't bad in itself, but there isn't much conflict in the situation because there is no secondary goal.

The second case gives a secondary goal: collecting halite. By allowing the character to swing from side to side, the player has to make a philosophical choice: swing early and play it safe, avoiding the enemy but collecting no halite, or leave late and collect the halite, but risk missing the jump and colliding with the next enemy.

Additionally, the player has to make decisions as to whether they should jump to collect halite from the opposite wall, even when there is no eminent danger. Again, they can play it safely or with more risk. And they can vary the amount of risk they are prepared to take depending on how responsive their fingers have been thus far. (Ultimately, it is a variation on the twitch genre, but one that gives additional options to the player without explicitly appearing to do so.)

Once the player is at the bottom, we can design the ascent, which can be via the taut rope that now exists. While climbing up a rope isn't a particularly strong game mechanic, it doesn't need to be interactive at this point, so switch to a cut-scene.

The Second Approach

Revisiting the original question, could the winch break down after an easy descent? This would make the game about escape rather than collection. It's a conceptual difference that may or may not be important to you. For a small casual product like this, collection is a quicker game to play in spurts with an easy-in and easy-out approach. An escape has a long build up, but the only real "win" state is if you manage to exit the shaft. Getting 99% of the way out isn't good enough to win, but collecting 99% of the halite *is* good enough. Take a look at Figure 3-3, which looks at pay-off graphs.

But that aside, how would a player *escape* from the bottom of a shaft?

- Climb up the rope

- Climb up the walls, using the rope as a safety net of sorts

- Use the spaceman's jetpack

Since the direction of travel along a rope is essentially one-dimensional, there isn't much scope for control. You could climb up or down. In doing so, the conflict is avoiding moving obstacles[12] or it is time-based (e.g., escape before the oxygen runs out). We'll consider both shortly, although it appears to be the reverse of the descent idea that we considered in our first approach.

Climbing up the walls is possible. The spaceman would climb up one wall until he hits an obstacle, and then jump across to the other wall. In the process, he'd fall slightly under gravity, losing ground, and continue to climb up on the other side of the wall until another obstacle befell him, as shown in Figure 3-5. While the interaction of climbing isn't very interesting (it's essentially button bashing), you could make the player climb automatically; the control is to trigger the jump at the appropriate points.

---

[12]There can be no static obstacles in a 1D game because there's no second dimension that you can extend into in order to avoid them!

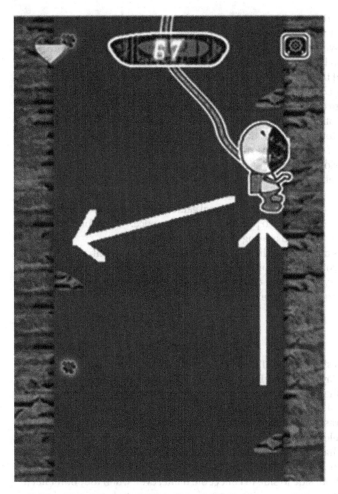

Figure 3-5. Climb up, fall down

Using the jetpack is a charming idea, but flawed. If he's able to use the jetpack on the way up, why didn't he use it on the way down and save himself all the trouble!

So currently, the game mechanic is timing-based, regardless of whether the player climbs the rope or down the walls. We should bear this in mind when considering the obstacles.

The Obstacles

Every hero needs a villain, so we need a nemesis to try to prevent the player from easily achieving the goal. This could be through static protrusions or creatures that move.

In both cases of movement, we assume static protrusions. This means that the player reacts to the level as if it were a classic reaction tester or twitch game. The complexity of the level is controlled easily by codifying the gap between successive obstacles.

If we added moving creatures to the mix, we would run into problems very quickly. Because we can't change the static obstacles, the player is forced to jump at certain points within the level. (They have a margin of error, for sure, but they need to jump before the next obstacle appears.) So if the player is forced to jump and a moving creature hits their path, the character would take damage, which the player could think unfair. Given that we can fairly increase the complexity by reducing the gap between obstacles, there isn't the need to create an extra (unfair) obstacle into the game just yet.[13]

But if we can't have both static and moving obstacles, what about just moving? In this case, the climb up or down would be straightforward, with the player attempting to anticipate the movement of the creatures to determine when, or if, they should jump. To me, this is too complex to develop effectively, or communicate to the player. In the classic game *Pac-Man*, each of the four ghosts has specific algorithms and movement patterns. An expert player can tell the difference between the ghosts, determine their next move, and then adapt the play strategy accordingly. Space Bounce is a casual game where, even if we were to craft such algorithms, the player is not likely to play long enough to notice.[14] Therefore, it is easier (from both sides of the table) to avoid moving obstacles in our first iteration.

While the arguments are evenly split between scramble down or climb up, I prefer scramble down because you're always progressing toward your goal, without the drop back that happens on every jump when climbing up. I also think that the collecting motif is preferable to escape for a casual game like this.

Pick-ups

As it stands, the game is a simple case of dodgems. Beyond basic reflex reactions, there are no decisions for the player to make. By introducing pick-ups, we change that.

Embedded in each shaft wall are halite crystals for the player to collect. These animate with a small pulse so that the eye is drawn toward them to indicate that they are worth collecting. In contrast, the static protruding obstacles do not move—a subtle but important difference in telegraphing the rules of the game world.

The game has now changed significantly. The player can still win by traversing all the obstacles and getting to the bottom of the shaft. But they can score more points by taking more risks and jumping from side to side to collect the halite, even when they don't need to move. This gives their score a point of difference over someone else's, and therefore a reason to play again. The player can also decide to take the pain (literally!) and impale the spaceman on a rocky protrusion, knowing that the sacrifice ensures that they can easily collect the halite crystal that immediately follows.

■ **Note** Since the player is able to make strategy decisions based around the gameplay, they get extra investment in the game and more impetus to find ways of beating it.

---

[13]Some games are marketed at the "insanely difficult and unfair" spectrum of the playing populous. As a casual game, we're not.

[14]It is left as an exercise to the reader to decide whether *Pac-Man*, if released now for the first time, would become a success.

The position and quantity of halite is randomized on each level so that everyone has a chance to get lucky with a high score.

Player Movement

I always argue that the very first thing a character-led game should do is define the character and its actions. If everything follows from that, you get a fully consistent game with no special cases in the level design that needs to be tweaked. A character that always jumps X meters forward, or Y meters high, lets the player learn these parameters to attain mastery. Any change in this logic and the player feels confused and/or cheated. Our first step is to design and define the player motion.

The first idea is bouncing. The rope hangs down in the shaft and the player presses a key to make the character bounce over an obstacle, as shown in Figure 3-6.

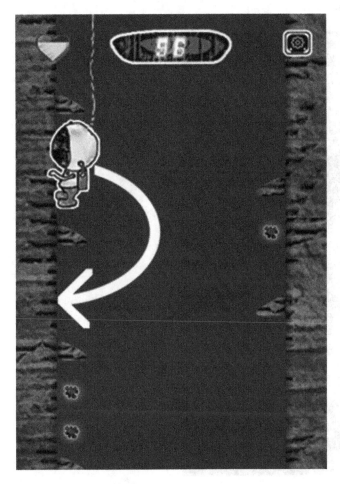

Figure 3-6. *Control by bouncing*

This looks nice, but it is not physically possible, because in order for the character to return to its stationary position against the wall, the rope needs to be positioned directly on the edge.

This would work fine if we were only considering a single wall, because there would be no way for it to work identically on the other wall. If we cheated and allowed bouncing from both walls, there's another point of realism that we'd have to ignore. That is, since the character is swinging from a free rope, they're only able to control the rope's direction of travel when they're able to exert force on it. The only time they'd be able to do that is when they are touching or holding the wall. If they are bouncing (almost) all of the time, the length of time when they contact the wall is very short. Since this is the only time that the player could realistically affect the characters motion, it would make for a very difficult game, even with a tolerance range. Since this isn't the game we wanted to make, let's look for other solutions.

The player could slide down the wall, which looks unrealistic unless the walls were tapered, as shown in Figure 3-7.

Figure 3-7. *Using tapered walls*

Since we are on a remote planet, we could use a story point to indicate that the gravity allows this to happen; although ultimately, any tapered edges would have to meet. For the taper to be visible, it'd need to move by, say, 20 pixels or more within each screen. On a 480×320 mobile screen, this would mean the two sides of the shaft would meet after 240 pixels, and so the game couldn't be more than 12 screens high. It's not a bad theoretical limit—and it's the best idea that we have so far!

Our next approach is to let the rope hang centrally and let them scramble down the side at the full extent of the rope. We're trying not to control the descent, but the side of the shaft that the spaceman is on. Moreover, it's to stop the character from swinging wildly from one side to the other. Visually, this would appear as shown in Figure 3-8.

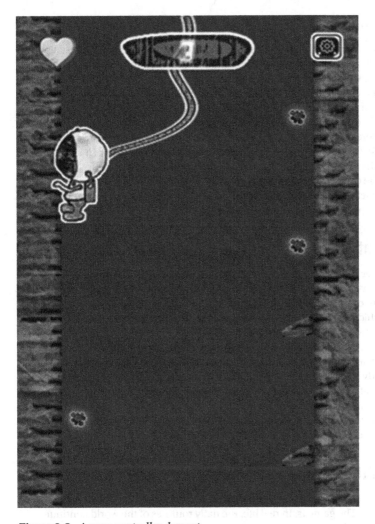

Figure 3-8. A rope-controller descent

So far, so good.

Finally, we could let the character climb down using foot and hand holds, as appropriate. This is tricky to do in real life, although it is easier in low-gravity environments. It also raises the point that if the player is able to climb down, they can stop and circumvent the obstacles at their own pace. Since that's against our ethos, we'll leave this idea for another game.

So we return to our penultimate idea and plan the screen design accordingly.

Character Positioning

Having now decided on how the character moves, and knowing that they stay fairly stationary on-screen, we need to consider the character's position within the frame of the screen.

There are two extremes: near the top and near the bottom. Knowing that the screen is always scrolling means that the nearer the spaceman is to the bottom of the screen, the shorter the length of time the player has to avoid the oncoming obstacles.

Since we have control of both the speed of descent and the gap between obstacles, it doesn't matter where the player is positioned. There is one decision to make (Do I jump or not?) and the decision is the same, regardless of the previous obstacles. (It is stateless.) Therefore, we position the character higher up the screen, as shown in Figure 3-8, so that there are a lot of the obstacles approaching, which psychologically unnerve the player, but with a few former obstacles still visible at the top to give the player a few moments of self-congratulatory pleasure before the next onslaught.

Character Control

It might seem strange to cover character control last. But once we know the range of the character's actions, we can determine the best way for the player to initiate those actions and with which input mechanism. With all the forethought beforehand, these answers are fairly self-explanatory, which makes our jobs as designers easier, and ensures complete consistency.

We know that the player can only swing the rope from one side of the shaft to the other, so they can only jump when in contact with a wall. This would imply a two-button control system: left and right. But since the player can't change direction mid-swing (since we've already stated, they need to push against something), they can only jump right when on the left wall and vice versa. Therefore, we can amend the original idea of two buttons (left and right) to a single button. This simplifies matters for a PC-based game, since any button can trigger the action. Furthermore, it greatly simplifies a touch-screen game, since it eliminates the need for on-screen controls.

Elements of the Game

Contrary to popular belief, the character that the player controls is not the driving element of the game. The game is. In real life, the daily routines of the world continue whether we're here to observe them or not. From a design point of view, then, we need to consider the state of the world and how the character fits within it.

In the Beginning... in the End

Knowing that the world exists without the character, it is a good idea to begin the game with an exploratory of that world. It doesn't need to take long, but showing the player the surroundings before requiring their full attention means that they can enjoy the subtleties of the visuals and ambiance as they prepare their fingers for the next level.

The method by which you delay the start varies greatly. Racing games have a countdown and a set of lights switching from red to green. Action games have a small section of the level in which nothing happens and nothing ventures into. Provided it fits the scenario and doesn't require an explicit button press,[15] you're good to go.

Similarly, the death of the character shouldn't trigger the end-level sequence immediately. In fact, letting the player savor the death sequence gives you fantastic scope to affect their emotions as a player. It is also one of the areas where you can legitimately cheat the player.

For example, a platform game often shows a character falling to their death. You can end this falling sequence at any stage, but you should always show it. Maybe it ends once the player hits the lowest level platform. Perhaps it's a bottomless pit; in which case, fade it out after a second or two. Consider the pacing of the game. Do you want to make the player suffer by forcing them into watching a five-second sequence?[16] Or should it restart almost instantly?

You can also use the death sequence to tease the player. While the character's death animation plays out, you could experiment and move the camera slightly, introducing a new health pack into the frame so that the player will believe it was off-screen when they received the deathblow! Or maybe there's a power-up. Or you could even show the next boss walking into frame, which makes the player believe that "one more go" is all they need to finish the level.

Remember that any cheating is done sensibly and within the confines of the existing game logic. This means that you could only introduce the boss earlier in the level, if it's usually generated randomly, or it's known that the boss could be anywhere. If the boss is waiting in a castle with a captured princess, then moving the castle to random points in the level, just to tease a dying player, doesn't make sense. However, if the power-ups are random, then it's reasonable to randomly spawn one—occasionally, just as the player is dying.

Designing Objects

There is no such thing as a static object in a computer game. Even if we don't have the time to animate it or allow it to be moved, no object is truly static. Even locked doors, for which we have no key, can be moved with a big enough gun! For practical purposes, however, we prevent most of our game world from moving or being destroyed, but that shouldn't stop us from creating consistent rules for each object.

---

[15]Because this takes you out of the state of disbelief —the world doesn't wait for you each morning to press a key!

[16]In *Cannon Fodder*, the final death sequence listed all the NPCs that had died during the mission. It was long, tedious, and unskippable. This added to the central message of "war is hell" and fitted well within that game, whereas in *Quake*, it would be out of place.

In Space Bounce, we have things to pick up and things to avoid. We need to create these in a way that the player can instantly know which is which, and why they are that way. This remains true of all levels, as new pick-ups and obstacles are added to the levels for the sake of variety. Conceptually, there is no difference between a halite on level 1 scoring 10 points, and a super halite on level 2 scoring 15, but the player must be able to determine that they are related items, and thus collect them without fear that it's a hazard.

■ **Tip**   One easy way to do this is to color-code the otherwise identical graphics. Alternatively, base each new object heavily on the one from the previous level, so its genealogy can be seen.

To do this, we create a common language for our game. This is a largely visual language. In our case, it says that a static object affixed to the shaft wall with an animating sparkle is desirable and can be collected, whereas a static object without any animation is a hazard. Similar techniques are used in first-person shooters, where a wooden door that can be destroyed has imagery depicting faded wood or broken paneling, whereas one that can't is drawn with metal reinforcement struts.

This is the maxim of "show, don't tell" at work. The more subtly you can communicate this information to the player, the more natural it feels. For example, a crate with a red-cross symbol[17] on its livery indicates that you'll probably earn a health pack if you open it. But the process doesn't stop there, because you also need to consider the actions and reactions of each object and with each other object in the level.

Designing Object Interactions

If something happens on-screen, then there must be a corresponding sound effect to accompany it. This is the Foley/Newton method that I mentioned in Chapter 1. In the first pass at implementing a game, only the actions that yield a genuine level progression warrant having its own sound effect, such as the case when a door opens. But for a fully polished game, there is an effect on any similar-looking objects that don't react, such as facades and decorative areas. And importantly, this sound must be different to telegraph that information to the player, because this guides them as to what to do next. Consequently, you should have at least three distinct sounds attached to a "door open action" event.

- The door opens.

- The door lock rattles; It doesn't open, but it could in the right circumstance.

- The door lock rattles in a significantly different way, so the player knows it can never be opened and therefore doesn't waste time looking for a key that doesn't exist.

---

[17]Although the Red Cross does not like game developers using their organization's symbol in games—especially shooting ones. It's normally better to switch to a green cross and/or a stethoscope logo to avoid their wrath. This can extend to all cases where a trademarked symbol is used. In short, be careful!

Other potential sounds for a door might include it being hit by a bullet, a character walking into it, a key locking or unlocking it, or it breaking. You might also care to add an introductory sound for some objects, before they are visible in the frame. Hearing a police siren, for example, leads you to anticipate that there is action nearby, and that maybe you should follow it. Naturally, you can introduce this sound, even if the police car doesn't exist within the game, because it's simply a mechanism to convince the player to move from one part of the level to another.

In the same way that all objects have an audio reaction for every possible game action, we need to consider a visual action. If a switch is flipped in-game, is there an animation to show that it changed state? Hint: there should be! In the first pass of the game, the switched image might change instantly or not at all. But for the final build, an animation should show the transition. It might also include some other visual cues to indicate that the switch has changed, such as a light illuminating on a nearby control panel. This is particularly useful when the switch is small or likely to be obscured by the character when the action happens.

■ **Caution**   So as to not overload the player with cues, their size and scope should be directly proportional to their rarity within the game. That is, something that happens all the time (such as menu button sounds) should be short and unobtrusive, whereas boss-level sounds and themes can be long and include many elements; for example, an anticipatory effect to announce change, the event, and a post effect when they die.

Another case for increased visual cues is in the gameplay elements themselves. I've already mentioned the halite sparkle animation that indicates which items can be safely collected. Look for others. Give the player enough information to help determine the result of their action, so they can't feel cheated if it goes wrong, while at the same time they can feel immersed and have a deeper understanding the game world. In a simple example, a sliding door could slide to the left or the right. How does the player know which way? A simple method might be to add an arrow on the door. A more progressive way might be to show the door runners above and below the door, which only extend to the left, indicating the direction of travel.

As with all things we've considered in the design, even one minor change could lead to a lot of extra work. Even adding a sliding door (because there isn't room to add a swing door in one particular location) could require these extra resources:

- Three audio effects (open, locked but openable, locked but unopenable)

- Graphics for the runners above and below the door

- Animation of a new style of switch used only in sliding doors to help differentiate them, thereby providing a direct case of cause and effect

- Graphics for an external indicator, perhaps a flashing light, to show that the door is open or opening

- Possibly some additional player input code that is the control mechanism to trigger the opening of the door

- A change to the training level to teach the player how to open a sliding door, giving them a chance to pick up on the visual cues you've provided

Detailing the Specifics

All we need at this stage is to know the basics of what actions happen, such as when damage occurs. We don't need to know by how much. That comes in the balancing phase. We should only have ideas at this stage, such as whether the amount of damage is relative to health, the size of the protrusion, or is a fixed amount. Start by writing down everything that can affect the player so that they can be categorized later. As with most of the design approaches we've covered, add everything that's possible and expand upon it to include all eventualities. It's better to have some events listed with a weight of 0 than to omit events that do have weight and disrupt the balance when they are added.

En Anglais s'il vous plait?

All of the examples and statistics mentioned here worked in the English language. For good reason: it's the only language I know! However, if your game is localized into different languages, do you need to adapt your game in any way? In Hangman, you would probably change the word list, but would that extend to the game logic? The point scoring system? Anything else?

■ **Caution**   Introducing localization into the game isn't just about replacing the text. A change in text may require you to modify the game logic, which in turn may affect the possible scores, which in turn may require separate high-score tables for each language.

For indie and small developers, it is common to write the game in your native language and only introduce other languages after release, once the game has succeeded in achieving significant sales. But language isn't the only form of localization that may be necessary. You might want or need to localize the currency. Even in films where Japanese actors talk amongst themselves in private in English, the characters still conduct commerce with the yen because that suits the situation. If you provide a way for the action to take place in another city, then switching currency may be necessary. This isn't as simple as looking at the exchange rate, however. Buying an in-game item with in-game currency[18] might cost £10. But the yen equivalent is Y1654.47. Do you round up? Round down? What happens to your nicely planned game when this happens? If you're expecting the player to swap three £10 items for one £30 item later on in the game, then does the

---

[18]Rather than purchasing something for real money.

same rounding error that turns £10 into Y1655 cause the game to break when it rounds £30 into Y4964, leading to a spurious Y1 profit available only to the Japanese players? Are you going to round off all the sub-yen and compound the error, as happens in salami slicing?

Once you have fixed the design for currency at a single point in time, you should then consider how money changes over time due to interest, inflation, and even currency fluctuations.

You might want to have constant rates for inflation and interest, so that every year—whatever happens in the game—$100 in the bank becomes $110 next year, and so on. This makes the gameplay easier to balance and therefore test and debug. Alternatively, you might look at in-game events and vary this amount according to its internal politics. This is one area where the game designer has the opportunity to infuse a message in the game. You might decide that your dystopian world has very high inflation and very low interest rates, meaning it's better to not save your money and this affects your buying power. Furthermore, consider the types of goods present in your world: Do they all appreciate in value at the same rate? A chocolate bar costing $1 now might cost $1.10 next year. But if the world (game or real) suffers a cocoa shortage, it could be $2 or more. Are you building that into the game? Is it sensible to do so?

Having some kind of money dynamics is essential in any game that takes place over three years or more. There was once an approximation that money doubled in value every ten years, but as I said, that is only an approximation, since the price of gold fluctuates wildly. In *Grand Prix Manager*, for example, the entire game was limited to ten years. This was mostly due to us (as programmers) being unable to predict the technologies that would be in use ten years into the future. But it was also due to being unable to effectively balance the finances after that period. The reasoning was that a player might forgive a consistent interest rate of 10% throughout the game's time frame, but wouldn't want the game to be so realistic that it simulated a stock market crash (such as happened on Black Monday in 1987, or the recession in the 1990s[19]) since the primary focus is on winning Grand Prix races. Granted, the ultimate goal is to have more money than everyone else, but you achieve that by winning races, not by second-guessing the stock market. Our USP was focused on racing, so we balanced the game accordingly so that winning races would ensure that you (financially) outpaced every other team.

As appealing as an automated solution sounds, the design can only be solid if you recompute all the numbers into the second currency. It's a lot of work to achieve that level of polish. The sad reality is that it's rarely worth it. The sadder reality is that it's usually expected by the vocal minority.

■ **Tip**   When using the dollar as a real-world currency unit, consider referring to it as US$ since large countries such as Australia, Canada, Hong Kong, and Taiwan (and smaller ones like Belize, Namibia) all use their own form of dollars. Naturally, for games based in Europe, the euro is standard and the primary choice; unless it's in the United Kingdom, which has its own currency—GBP or sterling.

---

[19]Or, if you're a student of economic history, the Friday 13th mini-crash of 1989, the dot-com bubble bursting in March 2000, the US bear market from 2007–2009, or the US Flash Crash on May 6, 2010.

Finally, localizing numbers (for money or scores) is also a necessary piece of work. The number two and a half may be written as 2.5 or 2,5—depending on locale.[20] While not a difficult change, it is a necessary duplication of effort to achieve a fully polished game.

Theory Pursues Practice

This section might also be called "hindsight" or "prototype and iterate," as the ideas are the same. To wit, it is very difficult to produce a set of rules about what you are doing and why the game works in the way that it does until after you have done it. At that point, you have the realization of the how and why it works. And at that point you will be able to go back over the game to polish the elements you missed, now knowing that you missed them. This iteration ensures a design consistency throughout the game, and is why it's so important to release early and often. By doing so you can iterate to ensure that everything necessary is in the game, everything that's not essential is thrown out, and any duplicated items are removed or modified so the game doesn't feel too similar.[21]

This is not a new idea. Indeed, the fifth century BC presented us with the great works of Greek theater... but it was not until the fourth century that someone[22] had managed to distill the learnings of what worked and what didn't into a book of theory that could be then studied and applied to new work.

Even if you don't get an early inclination of the game's through line,[23] decide on a path and follow it. Even if you don't stick to the path, it's more productive than wondering aimlessly, hoping that a path will show itself.

I have always found that plans are useless, but planning is indispensable.

—Dwight Eisenhower

Feature Creep

Perhaps beyond all others, feature creep is the one that causes games to miss their shipping deadlines. Or to hit them, but with bugs, omissions, and lack of polish. It's easy to see why. Every idea or feature we have inspires us to think of ten more, and it's very difficult to control those thoughts. Moreover, the larger the team, the more people you will inspire, and the more ideas you get back, and the difficultly is to tell them "No!"

---

[20]You can find information on which country uses which mark at https://en.wikipedia.org/wiki/Decimal_mark#Dot_countries, but as a rule of thumb, if it is (or was) part of the British Commonwealth or China, then use a "." to separate the decimal and fraction (e.g., 12.50) and a "," for thousands (1,000). Everywhere else uses the reverse.

[21]Portal is a good example of how a single mechanic can be repeated in many different ways, without feeling as if the designers got bored and simply decided to copy+paste the same puzzles into every level.

[22]Aristotle, in his book *Poetics*.

[23]A term created by Russian actor and theater director Konstantin Stanislavsky to describe how all of the characters' motivations and objectives are linked up through the source of the story, which forced the character through the narrative.

■ **Tip**   In each case, consider the pro and cons of each idea. How does it affect the other ideas? Remember, every time you add a new idea, you have to go back to every other idea to see how it's affected.

Alas, there is no magic bullet. You have to simply to "kill your babies," as I said at the start of the chapter, and save the ideas for another day.

Summary

In this chapter, you saw several different ways of how to approach a game design, via either a top-down or bottom-up approach. You also looked at three worked examples—Hangman, Mastermind, and Space Bounce—to examine the subtleties that exist within each (seemingly simple) feature, and how both mood and gameplay emerges from them.

We then returned to the Foley/Newton method to learn how each object should have animations and sounds that reflect each action that it makes and each interaction that it has with other objects for it to truly come alive.

Finally, we covered translations, game theory, and the harsh reality that not all features will make it into the game.

CHAPTER 4

■ ■ ■

Game Balancing

Finding the Goldilocks Zone

One of the most intriguing parts of game development is balancing. How do you make a game that is neither too easy nor too hard? How do you ensure that one feature of the game isn't so overpowering that it makes all other elements insignificant? Perhaps more importantly, who decides that? A game of any sensible size takes many months or years to develop, which means that all those working on it have an innate understanding of the interface and mechanics, so that *everyone* on the team finds the game too easy.

On the other hand, if you withhold the first version of the game from the testers so that they get a virgin view of your product, you have to ensure that it's complete. That is, the game must be able to explain everything that the player needs to know, without you (as the developer) having to stand behind the player saying, "That's not finished yet," or "We're going to add something to indicate that you need to jump over that box." The problem with that approach is that those elements happen only after the game has been polished—but you need them when the game is first tested, when it is without polish.

By adopting the MVP approach, you can first create just enough of a game for it to be tested in its entirety by a brand-new player. At this stage, it doesn't need to be particularly fun, but rather it should introduce the elements found within the game so that a player can achieve mastery in a safe environment.

To this end, there are two elements of game balancing:

- Level 1
- Every other level

Balancing Is About Level 1

The chronological first level of a game should be the first one developed and the last one finished. Let me grab a hot beverage while that sinks in!

The first level of play introduces the bulk of the game's features in such a way that anyone (player, tester, or focus group) can play it without external assistance. By the end of the first level, you (as a player) should have covered all the game controls and be comfortable using them. The player might not be able to perform pixel-perfect jumps yet,

© Steven Goodwin 2016

S. Goodwin, *Polished Game Development*, DOI 10.1007/978-1-4842-2122-8_4

but they can at least jump and do so in a controlled manner. The control system should also introduce you to other actions, such as changing weapons, opening the in-game menu, or using inventory items, should they apply to the game. There is little that is more frustrating than finding yourself in a life-or-death firefight and not knowing how to switch out of hand-to-hand combat mode!

The first level also introduces the language of the game. In this context, I mean the semiotics that the game uses to communicate its world to you. Is a flashing graphic something that should be collected, or avoided, or shot at? Are the green creatures the ones with which you should interact, or avoid, or shoot? Which parts of the world can be destroyed or manipulated? How is that telegraphed to the player?

If the game contradicts any established genre conventions or tropes, then this should be laid out in the first level. Is the current vogue for looking up in a first-person shooter to push the stick up or down, for example? Most of the time, the team has an honest and correct opinion on this by virtue of playing competitors' games in their spare time. But surprisingly, a large portion of game developers are not making products for their own demographic! For every team of twentysomething males making a testosterone-fueled shooter, there are two other teams making a casually licensed game featuring the latest teen craze. Even indies—often a bastion of the phrase "made by gamers, for gamers"—find it wise to improve cash flow by taking on work for hire in other genres. To do yourself, and your company, proud, you should apply as much polish to these games as any other. Therefore, you need to immerse yourself in the conventions of similar games that you haven't played before, so that you don't fall into the trap of adopting unconventional conventions.

That is why the first level should be built first.

But coming back to the second point, it should always be finished last. This is because the first level needs to inspire the player to keep playing. Everyone accepts that the first level is easy to complete, because its primary purpose is to set the scene for the game as a whole. But very few players accept a level 1 that is visually ugly, or has clunky animations or poor layout, since this doesn't bode well for level 2.

The Fluidity of Training and Levels

Throughout these discussions, we use the words *training* and *levels* as if contemplating a blockbuster first-person shooting game. That's certainly the image I have in my head while writing this, because it provides the easiest common ground with which to explain myself. However, there is no need to thoughtlessly skip ahead because your game doesn't have levels or training in the traditional sense of the words.

In some games, like the perennial example *Tetris*, level 1 is simply a slower version of level 2, so it might not seem like it is any different but it does provide a distinct expectation in the player's mind. The difference in difficulty between level 1 and level 2 need not be the same as it is between level 2 and 3, as I'll discuss later.

A less clear example might be an infinite runner, where your character keeps moving through the game world until the character dies. There's often no obvious distinction between areas. Nor are there any cutaways to give the player an indication that things are about to get more difficult. Instead, you can introduce the concept of a logical level, or pseudo level. Maybe the game is clearly considered a training level for the first 60 seconds, and the player is given an "invincibility cloak" for that time. Or you could adopt an implicit training section where the graphics and style are purposefully more "friendly" and inflict less damage on you. At the appropriate time, the graphics take a darker tone, telegraphing the change of state or level, so the player knows that the honeymoon period is over.

The concept of training is also fluid, because it doesn't need to be specifically stated that it's a training level. In a shooting game I wrote, where you played John McClane,[1] the training level was an actual shooting gallery in the police station with Sergeant Al giving you training orders. That was overt, but it fitted the mood of the game. In a puzzle game, you need to show (not tell) the player how the game works, if at all possible. You could train the player with simple versions of the real game, supported by additional voice-overs or graphics to indicate what the player must do in these scenarios. Let's consider some options in this regard.

■ **Tip** You should always encourage the player by allowing them to complete level 1, regardless of how badly they played.

A Training Level

To all intents and purposes, level 1 is for training; however, you decide how to define the training. It should introduce each item that the player needs to know for the basic game to play out. Furthermore, each element should be introduced individually, before requiring the player to combine them.[2] For the purpose of explanation, I use the theoretical platform game shown in Figure 4-1.

---

[1]Yes, the same one in *Die Hard*!
[2]Miyamoto has some advice on his creation of World 1-1 in *Super Mario Bros.* that is also worth considering at https://www.youtube.com/watch?v=zRGRJRUWafY

Figure 4-1. *The opening level of a fictitious platform game*

First, break down the actions within your game into categories such as these:

- The player character's abilities (e.g., run, jump, shoot)

- The abilities that the player reacts to (e.g., fall)

- The hazards that the player should avoid (e.g., monsters)

- The pick-ups that the player needs (e.g., ammo, health, gold)

- The weapons that the player uses (e.g., hands, gun)

These can then be further broken down and ordered in a logical sequence to guide the player through the level. This order starts with the easy, non-fatal actions and progresses to combinations that are more complex to execute. At each stage, you should be able to show[3] how each game mechanic works.

---

[3]Rather than "tell."

Abilities

Movement in a platform game is of vital importance, so start by showing the player that. In Figure 4-1, you see a wall to the left of the player and a gap to the left of the wall. This provides an (obvious) clue to the player that they are to head to the right, because it is a left-to-right game. This is reemphasized by the platform extending beyond the screen to the right and that the character is initially facing right. The player may run safely backward and forward to get a feel for the speed of their character, along with any available run or turbo modes.

■ **Tip**   Design your levels so that it leads the eye in the direction that you want the player go to and toward the goals you wish them to achieve.

Notice also that there are three walls. These are to demonstrate the limits of the jump ability. The left is too high, but is provided to both prevent the player from dying a stupidly banal death at the start of the game and to provide a guide as to how high the player can jump.

The second wall shows something that can be successfully traversed, with the height being level to the middle of the player's space visor. Again, by judging the obstacles in terms of the character, the player can quickly learn the rules of the game.

The final wall presents the first real obstacle to the game. The player should be able to see that it is too high to jump,[4] but that the platforms are all placed at equal levels to create an obvious stairs motif, indicating the player should climb them.

In the space of one screen, we have introduced the actions of run and jump in a simple and totally safe fashion, where it is possible to recover from any scenario—and the player will probably never notice they've done so! At worst, they'll consider it a simple prelude to what's coming next.

■ **Tip**   The best way to teach someone is when they don't know they're being taught.

You could even explain two more elements on the same screen by adding a collapsing floor on the top-right platform. This teaches the player about the different types of floors and explains why they're colored differently, and shows the safe height from which you can fall without taking damage. You'll also notice that if they fall, they do so to the right of the wall, allowing them to continue with the game.

Pick-ups and Weapons

Next, consider pick-ups. Not because they are the second-most important element of the game, but because I like the player to pick up two weapons before I introduce them to the hazards that they must shoot at. Two weapons? Yes, two, because this teaches

---

[4]The floor also extends to the right, indicating that this is the correct direction in which to travel.

the player how to change weapons, as well as shoot. For this I adopt a simple "walk over the object and you now hold it" philosophy. Similarly, if the weapons are created merely with increasing levels of firepower, then the player would automatically select the most powerful weapon with ammunition. If weapon selection is to be manual, then the weapons could appear in the top left of the screen as buttons or with an animating graphic labeled *Ctrl*, indicating the key that opens the full inventory panel.

If the weapons have different firing patterns, or need the player to hold the fire button down for a prolonged or more powerful burst, then this screen lets them experiment to learn that behavior. You might also decide to use this screen to demonstrate which elements of the environment can be destroyed and by which weapons.

You can also add non-weapon pick-ups on this screen to show how to differentiate between them and to give the player an idea of their relative abilities.

Hazards

Demonstrating hazards without taking damage is tricky. This is because, by their very nature, they damage you! Therefore, giving the player an easy option to shoot first and ask questions later is very preferable. Figure 4-2 shows our next screen.

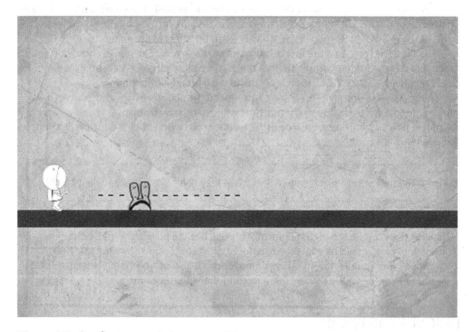

Figure 4-2. *Our first enemy, in its start position*

The dotted line (which is naturally not shown to the player) in Figure 4-2 indicates the path of the enemy. It starts by moving left, which gives the player a short amount of time to witness the screen and notice that the enemy moves to the left and then back again, letting them know that they'll be safe for a while. The player can then watch the enemy in safety for a while before choosing whether to jump over the enemy or shoot them.

This can then be enhanced by introducing two enemies on the screen at once to give the player practice at timing the shots, followed by screens where the enemies start by moving toward you in such a way that you don't know whether they'll stop and turn in time.

■ **Tip** To force the player into making the decision to jump rather than kill, you can introduce limited ammo into the initial weapons[5] and place ammo crates immediately beyond the enemies as both a reward and a reminder.

Once the player is able to cope with this, you can introduce enemies that can fire back! At this point, they should have the realization that the game allows them to combine the skills of jumping (to avoiding the missiles) and firing (to remove the attacker) without the method needing to be explained.

Explicit Cues

If your game isn't amenable to implicit game design in this way, then there are several ways to explicitly guide the players through. Some are more subtle than others.

The first and most obvious way is to introduce *Now collect the weapon* dialog boxes, along with a picture of the weapon, for example. These become quickly tedious, but serve as a last resort.

A second way is to introduce a buddy character, or ghost, that plays through the first part of the game, acting out the vignettes that you will play.

You could also introduce musical cues as the player approaches particular game elements: a positive upbeat sound for those elements that help the player, and deep or morose sounds for the enemies.

■ **Tip** Audio is a major part of the language of the game. It should be woven through the narrative whenever possible. This is fully explored in Chapter 7.

Finally, you might describe the actions of the world through color and visual means by changing the image whenever the game state changes. The more in keeping with the object, the better; for example, a blaster with a fully charged battery pack could show more lightning sparks than a dead one, or the graphic could be large enough for you to render a power meter along its side.

---

[5]In the same way, printers are sold with an ink cartridge that's only 1% full of ink!

Level 1 Is Still a Level

Just because the purpose of the first level is to teach, it doesn't mean that it shouldn't function as a conventional level. You should still increase tension as you move through it, introducing more hazards and bonuses in the process. Toward the end, these will overlap and require you to combine elements in a way that hasn't (necessarily) been explained. (As shown in our previous example, where you can jump and shoot at the same time.) This mimics the behavior of the game in a "real" level. In most cases, you want to carry over any points or weapons that you collected in the first level into the second level, so that it doesn't feel like a wasted exercise. In this case, ensure that players who jump straight into level 2 can do so without a disadvantage and that players who come from level 1 do not have an equally unfair advantage.[6]

The Other Levels

The second and subsequent levels should follow the same pattern as the first; that is, introduce new elements in a safe way first so that the player can become used to them. Also, there is no harm in reintroducing old elements so that they can become accustomed to them too. In drama, there is a principle called Chekhov's gun,[7] which says that any element introduced into a story, especially one that is seemingly unimportant, will have a use within that story before the end. Reintroducing a previous game device alerts the player to the possibility of its use and prepares the player ahead of time.

---

[6]If your training level involves giving the player experience with all the weapons and pick-ups in the game, you need to contrive a way of depriving the player of them before they progress to level 2.
[7]See https://en.wikipedia.org/wiki/Chekhov%27s_gun

All levels, including the first, should only be long enough to showcase what's necessary, what's new, or what's interesting. If you are writing a shooting game, for example, there's no need for the training level to include all 20 guns. Teach the three that are needed in the first few levels, and teach the fourth in the level prior to its use. Similarly, if one level is built around a sniper rifle, then let the player experiment with tin cans on a wall before meeting the boss enemy. Once the new feature has been seen, and the main objective (e.g., using the sniper rifle) has been satisfied, there is no need to continue with the level, so end it there and leave the player wanting more.

■ **Tip**　　The simpler the mechanic the level is trying to explore, the shorter the level should be.

Finally, make each level a self-contained experience that needs to be earned. If a level is merely the setup for the final level, then it will be impossible to lose since the finale must happen and therefore there is little tension or meaning to it. Consequently, it offers the player nothing and is a waste of time. Remove it or combine it into the finale, if necessary. Winning is no fun unless there's a challenge, regardless of level (except for training).

Balancing Is About Education

Throughout our discussions on balance, we are trying to codify the way in which the player can progress through our game without them finding it too hard or too easy at any point along the route. By introducing game features in a linear and sequential fashion, we can aid this. But, in essence, what we are doing is educating the user on how our game can be played. We can therefore reframe our approach and argue that balance is about education.

In the first instance, we need to teach the player the new features of our game and the emergent behaviors within our game. By introducing new elements to the game, there is a continued sense of learning and an increase in the challenge. While the player continues to believe that there is something else to learn or master, they will keep playing—provided all other variables are maintained (that is, it is still fun, and doesn't break its internal rules).

Second, we need to make the game increasingly challenging so that the player can use and hone these skills within the game. The key word here is *challenging*. Making the game unfairly hard is not necessarily challenging unless you are making a version of *Flappy Bird*.[8] Similarly, making a game excessively long (perhaps by having a large maze in the middle of a level) isn't particularly challenging. The challenge is in taking the learned skills and being able to apply them in ever more precise situations. Consider the case of jumping in a platform game. The player starts by easily making the jump, but over time, the distances get longer and so the required precision gives them less scope for error. Ultimately, the player's skills should be such that they move from a point where instead of it being possible to make a pixel-perfect jump, they find it impossible to miss it.

---

[8]Or *Super Meat Boy*, *Demon's Souls*, or any throwback game that mirrors the brutal games of yesteryear.

■ **Tip**   Once the parameters for jump (for example) have been set in stone, expand your game editor to show these parameters in-world, like *Super Mario Maker*, so that the designers can make progressively more challenging jumps based on data, and not judgment.

Finally, we need to ensure that there's a gap between their experience and knowledge, so that whatever the game demands of them, they can overcome it with their prior knowledge and mastery. This practice might come in the form of improved reactions in a twitch game, intellect through an understanding of the internal game logic,[9] or by an appreciation of deeper concepts, like gravity and how it acts on the jumping character.

As humans, we learn in many ways, but there is a generally agreed hierarchy on the best ways to learn.[10] From less effective to more effective, they are as follows:

1. Being told.

2. Reading for ourselves.

3. Audio and visual presentations.

4. Demonstration.

5. Discussion, usually in a group.

6. Practice by doing.

7. Teaching others.

In games, the explicit scenario of a training level that tells you "pick up the gun and shoot the can" achieves level 1-3. Watching a ghost character, or another player, run through the same feature scores 4. But once the player is able to use it, it's an easy 6. If the player hasn't had to sit through levels 1-3, then their only memory of the feature is more cemented at the higher level, which is the scientific reason why it's better to implicitly guide the player through a training level.

Balancing Is About Progression

All games start easy and progressively become more challenging. This is a gradual process. And while it has to start somewhere, there is no need for it to end. Many games, especially the classics, become progressively more difficult as the speed and number of enemies increase, until it's physically impossible for the player to win. There is nothing wrong with this style of game. However, an experienced player does not want 10 minutes of slow turgid gameplay, so we should provide a method whereby such a player can start at a more challenging position. Similarly, you should not make side quests optional if they unbalance the game by the giving players too many extra experience points or too much inventory.

---

[9]*Monkey Island* became easier and more logical once you understood the humor of the design.
[10]There are many scholarly papers on the reasons behind education, but John Dewey's "Theories of Education" is a good place to start.

Difficulty Factors

It's almost trivial to add a difficulty[11] screen to your game, listing easy-medium-hard levels, and use this parameter to control the game mechanics. Most affect the game resources in some way, with the following typical parameters:

- Speed of enemy movements

- Reaction times needed to respond to events

- Total time allowed to complete the task

- Enemy re-spawn time

- Damage taken from various types of shot

- Damage inflicted by various weapons to specific locations

- Number of safe zones

- Number of pick-ups (such as power-ups, ammo, health kits, and so on)

- Location of pick-ups, as harder levels might leave only the difficult-to-reach ones

The scores or bonuses awarded for such actions are rarely changed, because it's unfair to award fewer points for achieving the same goals.

■ **Tip**   Give the difficulty factors names to match the style of game. A British Army Special Air Service (SAS) attack squad would never consider "easy" to be a valid mission description, since no SAS mission is easy. Perhaps "namby-pamby mummies boy" would be more appropriate!

Controlling each feature can be as simple or as complex as you have the time to test it; that is, changing one number relating to the re-spawn time will have a domino effect to the way the enemies attack you, which affects the number of bullets used, which affects how much ammo is required in the level, and so on. You need to ensure that all difficulty factors are possible.

So, if the difficulty factor varies between 0 and 2, and gameplay experimentation results that the re-spawn time needs to interpolate between 18 and 10 seconds (according to whether the level is easy, medium, or hard), then the code doesn't need be anything more than this:

```
fRespawnTime = 18 - difficulty * 4.0;
```

---

[11]In this chapter, I use the term *difficulty factor* instead of "difficulty level" so that it's easier to differentiate between difficultly levels and game levels in the examples that follow.

This can be further improved by introducing other parameters, like the level, as follows:

```
fRespawnTime = 18 - difficulty * 3.0 - level * 0.5;
```

Note also that we've amended the impact that the difficulty factor has to compensate for the extra complexity introduced by the using the level parameter.

Another point to consider is whether we should provide a balancing mechanism for players starting at a non-easy level, particularly for puzzle games. After all, starting on easy and playing for 15 minutes will amass a certain number of points and bonuses. Whereas, playing on a medium level for 5 minutes is probably more involving and worthy of a higher score.

Difficulty Scales

Our formulas use a basic linear interpolation to compute difficulty. In the example, we determined by experimentation that enemies re-spawning after 18 seconds was quite easy, whereas 10 seconds was hard enough. It's also an obvious progression. Figure 4-3 shows some alternate scales.[12]

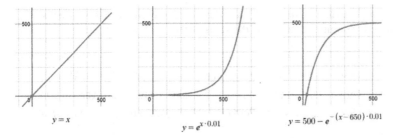

$$y = x$$

$$y = e^{x \cdot 0.01}$$

$$y = 500 - e^{-(x - 650) \cdot 0.01}$$

Figure 4-3. *Linear and non-linear difficulty scales*

After determining the end points, as we did in the re-spawn example, we can consider alternatives for how the game moves between them. Difficulty could grow gradually with a sharp increase at the end, similar to a typical boss level. Or it could ramp up quickly to get an early adrenaline surge, but then taper off as other gameplay elements are introduced. The choice is controlled by what else is happening within the game as the difficulty increases along the x axis of that graph. Kazunori Sawano, of *Galaxian* fame, says that "things gradually seem to get harder, but there's no apparent disjunction."[13] His games tend to react in a manner similar to the first part of the basic exponential graph.

---

[12]Generated by https://www.desmos.com/calculator (although other online graph calculation tools exist)

[13]See http://shmuplations.com/earlyarcade/

■ **Tip**　You can also vary the difficulty factor based on how well the player performs in the training level.

The most important point when balancing these scales is to avoid double jeopardy, if at all possible. This is where the player is at a natural disadvantage, but is made to confront a problem that was already difficult under normal circumstances. One such example is a level that causes the player to exhaust all of their ammunition in order to break through a wall, only to be confronted with a boss fight on the other side of that wall, but no ammo to help.

By Design

When an opportunity presents itself to incorporate difficulty in the form of risk/reward at the design stage, then take it. Nothing feels more natural. Several game styles tend themselves naturally to this.

It is difficult to think of a racing game without some element of rubber banding to ensure that the player can never get too far ahead or behind the other vehicles. In this way, the competitive element is never lost. This is a specific example of the more general case of a negative feedback loop, which can be applied in many cases. For example, controlling resources found in a real-time strategy game, issuing higher taxes in management simulators, and so on.

Fighting games like *Street Fighter* offer a risk curve that maps difficulty to the input control system. In games like this, you have the option of issuing a single key attack that actions immediately, or a multikey combo that takes longer to execute but can be more damaging. The balance between these is similar to the "press and hold the button to increase firepower" option in shoot-em-ups. In R-type, this is an analog progression, where for every N seconds the button is held down, the firepower increases by M%. In contrast, *Mega Man X* has a digital approach that increases firepower to 200% after N seconds, and 300% after M seconds.

Stealth games are one of the cases that have a more interesting risk curve inherent in the design, as shown in Figure 4-4. Here there is an increase of adrenaline and anticipation as the player moves into a position of stealth and hiding, followed by a sharp drop when they are discovered. The closer they get the precipice, without falling off, has an exponentially large payoff for the player, but with a fatal Boolean risk.

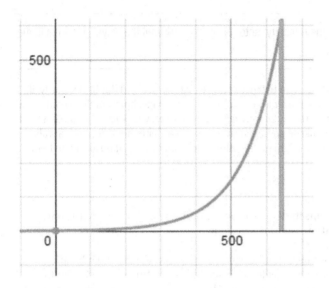

Figure 4-4. *A risk curve for stealth games*

If your design allows it, you can always modify the game design to accommodate for players with a wide range of skills. In a first-person shooter, for example, there might be unlocked doors in the easier levels that let you bypass the tight corridors that become risky in a fire fight. You could also take a deeper approach where difficulty is introduced by providing different solutions to the same problem. For example, an MMORPG (massively multiplayer online role-playing game) might provide two solutions for earning 100 gold: a simple one that involves grinding (i.e., dull and repetitive work) to make shirts, and a difficult one that involves complex and risky battles where the gold is won by the victors.

■ **Tip** By introducing extra elements in the design for more advanced players, you increase the longevity and enjoyment of the game for everyone.

Balancing by Implementation

The only point that needs be made at this juncture is to provide a means for non-programmers to control as much of the game balancing code as possible. Incorporating magic numbers into the code (as we did earlier) is very bad practice because the turnaround time for any particular change is large.

Instead, add a configuration file into the development environment that can be tweaked remotely, so a designer or tester can experiment with different values. If the configuration can be changed mid-game, then that's the best possible case. Otherwise, requiring a restart of a level (or even the game) is quicker than asking a programmer to recompile and redeploy a new version.

The implementation usually involves a text file parser, of your favorite design, and code to apply it to the global settings object.

```
file_value = load_field_from_config_file('config/game', 'game.respawn');
settings = new sgxDebugOptions();
settings.setOption('game.respawn', file_value);
```

You may wish to override the settings file with command line arguments, for example, for a more fine-grained configuration.

```
settings.setOption('game.respawn',
cmd.getOption('game.respawn', file_value)));
```

The code to read these settings is typically no more involved than this:

```
fRespawnMax = settings.getOption('game.respawn', 18);
fRespawnDifficulty = settings.getOption('game.respawn.difficulty', 3);
fRespawnLevel = settings.getOption('game.respawn.level', 0.5);

fRespawnTime = fRespawnMax - difficulty * fRespawnDifficulty - level *
fRespawnLevel;
```

Note the use of defaults for cases where no configuration setting value is present; it is included here as a safety precaution. As a programmer, you might also want to specify maximum and minimum values to limit user error; for example, re-spawning enemies with a 0-second gap is rarely a good feature!

Knowing that the configuration settings are conceivably integers, floats, or strings, you may need to write specific code for each to parse the input and validate it against known good input.

```
getOption: function(optionName, defaultValue) {
        var result = optionList[optionName];
        return result == undefined ? defaultValue : result;
},

getOptionAsInt: function(optionName, defaultValue) {
        var result = optionList[optionName];
        return result == undefined ? defaultValue : sgxAtoi(result);
},

getOptionAsBool: function(optionName, defaultValue) {
        var result = optionList[optionName];
        return result == undefined ? defaultValue : sgxBoolean(result);
},
```

■ **Caution**   Giving the development team the ability to change settings mid-game isn't difficult, but potentially fraught with danger if not explained well. If someone changed the re-spawn value to 30 seconds, while in-game characters are still using an internal variable requesting that they re-spawn after 18 seconds, this might be filed as a bug. Worst still, resetting a characters' "maximum time to live" down to 10 seconds, when it's already at 15, might cause issues if the code that checks for expiry is broken.

Developers working within the browser can also use a technique called *local storage* to hold state between sessions on a given user's machine. The code to read and write such data is simply this:

```
sgxLocalStorage.getOption = function(optionName, defaultValue)
{
  var result = defaultValue;

  if (typeof(Storage) !== "undefined") {
    result = localStorage.getItem(optionName);
  }

  return result == undefined ? defaultValue : result;

}

sgxLocalStorage.setOption = function(optionName, value) {
  if (typeof(Storage) !== "undefined") {
    localStorage.setItem(optionName, value);
    return true;
  }
  return false;
}
```

It is then a design decision on the priority order of the three settings. In Space Bounce, we use, in increasing order of priority, the configuration file, then local storage, and finally URL parameters.

```
var configurationDefault = true;
var sfxOn = sgxLocalStorage.getOptionAsBool("audio.sfx",
configurationDefault);
cmd = parseURLArguments();
sfxOn = cmd.getOptionAsBool(null, 'audio.sfx', sfxOn);
```

A Process

Balance occurs at multiple layers. Each layer needs to be play-tested, both in isolation (like a unit test) and as a whole (integration test.) At the lowest level, each element needs to be checked that it fits within a sensible range. This ensures that no single weapon, pick-up, or fighting move is so overpowering that it makes the others redundant. One way to achieve this is by fixing the ranges of each item in a graph similar to Figure 4-5, where you are only able to acquire and use the more powerful weapons when you've progressed to a suitable point in the game and the defensive parameters of enemies outweigh the attack capabilities of the other weapons.

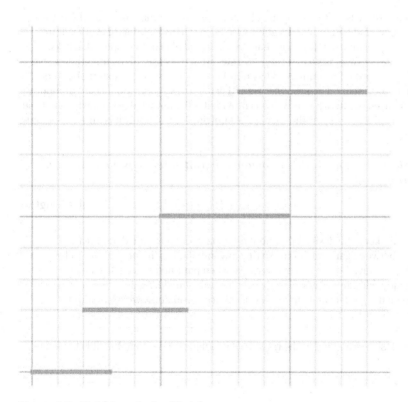

Figure 4-5. *Matching attack with defense*

A more literal approach to balancing is to introduce multiple parameters to every element. A role-playing game (RPG) has a series of statistics for each character. In the simplest game, this might be strength, skill, and stamina. You can then award 100 points to be spread between the three areas, according to the whim of the player. It is then the responsibility of the designer that the game requires comparatively equal amounts of strength, skill, and stamina, so that each character type has a chance of completing the game effectively.

Video games are meant to be just one thing. Fun. Fun for everyone.

—Satoru Iwata

Ultimately, there is a dichotomy in balancing a game. On the one hand, there are a series of numbers and equations that attempt to even the distribution of every feature and element of the game. On the other hand, there is the playability aspect that asks, *Is this game fun?*. Alas, there is no algorithm to detect that use case, so the integration tests are invariably performed by humans. They may be from focus groups, external testers, or your own departments. The producer should listen to everyone and discard or modify the feedback based on known bias. What is provided is the knowledge from which to base your balancing efforts, whereas the wisdom of knowing how to apply it is understood only through play.

Knowledge is knowing that a tomato is a fruit, wisdom is not putting it in a fruit salad.

—Miles Kington

In all cases, keep the design document up to date and relevant, detailing the relationships between game elements so that any imbalances in integration can be anticipated. This way, there is less of a surprise when parameters are tweaked and previously enjoyable gameplay suddenly become unbalanced. Again, there is no way to truly anticipate this, but it can help focus your efforts if you know where to start testing.

■ **Tip**   The design document is always a work in progress, so ensure that it is treated as such.

Summary

We began by looking at balancing on a grand scale, considering the role and execution of level 1 compared to level 2, and the concept of training levels and how they needn't be dull or full of written text explaining game concepts. Instead, you saw that by gradually feeding the player small problems in a piecemeal fashion, they learn the game mechanics by doing, which, according to the cognitive patterns of education, better cement the ideas in the player's memory.

Also, we examined the way that difficulty can be increased across a level (and the game in general) to keep the novice player interested, while still providing a challenge for the more experienced player. Accomplishing both ensures longevity for the game, which is always a good thing.

Finally, we looked briefly at the implementation details of difficulty scales, so that designers can tweak the magic numbers to perfection without interruption from the programming team.

CHAPTER 5

User Experience

The Crux of UX and Design

Very few teams have a dedicated user experience, or UX, person. Even fewer teams know what a UX person does. For our purposes, the UX is about making the journey that the user takes through the game from screen to screen as simple and as pleasing as possible. The player should be able to flow through the game like a proverbial breeze.

■ **Tip** The best user interface is the one that you never notice, because it should be naturally intuitive.

In Chapter 2, you learned about these screens. In this chapter, I cover how to effectively design and build them. If the player can begin the game in one click, then make it so. If you can add transitions between screens, then do so. Many UX elements intersect with interface design.

■ **Note** This chapter concentrates on the big picture and focuses on the common threads between all the screens and the way they fit together. In Chapter 6, you look at the in-game experience in more detail.

Basic Principles

There are several elements that are true of all games. I refrain from referring to them as "golden rules," so instead I use the word *principles*.

Before the Game

As developers, we generally have very little control over the UX before our game has loaded. But we can ensure that UX has at least been considered.

S. Goodwin, *Polished Game Development*, DOI 10.1007/978-1-4842-2122-8_5

To start, we need to generate an icon to exemplify our game. This might reference the main character (our spaceman), the gameplay (the mine shaft), or even just the genre in an abstract fashion. What's important is the size at which you create it.

Each platform has its own requirements regarding resolution. Often you need multiple icons to handle the myriad devices within the platform family; sometimes this includes variations in aspect ratio too. Furthermore, to achieve brand consistency, the same application icon should be used in the storefront and on your website. However, it is very likely that the required icon size differs for each purpose. At the time of writing, the largest size for an iPhone application is 180×180 pixels, whereas the version of the image required by the App Store is 1024×1024.

It is also likely that the icon will be used in other forms of promotion, such as on the box (for those making products fit for purposefully placing on shelves), in TV ads, or in print magazines. Therefore, ensure that the icon you originally draw is larger than you need—4096×4096 will probably be future-proof for a few years![1] Creating such an overly large image has the additional benefit that it is more likely to shrink precisely to sizes like 76×76 or 167×167, without creating the anti-aliasing effects that a smaller image would incur. This image should ideally be stored in a lossless format—preferably vector-based (such as SVG), but PNG is also a good choice.

■ **Tip** When designing icons for use in-game, make sure that they are user tested because they could be interpreted differently (i.e., wrongly!) by users.

The same rules apply to loading screens: create one as large as possible (at least 2738×2048 if you're supporting the iPad Pro) so that it can be used in all forms of media. Again, it is easier to scale the image down and look good, than it is to scale it up.

Game Flow

As soon as the player lands on the main menu screen, the first thing they want to do is leave it! They want a big button that starts the game and gives them the visceral thrill they've craved since exchanging their real-world currency for virtual data bits. Getting the user onto that game screen, or any others that they may wish to, is our primary concern. When Stephen Hawking was writing his book, *A Brief History of Time*, his publisher told him that for every equation he included, his sales would halve. Similarly, for every screen that you make the player click through, and for every second that they spend looking for the route there, their enjoyment will halve. This doesn't mean you need to cut features. If your game has difficulty levels, then you don't necessarily need to create a *Select level* screen. Instead, you can list all the levels on the main menu screen, partitioned in their own area, and click the button that begins the game at that difficulty level.

---

[1]Famous last words!

If there are too many levels to show, then you could show the five most suitable[2] with some scrolling arrows. Most of the time, the level they want to play is directly in front of them (costing only one click), while in rare cases, they might have to click an arrow a couple of times for the desired level to appear.

■ **Tip**   Always design for and streamline the most common use cases first. It's preferable to have 90% of your users needing one click and 10% requiring five, than to have 100% of users needing two clicks.

When planning a flow of how the user moves through the screens, consider the physicality too. If you're on a hand-held device, look at where your thumbs and/or fingers lie and place the navigation controls near them. This might be half-way up the screen, and not in the center or bottom right like most desktop games. To facilitate this, the interface should always be data driven, with the screens and widget positions loaded from a file (probably a different file for each platform). When developing cross-platform games, this data-driven approach ceases to be a "should" and becomes a "must."

In most cases, you'll want to keep the navigation buttons in the same location as the player moves through the screens. This might mean generating an interface template so that, should the position of the buttons need to move, you only need to amend one template and not ten separate interface screens.

Once the screens are all in place, consider the act of moving between them. It is very easy to switch them, but having a transition shows an extra layer of polish. Maybe the transition is a slide, a fade, or a custom animation. Doing so, however, implicitly requires that you're not using singleton patterns for the interface, since you can't have the exiting UI and the entering UI handled by one singleton.

To handle this case, the interface code needs a layer of subtle functionality. In Space Bounce, our UI code for the instruction screen is rendered with this method:

```
interfaceList[page].draw(surface, 0, 0);
```

Those final two parameters are the top-left x and y coordinates at which the interface should be drawn. It is rare for such parameters to be included in the first pass of an interface library, but by providing this functionality at the start, transitioning between different interfaces is not difficult at all. The process is made simpler by the fact that, while transitioning, the user can't interact with the UI, therefore we don't need to worry about offsetting the mouse or touch positions to match.

---

[2]What determines the most suitable level is dependent on the game. Often it'll be the last one that the player played, but left incomplete.

Branding

As much as we developers consider ourselves free-spirited creative types, there is the harsh reality that we can only be so while there is money coming in. It isn't just the money men and women that talk wistfully about the benefits of game branding. So should we. Branding isn't a dirty word, merely a way of providing a consistency of style that suits our game that leads to better immersion.

The features involved in branding include very few basic elements, but their reach permeates everything.

The typeface is the most obvious. Every piece of text in the game needs to be rendered with a specific font that is suitable to the game. Our space game would receive strange looks if the title screen appeared with the text shown in Figure 5-1.

SPACE BOUNCE

Figure 5-1. *Old-school stencil is the wrong font for a space game*

This is why the font shown in Figure 5-2 is adopted.

Figure 5-2. *A better font choice*

For additional styling, the letters A and O have themed graphics. If you do this, remember to replace the letters, wherever they're used, for consistency, and ensure that the words remain legible and their meaning understood. There is also a graphical echo on the word Bounce.

There are several websites that provide assistance in sourcing a suitable font, including dafont.com and Font Squirrel (`www.fontsquirrel.com`). Although many professionals might disagree, there is nothing wrong with following the tropes and using the Stencil font (as shown in Figure 5-1) in a military or war game. It is a quick and effective way to set the expectations of your audience. If you are an indie developer, then your work probably ends here, while those working in moneyed companies will spend the time to find a more unique typeface or even generate one themselves.

After choosing the typeface, you next need to pick a color. The art director will no doubt already have chosen a suitable color palette in which the whole game will be rendered. The important part of this equation is that it is consistent in all places. To that end, it is not unusual to create a small code wrapper to handle all text rendering in the game.

For example, instead of writing this:

```
surface.setCurrentFont(titleFont);
surface.setFontColor(sgxColorRGBA.white);
surface.setFontSize(24);
surface.drawText('Welcome to Space Bounce', x, y);
```

You instead call a method like this:

```
ui.drawTitle('Welcome to Space Bounce', x, y);
```

The ui class understands the typeface, size, and color required by the title so that consistency is ensured. This code may be expanded to include extra parameters, like the number of pixels between each line and the number of spaces at the start of each paragraph. It could also check the string for abnormalities (such as tabs) and remove them (or convert them to spaces.)

■ **Caution**   When choosing a color palette that features red and green, ensure that there is a color blind mode.

As a rule of thumb, there should be no more than four different styles of text on any given screen. They fit into the rough categories of title, text, emphasis, and interface. Adopting an abstraction as outlined earlier ensures that this limit is adhered to and that any changes made are reflected instantly across the game.

The next step in improving the uniform look of text is with items of data, such as score. Do you display the score as 2100 or 2,100, for example? Or 0002100?[3] It is simple to add a method to the magical ui class called drawScore, but complications occur later when the in-game score is updated to include some special effects (which require a customized text renderer, as you'll see in Chapter 6) but the code that displays the high score table is not updated. Such changes are to be noted in the design document and checked by QA.

---

[3]Including leading zeroes normally requires an understanding of the upper bound of the scoring system. This is rare.

The next element of branding involves the backgrounds for the menu screens, such as instructions or credits. Again, the art director dictates a style and theme, and source-suitable versions. Ideally, these screens are all different, as even subtle variations alert the player as to the purpose of those screens, and embiggen the experience.

■ **Tip** If you can't create distinct backgrounds for each screen, a cheap way of achieving the effect is to create one background larger than the game area and crop it in different locations. You might also decide to color tint an image or overlay the game characters in different locations.

Finally, we concern ourselves with the style of the widgets used by the interface. Since these are interactive, their appearance should give some clue as to their nature. (I have already suggested a separate font for them, whether this is by having a unique typeface or simply an alternate color, so they stand out.)

Visually speaking, the style should match the genre to draw the player into that environment. Our war game might color the edges of a button with camouflage, whereas a space game could use futuristic blue neon. There are very few cases where you would want to ape the UI of the host platform. One such rarity is in a game where you appear to hack into a computer network; it would be sensible to use the native UI design[4] in that case, since, paradoxically, it would make you believe it was really happening more than the fake movie-land vision of computer displays seen in TV shows like *CSI: Cyber*.

From a practical standpoint, we must next define the function of our widgets. A button in a traditional mouse-based operating system may cycle through up to six different states:

- Inactive

- Hover, with the mouse button still up

- Pressed, or activated

- Activated, but the mouse has moved out of the button area

- Released, with the mouse outside of the area (i.e., cancel)

- Released, with the mouse still in the area

Once the button has been released (with the mouse still in the area), it is activated and the action happens. Within our game, we have to consider if we're following this convention. A fast-moving game may prefer instead to trigger the action upon the pressed down event to save time waiting for the mouse up message to appear. In doing so, we remove the ability of the canny player to "undo" their action by moving the mouse outside of the area before releasing the button.

---

[4]Check the technical requirements of the platform first, as some platform holders do not approve of this.

■ **Tip**   If both types of button (trigger on pressed and trigger on released) are required within the same interface, then be sure to visually style them differently.

By adopting a "trigger on pressed" approach, you then need to implement appropriate code to handle autorepeat, if it is to be supported. Conversely, you need to consider whether this is useful in cases where a "trigger on pressed" button might trigger a new screen. At this point, the old widget has gone and a new widget might appear in its place, although the mouse button is still depressed. Should the new widget get triggered? Common sense says it shouldn't, but your code might think otherwise! For this reason, it is usual to trigger all widgets on the released message and all in-game actions on pressed.

When the game is destined for touch-based devices, the hover state can't exist, so we need to be careful about using it. So be certain that the game will never migrate to touch screens, never trigger an action, or provide necessary information based on the hover event; otherwise, you'll have a lot of frustrating work rebuilding the user interface to avoid it.

Interface Conventions

In most games, the interface is an accepted nuisance.[5] You are forced to click buttons to choose a difficulty level or select a character, for example. The task here is to make the interface as effortless as possible.

The first step toward this goal—ensuring that all UI elements are visually similar—has already been covered, so we can swiftly move on to their placement. By ensuring that all buttons or hot spot areas are in the same place on every screen, the player can quickly navigate to the game.

The relative position of buttons like OK and Cancel also come under this heading, although each platform has a different belief. It should be OK–Cancel, because Western languages read left-to-right, and OK is the first thing you read and the most common action.

Conversely, with 90% of the population being right-handed, the easiest area to click or touch is the right-hand side of the screen, meaning that the default action (which is invariably OK) is on the right.

Sometimes you'll see the buttons aligned vertically, but the issue remains whether OK is on the top or on the bottom, as similar arguments can be made.

In short, it doesn't matter which you choose, as long as you are consistent. Place the widgets in groups with others of a similar function, then move any potentially fatal widgets (such as a Quit button) away from the herd and include an *Are you sure?* message box when they're clicked.

---

[5]Strategy and management simulations are an exception insomuch as so much of the gameplay relies on the player being able to navigate the UI that it needs a dedicated person to ensure consistency.

Visual Dynamics

If there is a golden rule in screen design for games, it's this: make something animate on every screen. It doesn't matter how big it is or how important, just ensure that there's something dynamic. This will make the screen come alive (literally and figuratively) and prove that the game hasn't randomly crashed!

The dynamic element can be an animation of an in-game character (which requires no more assets), or an occasional sparkle animation appearing by the title or next to other static graphics. It could be a moving or scrolling background. It could be two backgrounds, one with transparency, to produce a parallax effect. It could be a ticker tape along the bottom of the screen, relaying instructions or the game's high scores.[6] Or it could be anything else. Just add something. Anything. And make it move!

This idea of animation extends to the idle state, since nothing is ever truly idle. Even a person standing still will sway slightly, which means that in a first-person shooter, the hand holding the weapon would also move slightly. (And move more vigorously when they start running.) The introduction of a simple idle animation requires that you introduce animation code into the platform, which is a big step up. Consequently, it is a very small step to extend this code to trigger an alternate idle animation (such as head scratching or looking around) for when the character is inactive for a long amount of time.

■ **Tip**   All animations should have a minimum of three frames. Any fewer and it appears to merely oscillate, making the determination of direction impossible.

If there is an extension to this rule, it's "make *everything* animate." In this case, we're not trying to re-create a circus, because items don't need to animate all the time, but when a button is pressed, for example, the transition from up to down should take a few frames. Or selecting a radio button should cause its tick mark to slowly illuminate. You can handle this in code or with art assets; it doesn't matter as long as your code is strong enough to handle all use cases (such as when the player presses the button while it is animating), as it's another step change of improvement.

And, as described earlier, if you can introduce dynamics as the screen transitions, that's even better!

The Curse of the Web

While the World Wide Web has provided us with many benefits. It has also raised the bar in terms of what a good UX is. Many web companies have specialized developers looking at better and faster ways of getting the web-browsing public from the home page to one that reads "Buy this now." As game developers, we can learn from this, and appropriate their ideas as appropriate.

---

[6]Online games could display public tweets about the game, if the developers can trust their public to not write abuse!

Unfortunately, the web has provided us with many kludgey, broken, and awful interfaces! Many of them on popular, million-user web sites. Amazon and eBay, for example, have so many menus, buttons, side panels, and subside panels that a novice would not find it intuitive at all. Both sites have become successful *despite* their UX, not *because* of it. Therefore, don't judge your UX by how it compares to a web site you like, judge it on its own merits and the primary criteria of how long it takes the player to get into the game.

Similarly, don't use your favorite games as role models for design, because you'll suffer confirmation bias, which is where you agree with, interpret, or recall information that agrees with your pre-existent beliefs or ideas, in preference to any new ideas or possibilities.

Testing

Once the UI has been designed and implemented, you must test it. Repeatedly. If necessary, hire a user researcher to carry out real-world user tests with real-world users. Frequently, the development team is so comfortable with the interface that they believe it is already perfectly suited and complete. However, it rarely is. Since the team built the interface and knows its nuances, quirks, and issues, the team members often avoid them.

They also know the route through the menus or widgets to any specific part of the game. However, when the player approaches the same navigation, they won't have that foresight. Nor will they necessarily understand the semiotics present within the interface; that is, is the tab rendered in blue active or inactive? Or disabled?

As with all elements of the process, the sooner you can find issues, the sooner you can fix them and the lower the cost of doing so. For UX and UI elements, the first opportunity to test is at the pen-and-paper prototyping stage. This test process is iterative and should happen many times throughout the process, continuing with user research up to (and often after) release.

Coding for Design

When interfaces become dynamic in the way we want, where buttons take several frames to change state, we need to develop our code in such a way that it can accommodate this. We now look at some methodologies for doing so.

Separate Draw and Update

The approach taken in Space Bounce is to separate all actions into two parts: draw and update. Every object in the game has both of these methods. The draw method renders the object using the current state, but is not allowed to change it in any way. (In C++, this is thought of as a const method.) This is its signature:

```
function draw(surface) {
  ...
}
```

Whereas the update method is thus:

```
function update(surface, telaps) {
  ...
}
```

The telaps variable reports the time elapsed since the previous invocation of update. This is so the update method can change its state according to the strict rules of time, regardless of the frame rate. This value is measured in seconds, so we can easily vary the size, color, or animation frame based on it, thereby producing a gradual change.

■ **Note** Synchronous blocking functions make it impossible to create smooth or gradual changes to the graphics, or to effectively handle changes to multiple objects at the same time. Therefore, everything should be run asynchronously from an event loop with callbacks triggering completion—even though some platforms seem to advocate the opposite!

Taking a simple example, Space Bounce has a Game Over image that grows over time. The game is still playing in the background, so the halite sparkle animations can be seen, but the character is dead,[7] so the player's only choice is to watch the animations.

The update method is fully hierarchical, so the main platform update loop calls the game update loop (from SGXUpdate), which in turn calls the update loop of everything it knows about, such as the level and player. This hierarchy extends down as far as necessary. When the game over sequence needs to start, we use code similar to this:

```
game_over_time_elapsed_total = 0;
```

So in the update, we can call this:

```
game_over_time_elapsed_total += telaps * speed_of_animation;
```

This gives us a floating-point number that indicates the progress of this specific animation. As developers, we can choose any start and end points that we like, but 0 to 1 is fairly typical, so we can render the Game Over graphic with this:

```
t = game_over_time_elapsed_total;
var width = t * gVars.textures.gameOver.getWidth();
var height = t * gVars.textures.gameOver.getHeight();

surface.setFillColor(sgxColorRGBA.White);
surface.setFillTexture(gVars.textures.gameOver);

var x = (surface.getWidth() - width) / 2;
var y = 50;
surface.fillRect(x, y, x + width, y + height);
```

---

[7]As covered in Chapter 2, the player is not the center of the game.

You should be able to see how easy it is to now change the speed of the animation without affecting any other code or objects. This is much more visually pleasing than it suddenly appearing.

As a bonus, if you pass 0 into the update methods, you can make the object appear to be in stasis. This is very useful when you want to create bullet-time effects, or if you want to pause the game (triggering the in-game menu) but still want certain objects to animate in the background.

Do not try to skip the update loop if the time elapsed is zero because there are many cases where this produces inaccurate results. The first such case is that any child objects will not get an update message, which they may be relying upon to animate, when the game is paused.

The second case is very subtle. If you are building a game where all moves need to be predictable, then ignoring time_elapsed (or writing code that doesn't consider the value) will break. Imagine an enemy moves with code like this:

```
if (sgxRand() > 0.5) {
  x += 1;
} else {
  x -= 1;
}
```

They move a different number of pixels, depending on whether the method is called twice with a time elapsed of 0.1s, or once with a time elapsed of 0.2s, since the random function was called a different number of times and the distance moved is not time-compensated.

■ **Tip**   Always seed your random-number generator with the same value so its results are predictable from one run-through of the game to the next. This is essential to test consecutive runs of development builds, but often useful in release to eliminate potential edges cases breaking the game when a hitherto unseen random number sequences destroys game logic.

The correct method is to use time elapsed as a compensator, with code such as this:

```
movement_time_accumulated += time_elapsed;
movement_time_step = 0.1;
while (movement_time_accumulated > movement_time_step) {
  // Do random stuff here
  movement_time_accumulated -= movement_time_step;
}
```

Keeping a predictable game is also useful in playback scenarios and for testing, which you'll see in Chapter 10.

■ **Note** By threading telaps throughout the code base, adding time-based events is now trivial because the data is sitting there waiting. Furthermore, since all effects have a time element, it is trivial to add them.

Auditory Effects

The same gradual transitions that we advocate for visuals will also help polish the audio. When switching between two screens, we'd rather the audio fade out rather than abruptly change to the next tune. If your audio library supports callbacks, you can initiate the sound with this:

```
musicChannel = sgx.audio.Engine.get().playSound("music");
```

Upon the trigger of the change screen event, you call this:

```
if (!transitioning) {
  transitioning = true;
  musicChannel.startFadeOut(0.4, function(e) {
    changeScreenTo('credits');
  });
}
```

In this way, the transitioning variable acts as a blocker, preventing duplicate calls to the audio engine, and as a mini state machine to let you know what's going on.

If the engine doesn't support callbacks, you need to manually poll the music channel to see if it's still playing, and change the screen in that way.

One final complication occurs if the audio engine can return an error, such as null, when the sound can't be played. (This can happen when there are no audio channels available or a soundcard doesn't exist for some spurious reason.) In this case, you either need to explicitly handle this case:

```
if (!transitioning) {
  transitioning = true;
  if (musicChannel) {
    musicChannel.startFadeOut(0.4, function(e) {
      changeScreenTo('credits');
    });
  } else { // no channel exists, so change immediately
    changeScreenTo('credits');
  }
}
```

A better method is to abstract or amend the audio engine so that it always returns a valid channel. If the underlying engine fails to return a valid channel, then the wrapper can create a "null channel" that has methods identical to the usual channel and mimics their behavior. In this example, the startFadeOut method of the null channel would simply invoke the callback, so the first (cleaner) version of our code is all that's needed to run both cases.

Pretty State Machine

When moving from a Boolean interface of on and off to a tri-state one, we start to see code complexity grow. If we need to handle all six button states mentioned earlier, then the code gets very messy, very quickly. The natural solution here is a finite-state machine. This is a way of modelling a system that can only be in one given state at one time, with full descriptions of how it may move between those states.

Fortunately, these are not difficult to build. Even a basic one will last you for most (if not all) of the project. The one I used is fewer than 70 lines long. In essence, you need to consider each state as having four methods: onStart, onEnd, and the two we've already explored, onDraw and onUpdate. So now, instead of switching between two states, you can switch between six. Believe it or not, this makes things easier because most of the states are transitioning states in which you do not need to include any code, because while it is transitioning, you do not want to affect the object's state.

■ **Tip**   If you're building your own state machine, consider changing the state only at the end of the draw cycle, since any change within the code of update_state_old will next invoke draw_state_new, instead of giving the state a chance to prepare itself via an initial update_state_new.

Game Screens

By now, you should know all the separate screens leading up to your game, where they fit, and what content they contain. We conclude with a number of code examples and ideas on how to improve upon them even further.

The Title Screens

These are the pimp screens detailing the licensor, publisher, developer, and assorted third-party companies that need accreditation for their work. The first minimally viable option is to load all the screens into memory:

```
(function ctor() {
  var title_screens = [];

  for(var i=0;i<3;++i) {
    title_screens.push(loadTexture("resources/title/image" + i));
  }
})();
```

Display them, like this:

```
function draw(surface) {
  surface.setFillTexture(title_screens[idx]);
  surface.fillRect();
}
```

And cycle through them upon a mouse click in the update loop.

```
function update(surface, telaps) {
  if (sgx.input.Engine.get().mouseLeft.wasPressed()) {
    if (++idx == title_screens.length) {
      changeState('mainmenu');
    }
  }
}
```

This, however, may not match the legal requirements, as some licensors and publishers require that their logo display for a fixed period of time, and have any skip feature disabled. Even if it weren't a legal concern, I still advocate that the developer's title screen should be fixed in recognition of their creative and hard work on the product.

We should therefore expand our code to include a minimum duration of screen time, during which the screen cannot be skipped, and a maximum duration for when it changes automatically. Furthermore, these values should be set according to each screen, to handle vagaries in requirements.

```
var minDuration = [ 2, 1, 0 ];
var maxDuration = [ 5, 4, 3 ];
```

Although some might argue that an MVP would only include a single pair of numbers, making minDuration identical in all screens, the effort in providing this functionality adds so little development time that it is worth planning ahead. Also, if you have the choice of generating these numbers computationally or via a data set, always use a data set. If these timings change, it will be from management, who is more likely to request an extra half-second be added or removed from certain screens arbitrarily. Rebuilding a formula each time that they make such a request is an unnecessary time sink.

The update loop now needs to utilize the time elapsed variable to look like this:

```
function update(surface, telaps) {
  timecum += telaps;
  changeScreen = false;
  if (timecum < minDuration[idx]) {
    // do nothing, we're not allowed to skip it yet
  } else if (timecum > maxDuration[idx]) {
    changeScreen = true;
  } else if (sgx.input.Engine.get().mouseLeft.wasPressed()) {
    changeScreen = true;
  }
```

```
if (changeScreen) {
  if (++idx === title_screens.length) {
    changeState('mainmenu');
  }
}
}
```

But while we've fulfilled our legal requirements to the business, we haven't fulfilled the quality requirements to ourselves! It still looks amateurish because the images change instantly. Almost all graphic engines have a way of applying alpha channels and color filters to textures to lighten or darken them. So by tinting the image according to the time elapsed, it can appear to fade in.

To do this, we reuse the accumulated time variable timecum (which is equal to all the previous telaps values added together) to make the screen fade up in 1/3 of second, like so:

```
color.a = sgxMin(1, timecum * 3.0);
color.r = color.g = color.b = color.a;
surface.setFillColor(color);
```

Note that we clamp both the alpha and the color range between 0 and 1.

From here, it is a simple matter to add a state machine into the code to separate the cases of fading up, waiting for a key press, and fading out again. Since the fade up action evokes a sense of anticipation, it is generally slower than the fade out, where our first line is instead

```
color.a = 1 - sgxMin(1, timecum * 5.0);
```

Note that fractional numbers are written into the code in both cases, but never used. This is an aide-memoire that the numbers are indeed floating point, and that it is permissible to tweak them by small fractions without fear of breaking anything. This is useful if you have an overly fussy producer as it lets them make changes they think are important without interrupting the programmers! (We'd also move them into configuration files for external tweaking, but they serve here as educational examples.)

Main Menu

The main purpose of this screen is to navigate as quickly as possible into the game. Having already optimized this UX flow, the changes we make affect the underlying implementation. In Space Bounce, our buttons are as follows:

- Music on/off
- Sound on/off
- Instructions
- Credits
- Start Game

It would be very simple to look at the index of the widget to determine which button had been pressed. However, this can cause problems when widgets are added or removed, as you'd have to rearrange all the code to compensate.

Instead, attach a user-definable attribute, called user_data, to every widget and use that instead. Since the user_data attribute can be controlled by our application, without the system touching it, we can use any data type that best suits. One suggested implementation is to use bit masks, with the most significant 16 bits indicating the style of button (e.g., a Boolean button that triggers a screen change, or a toggle that doesn't) and the least significant 16 bits to indicate the identifier for the button.

```
onGUIWidgetSelect: function(widget, position) {
  var uid = widget.getUserData();
  var widget_type = uid & 0xff00;
  var widget_id = uid & 0x00ff;
  var newState = undefined;

  switch(widget_type) {
    case 0x0100: // change state
      if (!transitioning) {
        newState = newStateMap[widget_id];
        transitioning = true;
        musicChannel.startFadeOut(0.4, function(e) {
          changeState(newState);
        });
      }
      break;

    case 0x0200: // basic action
      musicChannel.toggle();
      break;
  }
}
```

Note that we utilize the closure functionality in JavaScript to make the newState variable available within the callback. Since all code should be written with an asynchronous mindset, this is a boon to development. Note also that it is perfectly acceptable to have a group with only one button in it, as we do when toggling music, as this eliminates the need for nested switch statements.

▓ **Tip** Never label a group or an ID with the number 0, as any broken data will invariably default to zero or false (or undefined, which can evaluate to false), causing false positives.[8]

---

[8]In the first builds of *Grand Prix Manager*, Damon Hill was winning almost every race, despite the code being balanced such that he shouldn't be able to. The bug was ultimately tracked down to the fact that his car was number 0, and when another car spun out of the race one of its fields was set to 0 (false) and giving an extra and occasional boost to Damon's car!

Within this code, we're still using the transition variable to block repeated clicks on the same button. We could have achieved the same effect by disabling the button after it was clicked. If you take this latter route, then it is wise to have two states on the button: disabled and grayed. The first stops it from being actioned in any way, such as by clicking on it, while the second changes its visual appearance. In this way, you can prevent the events, without diminishing the appearance of the game with gray buttons suddenly appearing as the screen slides out of view.

Instructions and Credits

Ostensibly, both of these screens show static data as described by the design. Our first draft would probably be a single texture. Initialized with this:

```
var creditsImage;
(function ctor() {
  creditsImage = loadTexture("resources/credits");
})();
```

And handled with draw-update pairing, like this:

```
function draw(surface) {
  surface.setFillTexture(creditsImage);
  surface.fillRect();
}

function update(surface, telaps) {
  if (sgx.input.Engine.get().mouseLeft.wasPressed()) {
    changeState('mainmenu');
  }
}
```

Note that this does not provide any facility for text translation, nor for animations or multiple screens. But it does provide an MVP, and this is all that might be necessary to release the game. To improve upon this, the static textures could be replaced with an array of textures that you can cycle through by using a variation of the title screen code.

However, this is still only a minor step forward. Or even a step back, since there is no facility in that code to go backward to the previous screen! Solving that is our next task.

We can start our improvements by asking the player to click the screen to turn the pages forward or back. Drawing the turn-page button images directly onto the screen texture, and checking for the clicked position in the update loop, can save time and effort.

```
function update(surface, telaps) {
  var xpos = sgx.input.Engine.get().getMouseX();
  var middle = surface.getWidth() / 2;

  if (xpos < middle) {
    page = sgxMax(0, page-1);
  } else {
```

```
    if (++page == page_count) {
      changeState('mainmenu');
    }
  }
}
```

This can be further enhanced by introducing a transition state that slides one page off, and the next one on. For this, we have two variables (page and other page[9]) and an accumulation of the time that the page has been turning, which is used for positioning the page image on the screen.

```
function update(surface, telaps) {
  if (/* we are turning the page */) {
    pageTurnTimecum += telaps * turn_speed;
    if (pageTurnTimecum > 1) {
      pageTurnFinished = true;
      page = otherPage;
    }
  }
}
```

You can use this to render both pages, like so:

```
function draw(surface) {
  x = pageTurnTimecum * surfaceWidth;
  surface.setFillTexture(pageImages[page]);
  surface.fillPoint(x, 0, sgx.graphics.DrawSurface.eFromTopLeft);

  x -= surfaceWidth;
  surface.setFillTexture(pageImages[otherPage]);
  surface.fillPoint(x, 0, sgx.graphics.DrawSurface.eFromTopLeft);
}
```

From here, there are two types of obvious improvements that we could make. The first is to use an effect that makes the pages look curled, as they would be if we were turning the pages in a book. The second is to replace textures with proper UI screens that contain animations or the buttons necessary to navigate between multiple screens. Since this is a space game, where paper will probably have been surpassed, the former isn't in keeping with our theme, so we'll implement the second idea and adapt our texture rendering code to use a UI object instead.

---

[9]We don't say "next page" because we want to reuse the same code when turning the page back to the previous one.

■ **Tip**   Once the basic instruction pages are present, you have the opportunity to be truly creative, since if an idea doesn't work, you still have a fully functional game that can be released. In a maze game, for example, you could present the instructions in maze where you can go right *or* down, to different instruction pages, and use the clues on the first page to guide you through.

The rendering of a UI page—rather than a texture—is a direct translation of the original. This is only possible, however, because we had the foresight to include x and y coordinate offsets in our interface-rendering code.

```
function draw(surface) {
  x = pageTurnTimecum * surfaceWidth;
  interfaceList[page].draw(surface, x, 0);

  x -= surfaceWidth;
  interfaceList[otherPage].draw(surface, x, 0);
}
```

Since we now have an interface on-screen, with proper buttons, we also need to introduce a state to prevent the buttons being used while the transition is in progress. We've seen that code previously, so we don't need to replicate it.

One observation to make here is that we're using buttons on the interface to switch between screens. If your game is released solely on touch-based devices, then a swipe motion would be better because that's more in keeping with the interface that the player expects from that device. Since ours is a browser-based game, we'll adopt buttons since they're universal.

At this point, it looks like there's little more that can be added. However, since our game is about jumping we could add our spaceman jumping across between the screens. We already have the graphics and pageTurnTimecum, so we only need to add the rendering.

```
function draw(surface) {
  playerWidth = gVars.textures.player.getRegionWidth(0);
  x = sgxRescale(pageTurnTimecum, 0, 1,
        -playerWidth, surfaceWidth + playerWidth);
  surface.setFillTexture(gVars.textures.player, 0);
  surface.fillPoint(x, 0, sgx.graphics.DrawSurface.eFromTopLeft);
}
```

103

Everything here has been seen before, except the rescale method that turns the time accumulation value from a value between 0 and 1 to a screen position. Notice how the position starts at -playerWidth (which means that the player is invisible at the left extent) and ends at surfaceWidth + playerWidth (which means the player is invisible at the right extent). This provides a clean way to introduce and remove the character without any special code or animations. Also, it means that the spaceman is traveling slightly quicker than the background, giving a more interesting visual parallax effect—for free.

Summary

The keywords for this chapter were *consistency* and *flow*. Consistency covers branding, font choice, the six states of a simple button, and the adoption of interface conventions and visual dynamics to cause the least surprise to a player.

Flow covers how the player moves from one screen to the next with the effortless ease of a flowing stream and how to navigate an individual screen. You looked at polishing these interactions and transitions, and the widgets included on each of them.

Once you learned how to move between screens and how to make them more interesting, we went over the practicalities of what these screens needed, including the title screens, main menu, instructions, and credits.

CHAPTER 6

In-Game Visuals

The Importance of Being Pretty

For most people, game polish and shine imply visuals. And that implies artists. While there is a lot of work for the artists to do in this area, it is not exclusively their domain. After all, if it were, the only words in this chapter would read, *Dear artists —please work harder and make it prettier!* It's a comment with zero substance, for sure. Instead we'll look at concrete examples of how traditionally simple visuals can be improved with a little code, a little art, and a little combined effort.

■ **Note**   This chapter concentrates on the in-game experience. To see how this fits into the larger picture, go back to Chapter 5.

The Game Framework

The draw-update approach shown in Chapter 5 provides almost everything needed to support better visuals in our main game. The one element that's missing is that of a viewport, through which you exhibit the game world to your player.

Room with a Viewport

All rendering of our game should take place through a viewport. This is a window on the total game world, indicating exactly which portion the player is able to see. This is exactly the same way that a camera's viewfinder shows you which part of the world you're photographing—if you move the camera, you change the view. In Space Bounce, the shaft appears as shown in Figure 6-1. However, due to screen size constraints and reasons of gameplay, you only show the player the portion indicated within the rectangle.

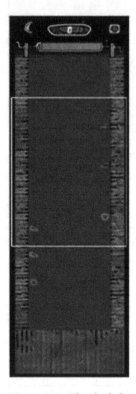

Figure 6-1. The shaft that exists in the world and what's visible on-screen

To ensure that the correct portion of the game is shown on-screen, you create a rectangular viewport through which your world is viewed. (Using the camera metaphor, assume its viewfinder is focused on the center of the viewport.) Its coordinates refer to the absolute world coordinates (world space), with the top-left corner of the viewport rendered at the top left of the screen. Consequently, all the game objects are offset by the appropriate amount with code, such as the following:

```
surface.fillPoint(viewportRect.left - x, viewportRect.top - y);
```

In this manner, all of your game objects can move uniformly up the screen in unison by moving only one object, the viewport.

However, this approach can be taken further, since it is not necessary for the viewport and the world to have the same scale. That is, your viewport on the world could be 1024 pixels wide, whereas your screen is only 320. In this scenario, your code needs to do more than simply offset the point; it needs to scale it too. 3D games require this functionality from the start, because it is included in every 3D API. Today, you only need a uniform 1:1 mapping. But it is a consideration for the future.

___

■ **Tip** If you have the opportunity to render your 2D game with a 3D engine, or understand how transforms can handle non-uniform mappings, then do so. It enables you to create special effects with scaling and zooms that take almost no extra effort. Creating such effects by any other method would be prohibitively time-consuming.

___

Knowing that you should use a viewport, the next step is to control it. Each time the game updates, you must update the position of the viewport to show an appropriate part of the world. Although I have said many times that the player is not the center of the game world, when it comes to controlling the viewport, the player is a very large part of it. After all, what's the point of a game when you can't see any part of the player?[1]

In the first version of our game, we prepare the viewport, as follows:

```
viewportRect.left = 0;
viewportRect.right = surface.getWidth();
viewportRect.top = playerData.getViewportPositionY();
viewportRect.bottom = viewportRect.top + surface.getHeight();
```

And let the player determine the y coordinate, as follows:

```
getViewportPositionY: function() {
  return y;
}
```

Since we have a 1:1 mapping between world coordinates and screen coordinates, we don't need any scaling in the viewport. And since the world is exactly as wide as the screen, we don't need to offset the x coordinate.

With this code, the player is always drawn at the top of the screen (regardless of how far down the shaft he is) and the world moves around him. But this is only version 1.

So far, it looks like we've written a lot of code for no discernible gain. However, let's amend the viewport calculation code inside the game's update method.

```
var y = playerData.getPositionY();
if (y < 192) {
  y = 192;
}
viewportRect.top = y;
```

So far, we've changed the method name on the player, since we don't *really* want the player to control what's seen on-screen; we only want the player to influence it. Next, we cap the y coordinate to 192. In our world coordinate system, 0 is at the bottom of the shaft. Consequently, when the player gets within 192 pixels of the bottom, the viewport remains unchanged—meaning the world appears still as the player falls within it.

___

[1]A common problem in developing first-person shooters is that there is no player visible on-screen, so only the arm is drawn. Since this is generally drawn after the scene, it doesn't interact with the world.

This is a highly effective technique used in many platform games. Even when the character appears fixed in the same spot, the reality is that both world and character are moving together, at the same relative speed. You know that this technique is used is when you see the character walk onto the screen. The world is static, but it starts moving as soon as the character reaches a given position.

We can improve this code further by positioning the player a small way away from the top of the screen. Maybe we want the viewport to be 10 pixels above the player's head at all times, unless he's reached the bottom, in which case we clamp the viewport to 192, as before. To achieve this, we would amend it as follows:

```
var y = playerData.getPositionY();
if (y < 182) {
  y = 192;        // clamp to the bottom of the shaft
} else {
  y += 10;        // 10 pixels above the players head
}
```

This is left as an exercise for you to determine what happens if the 182 was actually 192.[2]

It is also left as an exercise to consider how you would implement alternate viewport control algorithms. How would you position the camera in a two-player version of the game? If the character could fall outside the game world, you might want the camera to follow the character for a while, but then slow down and stop, focusing on a fixed point in space as you watch the character disappear from the screen.

Of Image and Collision Data

At first blush, each object in the game needs only an image. However, if this object is to interact with others, it needs something else: collision data.

Even in a simple game like ours, there are benefits to be had by creating separate collision objects for the graphics. In Figure 6-2, for example, you see how the tools pipeline can generate the collision data automatically.

Figure 6-2. Generating collision data

---

[2]If 192 is used, there is a glitch near the bottom of the shaft as the viewport jumps from 203 to 192 in a single frame. Because this only happens at the bottom and therefore takes time to test, it's the sort of problem that can go unnoticed unless end-to-end testing is carried out.

First, the transparency of the image is used to determine the outline that is deadly to the character. (After all, if the character was "impacted" at the location of a transparent pixel and lost health, the player would feel cheated.) The deadly pixels are then encoded into binary for optimal storage, so the collision detection routines need only need a few bits of data via an "and" mask to see if a collision has occurred.

■ **Tip** It is typically better to do this offline, rather than try to compute collision maps in-game, because you can prepare the data in the exact form in which you need it for the game engine.

In games that are more complex, this benefit increases exponentially. A 3D mesh, for example, may have thousands of polygons, so checking each of them for a collision is very time-consuming. Instead, a low-polygon mesh can be created exclusively for collisions; it has a very low memory footprint and a high compute speed. Furthermore, the rendering mesh consists of arbitrary faces, whereas the collision mesh contains only regular spheres, making ray and volumetric tests very quick indeed.

About a Player

Having now realized that the viewport logic is only influenced by the player, we need to ensure that the rest of the game code follows suit. Originally, the player would implement a method, such as shown in the following:

```
isGameOver:function() {
  return y == 96 ? true : false;
}
```

This causes the level to display the Game Over message and offer a restart. However, the game need not end because the character is dead. Instead, it can continue for a few seconds, letting the player relish the death animation, before displaying the restart level option. So we invoke the state machine, as follows:

```
switch(substate) {
  // etc...
  case GAME_IS_PLAYING:
    if (playerData.hasPlayerExpired()) {
      setSubstate(GAME_IS_WATCHING_PLAYER_DIE);     }
  break;
  case GAME_IS_WATCHING_PLAYER_DIE:
```

And modify our player code to match the intention of the method, and not the name:

```
hasPlayerExpired:function() {
  return y == 96 ? true : false;
}
```

Notice that there is no difference in the internals of the method; only it's naming. However, isGameOver is incorrect. The game is not over because the player has died or reached the bottom. The *player* is over, not the game.

> *There are only two hard things in Computer Science: cache invalidation and naming things.*

—Phil Karlton

This naming ensures that all developers understand the precise intention behind the method for a high-quality code base. I'll cover more on the internal polish of code in Chapter 9.

Object Metadata

Wherever possible, you want to attach metadata to your objects in the asset pipeline. (See Chapter 11 for more on this.) This ensures a data-driven approach, whereby the game can be modified without affecting the code, allowing the changes to be made by developers of all disciplines.

For example, each texture file can contain more than one image. Our main character has six distinct regions depicting his climb-left animation, as seen in Figure 6-3.

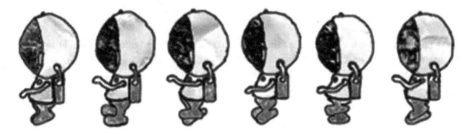

Figure 6-3. The spaceman character, presented in regions

From the artist's point of view, having all the images in a single file makes it easier to manipulate in the art tools, while the programmer has fewer assets to keep track of. From the computer's perspective, however, this can be a lot quicker on some platforms, because there is no extra time spent uploading each new texture from the computer's main memory into the graphics card, since only the region coordinates (called *UV coordinates*) need to be uploaded for each animation frame. Browser-based games probably won't see much improvement, but WebGL, DirectX, OpenGL, and anything on a console certainly enjoy the benefit of using regions.

Textures can also benefit from metadata describing the material that they represent, such as concrete, tile, or wood. In games where bullets are fired into surfaces rendered with specific textures, it is necessary to know which ricochet sound sample to play and which bullet hole to draw. By holding this metadata in the texture, this is easy to determine.

Animations also benefit from various elements of metadata. Events such as sound effects can be cued on specific frames in the animation to ensure that the audio is properly synchronized. The most common effect is that of footsteps, but it could also include deaths screams or gun reload sounds.

■ **Tip**   Don't trigger the sound on a given frame, since the animation system might play the same frame twice if the animation frame rate differs from that of the screen update. Instead, trigger on the rising edge as playback moves from frame A to frame A+1.

The other piece of useful metadata is references to the transitional, or glue, animations. In fact, these are probably the most important animations in the whole game! When moving between the stand and run animation, for example, it is usually necessary to include a short two- or three-frame animation of the character breaking into the run. This is to prevent the animation from "popping" between two distinct poses. You notice this a lot in games if you cause a character to perform an action midway through their current animation sequence. It is generally impossible to find the time to create an animation that transits from every animation to every other animation, so you should start with the most frequently seen. These are usually the ones to and from standing, run, prone, and jump.

■ **Tip**   If possible, trigger your animations from the AI code, not the other way around. In this way, the character will appear intelligent because their animations are always smooth and look preconsidered.

The Game Interface

Within the game, there are several elements comprising its interface, but this is the main case where less is definitely more. Every widget that you place on the screen is one more interruption to the game at hand. If you're building a simulator of some description (a flight sim, management game, and so on), then the interface *is* the game. But platformers, shooters, and the like need as much screen real estate as possible to increase the immersion of the playing experience.

The obvious solution is to reduce the size of the graphics on the interface, but this is usually answering the wrong question. The question is actually *How can I remove the need for this information on the interface?* The first version of Space Bounce had a depth counter, which was a fun way of comparing your progress on one attempt to the previous. However, at best, it added only minor value to the gameplay, and at worst, was a distraction, as your goal as a player moved from trying to collect as much halite as possible to descending as deeply as possible. It was removed with no impact to the game. All interface elements should consider the optimization trilogy of RRR—remove-relocate-represent.

Removing the Interface

If your game has multiple modes, then you should definitely hide the elements that do not apply to the current play mode; so if your first-person shooter has a driving section, there is no reason to show the speedometer at any point that you're not in a vehicle.

Look at your interface to see what can be removed from or moved into the game world. In a shooting game, you might have the following:

- *Health*. This is more important to most players than the score in a first-person shooter, so it usually needs to be represented somewhere. By applying this information into the game world, a deeper experience can be created. Maybe this involves the player dripping blood on the floor or moving more slowly when they have less health.

- *Ammo*. Another important first-person shooter staple. Could it be represented visually by having a bullet counter on the gun? Or by rendering the bullets left in the chamber of a six-shooter?

- *Time*. If there's a time counter in the game, how often is it used? A little at the beginning and a lot at the end, most likely. You could adapt its presence, size, and appearance via context, and introduce audio cues to indicate when time is getting close to running out. In a first-person shooter, you could you place the time on the player's watch, which is visible throughout, or incorporate it into clock towers (and the like) within the level. Audio cues such as clocks striking the hour fit well here.

- *Compasses and mini-maps*. These often appear together, despite one being generally redundant. If you know your next objective, then the only piece of information to which you need regular access is the direction of that objective. The map is a nicety, but once you've seen the map once or twice, you know the lay of the land (pardon the pun!) and can effectively navigate around the nearby obstacles, so the only information it conveys is the general direction in which you need to head. When the map also displays incoming enemies, as it would with radar, it's easy to move this into the game world by showing the display on a piece of equipment that the player carries. Again, you can also use audio cues to indicate when there is someone, or something, behind you.

Relocate the Interface

When you have removed all unnecessary elements, you can then look to see if any can be relocated to a secondary UI panel. Ask yourself, *Which of these features will be used throughout the game?* and *Which of these features might only be used once?* An option to review the level objectives might be necessary, but it is often a minor feature and so could move into a secondary in-game menu, where pressing two or three buttons is not going to affect the gameplay significantly.

An inventory or mini-map is a potential candidate here because it is something that could be opened temporarily based on a single click or key press. The game context indicates how long this might be. It could be programmed to disappear after 10 seconds, or it could wait until the player has moved 20 meters through the level, which indicates that the player has learned it sufficiently to play without the map for a while. The same could be true of time. Even levels that are entirely focused around time could work with the clock only appearing at vital points.

There are two types of in-game menus. The first relates to options that affect the gameplay. This might include inventory selection, reloading, map review, and so on. The second type pauses the game when invoked (thereby eliminating the need for a separate "pause game" button!), so the player can handle all non-game interactions, such as load and save, controller settings, video configuration, and an exit to the main menu.

Switching audio on and off is often considered a secondary feature, because people generally only ever play with the audio on or off; it is rarely changed frequently or mid-game. However, there is also an argument for keeping it on the main game screen, since people who like the audio on still need to mute it occasionally so that they can listen for important real-world events (such as train announcements and dinnertime!).

■ **Tip** Consider having separate volume controls for music, effects, and voice so that the player can adjust each to their own sensitivities.

Represent the Interface

Once there is nothing else to remove or relocate, consider which features could be better represented visually. A screen that reads *Health: 100%* is certainly informative, but it still takes a human a short while to parse. Having a health bar, with markers indicating immanent death, is better. Similarly, a face that becomes increasingly bloodied as you're being beaten works well.

The same approach works for devices like speedometers and clocks that have real-world visualizations. The latter being an interesting point in itself. Most people are now so accustomed to digital time, that it's become the primary means of communicating time to the player. However, to demonstrate the *passing of time*, it is the worst interface imaginable! Watching a sweeping second hand traverse the edge of a clock face gives you a much better connection with the time you're spending (wasting?) on a particular task. So if possible, and suitable, spend the time writing an analog clock.

On Different Devices

For all the complexities of console development, the one area that isn't difficult is the screen design, because one size fits all. There are a fixed set of possible screen resolutions,[3] and you, as a developer, simply support them as necessary.

For mobile and browser-based games, you have to contend with myriad different devices with differing resolutions and aspect ratios. A truly polished game handles them all. How you do that depends on available time, game genre, and so on.

For shooting games, you can usually specify an appropriate viewport and the game world will be rendered effectively on all devices. You then need to codify the user interface with a set of relative positions and sizes so that all UI elements are visible by being positioned on-screen and are large enough. For example, instead of writing a UI configuration file like this:

```
{ x: 205, y: 5, field: 'score' }
```

You may instead include meta-information like this:

```
{ x_align: 'right', x_offset: 20, y_align: 'top', t_offset: 5, field: 'score' }
```

In this way, the text always justifies to 20 pixels of the right-hand side of the screen, regardless of how wide that screen is.

If you are intending to support a wide range of devices, then you need to create several versions of this file for small screens, medium screens, and so-stupidly-big they-wont-fit-in-your-pocket screens! At game start, the device capabilities are checked and the appropriate file is loaded and used. These capabilities should include the screen resolution and the DPI (dots per inch) if available, and on both axes. This may also require the loading of larger or smaller typefaces and interface graphics, so that the images don't become unreadable on smaller screens.

■ **Tip** Always determine the minimum supported resolution near the start of the project, often determined by the size of the user base. For any project that is non-trivial, the development time usually means that a mid-range device today will be considered the low-end device upon completion, so worry less about spending excessive time supporting them.

For larger screens and those with non-standard aspect ratios, you often have to letterbox your game with black borders. While it might feel defeatist to be wasting so much screen real estate, you can be sure that the graphics will appear as the artist intended. If you're keen to go one further step, then you could use these black borders to include the heads-up display or other interface features that otherwise would obscure the main play area.

---

[3]Ranging from 480p to 1080p

The Input Interface

So far, we've been concerned with minimizing the interface that the player sees and hears. Let's now consider the interface that the player uses to feed information into the computer—usually the keyboard, mouse, controller, or touch screen. The control system is the most important connection between the player and the game. Get it working as soon as possible. Hone and tweak it throughout the life cycle of the game by the most game-savvy players you know. (Yes, *players*, not developers!)

The same rules apply: remove, relocate, represent.

Work through each key shortcut, button, or hot spot to determine if it's truly necessary. At the start of Space Bounce, there were two buttons: one to jump left and one to jump right. Each was assigned a separate key. The buttons were fairly large to ensure that the player always hit them, and so was never frustrated by missing a jump. But since a good button size was never formally decided, they were removed, and the jump direction was determined by whether you touched (or clicked) in the left-hand side of the screen or the right. It's difficult to get a button larger than half the screen.

But you can!

It quickly became clear that after adopting the rule "you cannot change direction mid-flight," the only time that jumping was permissible was when clinging to a wall. And when clinging to the left wall, there is only one direction in which you can jump: right. At this point, the whole screen became a button to trigger whichever action was contextually accurate.

■ **Tip**　Web-based games are often played on tablets and rely on touch areas more than key presses. You should always provide key equivalents for the desktop players, provided you don't give them an unfair advantage in doing so.

Gradual Changes

By far the most important element of improving the game is to do so in stages. Small stages. Each one raising the standard of the game, as a whole, by a little bit. By doing so, you ensure that you can always release something complete and good, without ever getting bogged down in a sprawling mess of a 100 ideas that you want to do. Each "just takes a moment," but ultimately sucks all available time into its development.

This section covers a number of basic features present in many games to show a simple progression from basic functioning components to more polished versions. This is not to say that you should read the last paragraph for each section and build that feature first; far from it. Indeed, that would miss the point of building out the features gradually so that you can learn what works for your game and how to incorporate those ideas into other areas. Instead, work through each to see how a feature, such as the score, can begin life as a simple text routine at the start (when you only need something functional as you test the gameplay) to something with multiple textures and effects by the time that you've finished. By following the journey, you also witness the domino effect of making such changes in order to get an appreciation of how work can produce unintended consequences that can delay a project.

Furthermore, the code and ideas presented here are meant as suggestions and guides; by no means do they represent the end of the journey. There can never be too much polish. You will probably imagine many more improvements to those I've suggested.

Interface Buttons

While it is a bad idea to change the look of the standard interface widgets within a game, there are often improvements that you can make across the board.

First, for mouse-based platforms, you can utilize the hover functionality (not found on touch-screen devices) to modify the button slightly when the player is over it. This highlights the fact (pun intended!) that the graphic on the screen is interactive and available for use (a fact that may not be obvious during the first play through.) It doesn't need to be anything more than a separate frame with a slightly lighter button face.

Additionally, you could provide tooltips, which are small textual descriptions describing the action of the button. Again, these require a platform with hover capabilities. To prevent the play area form being obscured, they are unlikely to appear mid-game.

Finally, although changing the button style in mid-game is bad, having a color tint to reflect the player's livery is a nice touch—particularly in a multiplayer game where the in-game menu is colored differently so that you can see who has control at that time.

The Background

As the spaceman drops down the shaft, no one is looking at the background, so the first version is usually as follows:

```
surface.setFillTexture(gVars.textures.backgroundShaft);
surface.fillRect();
```

Filling the whole area with a single texture is more interesting than a black background, but it still looks like the background of a computer game screen rather than the rear wall of the shaft—no matter how nice the graphics. So, more can be done. Mostly obviously, it could scroll using the viewport area as a guide.

```
var bgy = viewportRect.top % screenHeight;
surface.setFillTexture(gVars.textures.backgroundShaft);
surface.fillRect(0, bgy-screenHeight, screenWidth, bgy);
surface.fillRect(0, bgy, screenWidth, bgy+screenHeight);
```

Notice that the background texture fills the screen, but nothing more. Therefore, as soon as it starts scrolling off the top of the screen, we need to draw a second version underneath it to continue the illusion and hide the gap at the bottom of the screen.

■ **Note** This also requires that the texture tiles perfectly on the y axis, so that the top edge matches the bottom.

While this is nice, we can achieve a much nicer effect by scrolling the background at a slightly different speed to the main walls. In our game, the background has no interactive effect on the gameplay, so we can do anything with it we like. A slightly slower movement gives the impression of depth and distance, as it produces a parallax effect. Our rule about having something move on every screen works well here since two things need to move at different relative speeds for motion to be perceived. (Do you remember the viewport moving at the same rate as the character?) One method for achieving this slower scroll is by starting the background at a different Y position, and moving it onto the next Y position at a rate different from viewportRect.top.

```
var bgy = (viewportRect.top/2) % screenHeight;
surface.setFillTexture(gVars.textures.backgroundShaft);
surface.fillRect(0, bgy-screenHeight, screenWidth, bgy);
surface.fillRect(0, bgy, screenWidth, bgy+screenHeight);
```

This does have one minor problem insomuch as the background of the shaft extends into the sky. We can eliminate that by drawing a special sky texture over the appropriate area, obscuring the shaft background that has previously flooded the screen.

```
var skyHeight = gVars.skyPositionY - gVars.shaftHeight;
var bgy = viewportRect.top - gVars.skyPositionY;

if (bgy > -skyHeight) {
  surface.setFillTexture(gVars.textures.backgroundSky);
  surface.fillRect(0, bgy, screenWidth, bgy + skyHeight);
}
```

This was one of those times where the quicker option—from a development standpoint (rendering more textures than necessary and overfilling the screen)—was taken.

Our final addition comes in the form of an Easter egg![4] A 100-million-year-old egg to be precise, because we're going to add a moon to the sky. Normal developers would draw it to the background sky image and be done with it. Special developers would render it separately, as follows:

```
var moonX = 30;
var moonY = viewportRect.top - gVars.moonPositionY;

surface.setFillTexture(gVars.textures.moon, 0);
surface.fillPoint(moonX, moonY, sgx.graphics.DrawSurface.eFromTopLeft);
```

For those polishing their game as much as possible, there are two other improvements possible: positioning the moon at the appropriate position in the sky and adapting the moon to show its phase (full moon, new moon, etc.) according to the current date!

---

[4]An addition that only ardent players will notice. This is fully covered in Chapter 10.

Personally, I don't want to obscure the score by allowing the moon to be positioned near it, so I've ignored the first idea. But for the second, I found some freely available code online[5] to compute the moon's phase, and then I used a black circle the same size as the moon texture to obscure the necessary part of the moon. Since the sky is also black, you don't notice the overlaid texture. The new moon texture therefore has two regions and appears as shown in Figure 6-4.

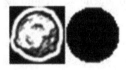

Figure 6-4. Moon texture, with secondary eclipse region

From here, there's a basic calculation to eclipse the moon.

```
// phase: 0=new, 0.5=full, 1.0 waning
var phase = SunCalc.getMoonIllumination(new Date()).phase;
var moonWidth = gVars.textures.moon.getRegionWidth(0);

if (phase < 0.5) {
  moonX -= phase * moonWidth * 2;
} else {
  moonX += (1 - phase) * moonWidth * 2;
}
surface.setFillTexture(gVars.textures.moon, 1);
surface.fillPoint(moonX, moonY, sgx.graphics.DrawSurface.eFromTopLeft);
```

It's not scientifically accurate, but close enough for now. With more time, I could have created 30 different moon images—one for each day of the month—for a more accurate reflection of the moon's phase.

■ **Caution**   Review the license agreements very carefully when taking source code from web sites. In most game projects, you will only be able to use MIT and BSD 3-clause licensed code. The *Game Developer's Open Source Handbook* has a lot more guidance in this field.

---

[5]See https://github.com/mourner/suncalc

Scoring System

While the primary goal of the character in this game is to collect trilithium halite, the goal of the *player* is to obtain a high score. Any game that has such a primary driver should devote the most polish to that area of the UI. It is the area they'll see most often, and it's what they'll objectify. To that end, let us walk through the six phases of polish we added to the visuals of the scoring system in Space Bounce.

During development, all we needed to know was the score and that the game was awarding us the right number of points, so our code was simply:

```
surface.drawText(data.score, 205, 5);
```

This is clearly inadequate, since the color and style of the text is governed by whatever has come before it. So we created a method that would handle any given style.

```
GameStyle.drawText = function(surface, style, value, x, y) {
  if (style === "score") {
    surface.setFontColor(sgxColorRGBA.White);
  } else {
    surface.setFontColor(sgxColorRGBA.Red);
  }
  surface.drawText(value, x, y);
}
```

This helps eliminate some simple bugs that might occur when the machine reaches this method via a different code path to normal, but it's nothing that couldn't have been achieved by other methods.

The next step is the realization that the information drawn on screen might not be the same as the data presented in the computer's memory.[6] If our score is 100 and we've just been awarded 10 points, our score is 110, and that is what should appear on the high-score table. But, if we decide to gradually increase the score on-screen in increments of one, then we need to store both pieces of information.

For this, we create a new class, GameStyleText, which holds the following:

- The current value

- The target value, toward which the current value gravitates

- The rendering style, color, and typeface

- A draw method

- An update method with the usual telaps parameter

- Set and change methods to modify the value. This ensures that we never change the value directly, like good OO programmers!

At no point do we refer to the value as the *score*, since we may wish use this method to represent other parameters in the game, such as bonus.

---

[6]It's a similar argument to why the rendering mesh should be different from the collision mesh.

Consequently, we can use the update method to create some visual interest when the score changes. In this implementation, we are ignoring telaps for the simplicity and brevity of example.

```
function update(surface, telaps) {
  if (targetValue > value)  {
    ++value;
  } else if (targetValue < value) {
    --value;
  }
}
```

The motion of the numbers will certainly catch the eye, and there's no reason why the routine can't be improved to count first the units, then tens, then hundreds, and so on. This is left as an exercise to you, the reader.

An alternate route is to render the numbers slightly larger whenever the score is changed. This improves on the previous solution because multiple changes are visible if they are awarded in quick succession—something that wouldn't happen with the counting solution. We start with the following change method:

```
change: function(newValue) {
  targetValue = newValue;
  value = newValue;
  attackTimecum = 0;
  decayTimecum = 0;
}
```

We have introduced two variables in the form of attack and decay. They take their names from the ADSR envelope used in audio synthesis, which represents attack-decay-sustain-release. We're interested in the first two parts: How quickly does the number grow on-screen to show the new score (the attack)? and How quickly does it revert to its usual size (the decay)?

■ **Caution**   Depending on your use case, you may wish to check for the instance where the change method is called with an identical value. That is, do you really want the score flashing if nothing had been added?

When adding scores, it is preferable to have the size increase quickly, since it's important, and decay much slower. This is contrary to giving the player a bonus, where it's better to increase it gradually so that the player gets to see the effect longer.

These ideas lead us to amend the code to the following:

```
function update(telaps) {
  if (attackTimecum < 1) {        // growing
    attackTimecum += telaps * 15;  // speed of increase
  } else {                         // collapsing
    decayTimecum += telaps * 5;    // speed of decrease
  }
}
```

We can then amend the render code to see how far through the attack or decay cycle we are (between 0 and 1) and compute an appropriate size for the text as somewhere between 20 and 30 pixels.

```
var pulseMinSize = 20;
var pulseMaxSize = 30;
var pulseDelta = pulseMaxSize - pulseMinSize;

var pulseSize = pulseMinSize;

if (attackTimecum < 1) {         // growing
  pulseSize += attackTimecum * pulseDelta;
} else if (delayTimecum < 1) {   // collapsing
  pulseSize += (1-delayTimecum) * pulseDelta;
}
```

We would then like to draw this with the following:

```
surface.setFontCharacterSize(pulseSize);
surface.drawText(value, x, y, sgx.graphics.FontParameters.AlignMiddle);
```

Well, we would *like* to. Unfortunately, there is no method for setFontCharacterSize, so this seemingly simple addition requires several extra changes. First, we need to switch from the standard font routines supplied to a custom renderer where the characters are drawn using textures whose size can be changed. (Or we extend the library code and implement the same functionality, which is preferable but not always possible.)

Next, we need to write our own code for aligning this text to the middle of the screen. This involves three passes, one to compute the width of the string, one to determine the new start X position, and a third to perform the rendering itself. The first and third passes are almost identical. To wit:

```
width = processScore(value, x, y, false, pulseSize/20);
x -= width/2;
processScore(value, x, y, true, pulseSize/20);
```

But even this is not completely perfect! It's fine for our game, since each number in the font is of a fixed width. But imagine what would happen if the font was proportional: 111 would be more narrow than 888. A jump in score from 111 to 888, although unlikely, might be possible, and therefore the numbers will appear to jump slightly as the difference in widths would cause the text to shake.

A better (I dare not say *best*, as someone will disprove me!) solution is to determine the middle digit, center it, and place all the other digits around it. However, I don't think anyone will notice because the speed of the action, and so I have not written this code. Learning and accepting cases like this is the start of a road toward pragmatic programming. By understanding which code has a genuinely positive affect on the game, and which code doesn't, you can focus your time on the areas that need it most. But, if you really have nothing else to work on, I leave it as another exercise for you!

■ **Caution**   This is a good example of how an apparently simple request can escalate into lots of new code. Before committing to time estimates on such requests, the development team needs to first consider the complete design to understand the system capabilities, and then compare them to the design requirements.

The End Game

In character-driven games, the player sees the fail state a lot more often than the win state. So it makes sense to vary and polish this as much as possible. If you think how tired voice acting sounds once it's been repeated several times, imagine what it's like rewatching the end game sequence. Improving this involves adding two new states: an end game animation and the wait for a button press to restart.

The first part of the end game sequence is to keep the game in the background, ideally animating. We accomplish this easily by considering the end sequence no differently than the rest of the game but with a separate substate that prevents the player from controlling the character.

The second part introduces a small animation of the words *Game Over*. From a rendering perspective, the texture is rendered at a size directly proportional to the total time accumulated and accomplished by the code you saw in Chapter 5.

Once the image is full size and you're waiting for a key press, you can further enhance the sequence by fading out the screen slightly, indicating that nothing else is going to happen.

```
function drawScreenFade(surface, t) {
  var color = new sgxColorRGBA(0,0,0,/*alpha=*/sgxMin(t, 1)/3);

  surface.setFillColor(color);
  surface.setFillTexture(gVars.textures.backgroundShaft);
  surface.fillRect();
}
```

Ideally, you'd want to move these magic numbers into a configuration file or a data file generated by a stand-alone tool so that the more creative team members could make more involved fades.

There are many other improvements that are possible in this game, but this should give you an idea of what is necessary to achieve the minimum level of acceptable in-game visuals.

Summary

To make the game pretty, you learned about the visuals from every angle, starting from the game world and the mechanisms involved in using a viewport, to the player and its relationship to the game as a whole.

By examining the game interface, you saw how the optimization trilogy of remove-relocate-represent can aid the visuals by treating the interface as part of the game itself, not something that needs to be drawn on top as a distinct part of it. This minimization approach was also considered when looking at the input interface, and reversed when considering ways of improve the background image.

This chapter also introduced a lot more code here, not least with fully worked examples of how a simple score panel could be improved with visual metaphor and styling.

CHAPTER 7

Audio

Hear, hear...

Of all the disciplines, game audio is probably the most neglected. (Except maybe testing!) Every time you hear of a game developer who added the audio at the end of the project, you know they're a game developer who's neglecting the audio experience. There are probably many reasons as to why it's left until last, but the importance of good quality audio cannot be understated. The classic example of watching a horror film without the sound demonstrates how necessary audio is to establishing mood and building an environment.

What is also universally true, in the most part, is that the audio team is the smallest within the company. (Except maybe writing!) Logically speaking, the audio team needs a minimum of a sound engineer, a composer, an audio programmer, a tester, and a producer. The engineer will create or source the sounds to improve your game. The composer will write the title music, company jingle, and other themes within the game. The programmer will know how to make best use of the music and sounds when incorporating them into the game. And the producer should ensure that the brief is being kept and settle any arguments between the others!

Physically speaking, those five roles may be handled by as few a one individual.[1] Sometimes with that individual additionally being responsible for another discipline, such as general game coding. Indeed, it is very rare to not find at least one musically inclined person in every game development team. It tempts many teams, especially the small independents, to look inward first for their audio needs. This also points to the reason for including a producer—preferably an external one—in the audio team, because if the audio programmer has a personal interest in music they might overcompensate in this area to avoid the drudgery of bug fixing. Or they may have aspired to be a musician earlier on in life. Should the producer allow them to use their music at the start of the project, but ultimately decides to hire external composer, the programmer is liable to feel disillusioned. (Programmers are often sensitive souls!) Consequently, the producer needs to be direct from the start about the use of placeholder assets (such art, prose, but especially audio) to manage expectations.

---

[1]It's always better to have a different tester to the implementer. However, when testing the audio the composer and sound designer should be there (at least once after beta) to ensure that every sound that they've made has been correctly incorporated. Only they are able to hear a sound that's missing!

S. Goodwin, *Polished Game Development*, DOI 10.1007/978-1-4842-2122-8_7

Content

Most games use the same four categories of audio:

- Music
- In-game effects
- Voice acting
- User interface sounds

Depending on the genre and style, you may be heavily skewed toward one type of resource over another. You may also find that some audio resources don't fit neatly into one category, such as a musical motif that accompanies the company logo. Is it music because there's a melody and harmony, and it requires a composition? Or is it a user interface effect, because it appears only as part of the start-up splash screen? Regardless of whether or not you have an in-house audio engineer, you always need to clearly outline the requirements for each part of the project.

Music

Within the five letters of the word *music*, there are a seemingly infinite array of possibilities and opinions for what type of music you need. And how much. By already deciding the genre of your game, you have eliminated many options, and by knowing the make-up of your team, you can eliminate many others.

As always, the overriding key concept is *theme*. It must "fit" within the theme of your game. If you are building a game whereby you are trying to escape a jungle, then a music score involving futurist synthesizers and rocket effects is probably not going to create the right ambiance. Similarly, a game set in a serene underwater world will probably use music with a much slower tempo, and fewer intricate melodies. That is not to say it isn't possible to compose for a juxtaposition of styles, but it's harder to do so.

■ **Caution** Fitting within a stereotype makes it is easier to sound good, but more difficult to sound great.

In popular culture, there are several well-known cases of this. Prior to the release of *Star Wars* in 1977, most sci-fi films depicting space environs had electronic sound tracks representing a futuristic vision of high technology. The composer, John Williams, was able to show that a symphony orchestra was able to capture the same *feeling* with traditional instruments, without using the same sounds. He didn't try to re-create the high-tech sound of a synthesizer using the orchestra (nor should he, since the worlds within *Star Wars* have an old "worn in" feel about them; of a system living under an oppressive empire for decades), but instead created a new musical language for the film that inspired other sci-fi directors to consider large symphonic scores for their films.

If we exclude finances for a moment, the first two questions are *What music do you want?* and *Where will it go?*

Spotting

This is the process that the producer and the audio lead work through to determine what music is needed. This might be in form of formal compositions, or short musical phrases known as *stings*. It can begin at any time, and may take place several times during the course of a project.

In the first instance, it is necessary to work through the game design document to provide an overall feel and scope of the audio work necessary. The design will be adorned with verbal flourishes that will (subsequently) need to be documented so that the team knows what audio to expect. Naturally, there will be a lot of boilerplate audio, such as button sounds for the title screens and menus, but the spotting process will also highlight the various levels that need specific music, what the player should be feeling at each point, and even the approximate length of gameplay.

This same spotting process takes place for the audio effects in the game. Every object must be noted, along with every action it has, or could have. Observe everything, and later prune out those effects that offer little enhancement to the game, or would be too problematic to include. Instead of noting a sound for 'gun' you should have a list that includes every type of gun in the game as, even to the untrained ear, a handgun sounds significantly different to an M16 assault rifle, so separate effects are needed.

Even within an individual object, there may be multiple actions. A gunshot is an obvious effect, but don't get so carried away that you forget about sounds for:

- Reload

- Safety catches on and off

- Cocking

- Bullet ricochet (on what type of surfaces?)

- Bullet casings dropping on the floor (what type of floor?)

- Jamming

For example, if it's a shooting game, this process determines which weapons are used and which ricochet effects are needed, according to the types of surfaces those weapons' bullets hit.

Since you also need to consider *all* objects that act or react within the world, it's often better to work from the textures, meshes, and other assets rather than the design document. If there's a level featuring a jukebox, for example, is it playing when the character enters the room? Can the character stop it from playing? Can the character change the song? And so on. It is then the producer's responsibility to ensure that a level designer doesn't arbitrarily add similar objects, like radios, into the level, thereby increasing the work of the audio team. Similarly, if the image of a floor tile changes, it might no longer look like wood, in which case an alternate sounds for the footsteps, bullet ricochet, and casing drops would be needed.

After considering the objects in the world and the sounds they have (and how those sounds change), consider the player itself. What sounds do they have? Do events change them? These events could be akin to invincibility in *Super Mario*, or times where the player is taken to a mini-game. Considering the Space Bounce example, we might break this down as follows:

1. Preparing for the descent.

2. The winch/rope snaps.

3. The initial panic scenario, as the player begins to descend.

4. The gameplay itself, as the player falls.

5. Reaching the bottom.

As a team, you can then determine the music that you want at each section and how it is to be achieved.

The scope of music and effects within a typical game are fairly standard, so in order to help plan those spotting meetings, I outline the usual audio suspects and revisit the spotting process for music.

Pregame Music

It is popular, and usual, to have music over the title screens to better cement the user in the game world. If the first screen your player sees is a silent, static, image, the ideas of "game" and "fun" is very much diminished. A musical backdrop is simple to determine and prepare, since the screens are static in nature and so won't conflict with other audio since none is playing. Either it's a short musical motif to accompany the company logo, in which case it's timed to synchronize with the logo fading in and out. Or it's a long piece of music that loops for as long as the player is on the screen. This is usual for the main menu.

If you have the time, or money, you can easily improve the user experience in this area by varying the music between the main menu, the credits page, and instructions, for example. A simple fade out, and fade in, is all you need to show polish.

If you're able to go further, then each menu can have unique elements layered over the score. For example, if the character can be customized and has its own menu screen, then introducing the main character's theme would foreshadow those places in the game where it reappears. The Pod in *LittleBigPlanet* makes use of this idea in its menu system.

▪ **Tip** Repetition of musical motifs and themes adds meaning to the score, and experience as a whole. It can be used throughout the game, not just with the main character themes.

In-Game Music

The scope of the in-game music varies drastically among projects. It could be a minimalistic or ambient score that comprises of only a few notes here and there just to give the loudspeakers something do, or a fully layered orchestra whose score changes dynamically according to how well the player is doing in the game.

■ **Tip** When working on very "low-tech" platforms, an ambient score is easier to loop, since the loop point exists when there is nothing playing. By contrast, a fast-paced drum loop has no such gap.

To begin, you should break down each section of each level in the game to determine what the player is doing and what they are feeling. For puzzle games, this is often simply "solve stuff," making the spotting process very easy. It most likely includes a musical loop, with spot effects each time a puzzle element has been solved.

In a larger game, it might break down into the following:

- Exploration and/or navigation

- Escalation, as future events or locations are discovered

- Danger or combat sequences

- Stealth sequences

- Success or failure audio

Each one might deserve its own musical style, stings, and so on.

It is usually better to have some music than none at all, so having background music is a (technologically speaking) easy win. That is not a hard and fast rule, however. Any game set in the horror genre, or has large elements of suspense, would do well to ignore that rule and use the music to punctuate the scenes, and use silence to scare the player who know that *something* is about to happen, or jump out at them, but the silence will not give them any clues as to *when.*

Once you know the type of scenes that the music will support, consider how the musical transitions happen.

In the simplest cases, you might just have a tune that loops indefinitely while the level is being played, perhaps with overlaid stings to signify change. Alternatively, you might increase the tempo of the music as the level approaches its end. Most puzzle and casual games adopt this approach since it is easy to determine if the game is coming to an end or that the player is in genuine peril.

■ **Tip** Always add a second or so of silence at the end of any music that is intended to loop. This gives the player a gap of silence that reminds them to do something, and stops the audio becoming too annoyingly repetitive, like a stuck record or an alarm clock.

With some more effort, your composition might involve many interwoven melodies that are dynamically adapted, or faded in and out, during the course of the game, with an intelligent composition engine changing the score in real-time to match the players state within the game. This latter approach is common on role-playing games, where a standard theme might have different variations depending on whether the player is exploring or in battle mode.

A fully dynamic system is expensive to create from a technological point of view, and involving from an artistic one. Both composer and programmer need to work hand-in-hand so that every note played is correct, and is synchronized to the rest of the score. You can mix this either horizontally or vertically.

Horizontal mixing is when you take two pieces of music, and play them sequentially. (Or almost sequentially). You might trigger one when the onMusicComplete message is triggered, or use a playQueuedMusic method to allow the audio engine handle it automatically. A good audio engine makes the two sounds follow each other seamlessly, without a gap, making it sound like one continuous piece, as shown in Figure 7-1.

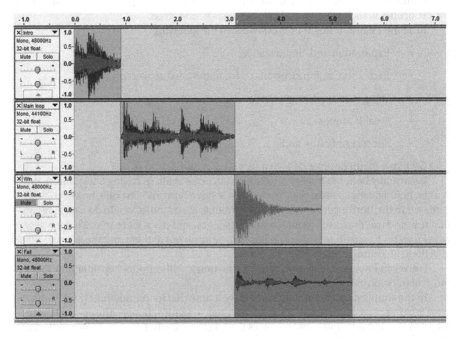

Figure 7-1. Horizontally queued music, without gaps, shown in Audacity. Note the muted "win" track.

A typical horizontal mix consists of the following four parts:

- An introduction
- A standard gameplay loop
- An ending for winning
- An ending for losing

During the spotting process, you may uncover several different "standard" game loops for use within a single level.

If you wish replace a music cue before it has completed playing, then you may instead need to adopt a vertically mixed solution, since it is often very difficult to know exactly where within a large WAV file where a second WAV file can start and still sound good. (And even if you know, does the audio engine and sound drivers have sufficiently low latency to change the sounds over without you noticing?)

On the other hand, you might need to fade out one piece, and just before it's inaudible, fade in (or start at full volume) the second piece. When a platform, such as HTML5, is unable to support effective audio queuing systems due to poor latency, it can usually still play back multiple audio channels using this method, and so this becomes the second-best option. The audio signature here looks like Figure 7-2.

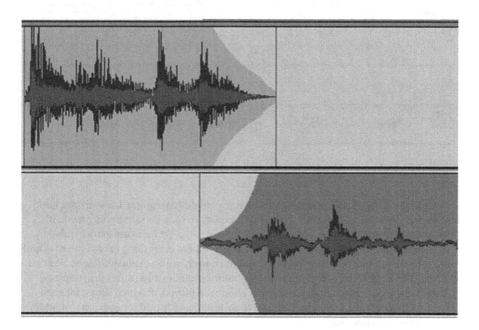

Figure 7-2. Fade out and fade in

As a last resort, you can simply stop one piece from playing, and start the next. This sounds unpolished in almost all cases, and very few platforms support a single audio channel and so is rarely a good option.

Vertical mixing, as shown in Figure 7-3, is when a single sound file contains multiple pieces of music already synchronized within it. All stereo music could be said to be vertical, as it contains two tracks (one for the left speaker, and one for the right) which are synchronized at the source. For a game score, you might have three or more pieces all held within a single file. Each piece would be on its own *channel*. The audio engine is then able to fade each channel in or out, creating an ever-changing ambiance with the game world, reflecting the player's state. Naturally each channel must work as a stand-alone piece of music, as well as in combination with any (and all) of the others. The way in which individual layers can be activated are triggered by logic in each of the particular game sections we saw earlier; exploring, combat, and so on.

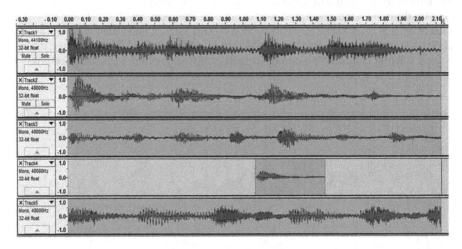

Figure 7-3. *Vertical mixing, with concurrent playing tracks, one of more may be muted*

Consider a traditional pop song in which you might have guitar, bass, drums, and keyboards, performing alongside the vocals. In order to keep song sounding fresh, it's likely extra keyboards will be added during the final verse. Or there are extra cymbals and hi-hats in the chorus. There might be a section where everything except the bass and voice is removed, before all the instruments return to create an explosive finale. You can re-create this approach by working with your audio engineer and sound programmer, to determine which combinations of tracks should be played, at which times, for each scenario. Often a battle sequence requires more energy, so introducing drums (or adding more drums) is a quick win.

Such techniques can be difficult on the "low-end" platforms (like HTML5), or without customized code, but is still technically possible.

> ▓ **Note** Older games often used in-built sequencers (called *trackers*) to make vertical mixing almost trivial to implement from a technical point of view. The trade-off was that it took more conversations between audio programmer and composer to get it right. Nowadays, more impressive fidelity can be achieved by preparing the audio in a recording studio, which, despite the more limiting mixing control, usually trumps the benefits of having a fully dynamic score.

Postgame

There are several places where a post-game screen can occur. Of course, it includes the *You win* and *You died* screens at the very end of the game, but it can also include interlude screens between levels. It never needs to be very complex, but having a short respite after each level, where you can display the current state of the game and let the player have an (enforced) break, is a good idea. It's also a good point to trigger some music. This could be dynamic with the game choosing one of three different themes, depending on how well you managed in the preceding level. Or it become a singular theme, such as a reprise of the introductory game music, or even just a sound effect of a cymbal crash.

Sourcing Music

In an ideal world, you'd have the resources to hire an audio engineer, either as a permanent member of your team, or under contract for the duration of the project. In this case, the solution to sourcing the music is easy since you simply assign them the work and they use their skills, knowledge, and ability to create work to your specification. For those with a more limited budget, there are still other options to consider.

The first consideration is to separate the concept of "music production" into its three primary parts. To begin, there is the act of composition—writing a series of notes that produce a melody. Then there is the production, which turns those notes into something that can be heard. And finally, there is the recording of that production.

Even a simple melody takes time and money to produce, so be aware that it will generally involve a significantly higher cost than using an existing composition. There are several ways to legally use an existing composition without incurring such high fees. The first is to use something old. In the United Kingdom, copyright in a composition expires 70 years after the death of the composer; or, when multiple composers are involved, after the death of the last remaining composer.[2] While this rule obviously includes the old masters, like Beethoven, Chopin, and Mozart, it also includes those that died in 1946, or earlier,[3] which includes more contemporary names like Gustav Mahler, Claude Debussy, and Erik Satie. In non-classical fields, the work of rag pianist Scott Joplin is now out of copyright, as is Fats Waller.

---

[2]Note that this only applies to the composition, not the performance. So you will still need to hire someone to play or program the music.
[3]If you're reading this in 2016.

■ **Caution** Copyright law is not only a very large topic, it's also a very local one. What is true in one country, is not necessarily true in another. The "70 years after death" rule varies too, with equivalents labeled as "50 years after death" or "50 years from death," or "30 years after publication" and even "Posthumous works first published between 1923 and 1977 ... are protected for 95 years." Since your game is likely to find its way into more countries than you have lawyers for, always err on the side of caution.[4]

The second way of using an existing composition is to license it. There are many companies, and individual composers, that are willing to license you a piece of music under a 'royalty free' basis. They include the following:

- `http://beatsuite.com`
- `http://incompetech.com/music`
- `http://purple-planet.com`

Generally speaking, you will pay a one-off fee for the right to use the music in your game, either on an exclusive or non-exclusive basis, without having to pay a royalty for each time the game (and therefore the music) is played. The cost varies according to the size of game, the number of platforms on which you are releasing, and so on. As a rule of thumb, exclusive[5] rights are usually twice the cost of non-exclusive. And, of course, if someone else has already licensed the piece, you will not be able to get it on an exclusive basis. In many cases, the composition will be licensed with an existing recording, thereby saving money in the performance.

Although many producers dislike the idea of licensing existing music, citing reasons such as *It's not original; It wasn't composed for our game, so it won't fit;* or *What if someone has heard it in another game?*, these arguments hold little water. There are hundreds upon thousands of wannabe musicians in the world, and the Internet has given them all a platform upon which to sell themselves. Consequently, the chance of someone else stumbling across the same piece of licensed music is incredibly small. The primary reason for a small indie not using licensed music is the time it can take to find something you like—especially if you have something specific in mind.

The third most common way of getting music is to use work released under one of the Creative Commons licenses. If there are thousands of works in the virtual vaults of music licensing companies, then there must be millions under a Creative Commons (or CC) license. These can be used without a fee, provided you follow the rules set out in the specific license.

---

[4]Only the briefest examples are available on the usual resources such as Wikipedia and `http://imslp.org/wiki/Public_domain`. Always consult with a lawyer for anything created within the last 150 years, just to be safe.
[5]As the name suggests, exclusively licensed works won't be made available to anyone else after you have secured rights on them.

■ **Note** The license dictates what you are allowed to do with this version of the music, but it doesn't prevent you from asking the composer to license the music to you under a different license. Perhaps for a fee. So CC music is the start of the search, not the end.

The following describes the most common Creative Commons licenses.[6]

CC0

This the same as a public domain license, whereby you can do anything that you like to the piece. It is quite rare to find good music under this license, but it is included here for the sake of completeness.

CC BY

CC BY is the Attribution license, which states: *This license lets others distribute, remix, tweak, and build upon your work, even commercially, as long as they credit you for the original creation. This is the most accommodating of licenses offered.*

It can be used in games because you can do anything to the work, provided the original composer(s) has their name involved. This attribution need not be in the game itself (although it's only fair to do so) and could be a README file, or included on the company or game website. If you are using a lot of CC music, then it's usual to attribute them on the website, so to not overfill the in-game screens.

CC BY-ND

CC BY-ND is the Attribution-NoDerivs license, which states: *This license allows for redistribution, commercial and non-commercial, as long as it is passed along unchanged and in whole, with credit to you.*

For most games developers, material released under this license is potentially unusable. That is because adding the music to a game might be considered as "adapting" it. The full license details this thus: *For the avoidance of doubt, where the Work is a musical work, performance or phonogram, the synchronization of the Work in timed-relation with a moving image ("synching") will be considered an Adaptation for the purpose of this License.*

It is tricky to know whether any part of the game would become synchronized to the music, or whether the composer would consider it so. Additionally, if you used the music only to accompany the title screens, it might also be considered synching. Even fading out the music early, or using just the chorus, might be considered as "derivative," so (without a lawyer on hand to assess your specific needs) it is best to find an alternate license. (Or contact the creator to ask whether you can license it another way.)

---

[6]As noted at https://creativecommons.org/licenses/.

CC BY-NC

CC BY-NC is the Attribution-NonCommerical license, which states: *This license lets others remix, tweak, and build upon your work non-commercially, and although their new works must also acknowledge you and be non-commercial, they don't have to license their derivative works on the same terms.*

This is identical to the CC BY license, except that you cannot use it in commercial projects. Even if the game is free-to-play, any commercial elements within it (such as in-app purchases) would mean that the game is commercial, and therefore breaking the terms of the license.

CC BY-SA

CC BY-SA is the Attribution-ShareAlike license, which states: *This license lets others remix, tweak, and build upon your work even for commercial purposes, as long as they credit you and license their new creations under the identical terms. This license is often compared to "copyleft" free and open source software licenses. All new works based on yours will carry the same license, so any derivatives will also allow commercial use. This is the license used by Wikipedia, and is recommended for materials that would benefit from incorporating content from Wikipedia and similarly licensed projects.*

This is identical to the CC BY license, except that you must share it, and any derivatives, under the same license. This means that you are allowed to create a version with fade or that only uses the chorus, but under the proviso that you included the new recording with the game in a way that it could be taken and used by someone else.

You can abide by this license by including an alternate recording in a file entitled *my game-the soundtrack.zip* on your website. However, there is some debate as to whether the "share alike" component applies to just the music file, or if it "infects" the rest of the game, requiring you to open the game. (Those who have experience in open source game development will appreciate the complexities of mixing GPL and non-GPL source code.) In this case, it is best to first ask the composer whether they'd create a license exception for your game, explaining the situation. Then, consult a lawyer, since the composer might have intended the SA to only mean the audio component, but in reality, the composer might have written some extra stipulations on their website that supersedes or augments the license that they applied to the work. It will then be a decision based on community commitment whether the lawyer argument trumps the desire of the composer.

CC BY-NC-SA

CC BY-NC-SA is the Attribution-NonCommerical-ShareAlike license, which states: *This license lets others remix, tweak, and build upon your work non-commercially, as long as they credit you and license their new creations under the identical terms.*

Although this is a combination of both the NC (which prohibits you from using it in commercial games) and the SA license (which requires you to release your changes to the world), this is technically no more limiting that the BY-NC license, since conforming to the SA component by releasing your audio files is not difficult. Naturally, if your lawyer has recommended against using BY-NC, they would also recommend against this.

CC BY-NC-ND

CC BY-NC-ND is the Attribution-NonCommerical-NoDerivs license, which states: *This license is the most restrictive of our six main licenses, only allowing others to download your works and share them with others as long as they credit you, but they can't change them in any way or use them commercially.*

In short, ignore it! There are too many potential issues in using this license. You should ask for an alternate CC version or simply find other music. There's a lot out there, after all!

In-Game Effects

The scope of in-game effects is staggering; it covers every single second of the game. Although this might appear daunting and necessitates an audio designer to create every sound from scratch (and therefore increases the expense), it is often unnecessary. Many games are able to make use of stock sound libraries that provide a set of standard effects like explosions, gunfire, screams, and so on. Like their partners in royalty-free music, these effects are either cash-free or sold for a fixed fee, allowing you (and everyone else) to use them in their projects without paying a separate royalty each time they are played. Some such libraries are found at the following websites:

- http://freesound.org
- http://freesfx.co.uk
- http://audiojungle.net
- http://www.soundsnap.com

While it is true that some keen game players will be able to tell when an M16 reload has been used in multiple games, most are too busy playing to care.[7]

The sounds in these libraries often come in two forms: dry and wet. The dry version is the raw sound, without any effects applied. This allows you and the game's audio designer to apply appropriate amounts of echo, reverb, and so on, to the sound so that it fits in the environment of your game. After all, the sound of a gunshot varies whether it is in a large church made of granite, or in a small wooden barn, or even underwater. The wet version of the sound includes a set of standard effects to make it usable in the majority of licensees.

Outside of AAA products or those with a dedicated audio programmer resource, it is rare to have a game audio engine that can take a dry sample and apply the necessary effects to make it sound correct based on the game world's surroundings, so your team needs to control where the various sounds can be heard, and therefore which ones need to be generated offline.

---

[7]The most famous reused sound effect is probably the Wilhelm scream, which has appeared in over 300 different films, but almost no one outside of the media industry knows or cares!

■ **Note**   Until the release of *2001: A Space Odyssey* in 1968, few people considered the possibility of sound in space. However, space itself is a vacuum, through which no sound can travel, so director Stanley Kubrick decided to forgo all sound effects when viewing space. He opted instead for music. This might be too much realism for a non-art project game, but certainly something worth considering.

Each sound might also need to be supplied in multiple environmental versions. A bullet ricochet might need variations depending on whether the bullet hit concrete, wood, metal, or carpet.

There should definitely be alternate instances of most sounds to provide some variety between repeated playback. The number of variations is directly proportional to the number of times the player is likely to hear it. So a musical sting for when player "picks up the final key" might have only one version, whereas a gunshot might have four or five. Not all of these versions need to be created by the audio designer, however, as it might be possible to change the pitch of the sample, or add some other effects, from within the game engine to create enough difference.

Voice Acting

Voice acting is something that is very easy to do, but hard to do well. Witness the number of professional game developers who are spending more on voice actors than an indie might spend on their entire game—and it still sounds bad! Painfully bad. There are two main elements to this:

- Bad script

- Bad acting

As you'll see in the chapter on writing, everyone believes that they can write dialog. Whereas in reality, most write cliché tropes that wouldn't engage a bunch of kids on a sugar rush. So unless you're proven in this area, either hire a writer or drop the voice component.

Bad acting comes down to the relationship between the actor and their director. In games development, the director is usually the audio engineer or the producer. It is the director's job to ensure that the actor understands the lines and the motivation for saying them. For example, is the word *mate* meant as a friendly gesture or a warning? Is the line sarcastic? If the actor is voicing an accent or dialect that isn't their own, do they understand the nuances of it? What is the correct pronunciation?[8] If you can provide a reference, then do so. It is also their job to ensure that the voice matches the character in feel and texture. It is up to you whether you adhere to the Hollywood stereotypes of using an English actor with a British accent to play the bad guy!

---

[8]Pronunciation changes according to location too. The word *bath*, for example, has an "ar" sound in some parts of the United Kingdom, and an "ah" sound in other parts.

■ **Note** Games, like films, let the player suspend disbelief for a while. Anything that pulls them out of this immersive situation breaks that spell. Even things as simple as having someone using British terminology (such as *bonnet* and *boot*) but speaking with an American accent (when an American would say *lid* and *trunk*) are confusing to an audience. (Even if they can't tell you why it's confusing.)

The director should also be there to ensure that the lines are delivered naturally, and not as if they're in some over-the-top melodrama. Or worse, delivered as if they are trying to mimic a more famous actor. This second case can have legal repercussions too, since only Bruce Willis sounds like Bruce Willis. If you use someone that sounds like him in a game, there might be a legal case that argues you're using his fame and credibility to bolster your game by implying he was involved.

Even a voice-over explaining a training level involves some level of acting expertise. While you might be able to get someone from Fiverr (`www.fiverr.com`) or VoiceBunny (`voicebunny.com`) (for example, or one of the many specific voice talent agencies representing professional actors) to record the speech for you, it's probably worth keeping it as text-only if possible, because bad voice acting shows less polish than having none at all.

User Interfaces

The audio in a typical user interface can be found from the same audio libraries as the in-game effects. You generally need only a few standard effects, such as for when buttons are clicked and when screens change. Most importantly, however, since these sounds will occur a lot, it's important that they are not particularly prominent or memorable because they quickly tire the ear. Unlike the in-game effects, it is usually best to not have multiple variations for these sounds.

■ **Tip** You can often make use of a general MIDI drum kit (as found in most PC sound cards) as an inexpensive way of making clicking sounds for buttons.

Preparation

Having acquired the audio resources, you next need to organize them. This is more involved than simply loading them into your game editor, however, as there are other parameters to consider.

Normalization

In the audio world, there are two main forms of normalization: peak and loudness. In each case, the volume of the original sound is changed so that the peak (or loudness) of the entire sample is at a given level. In Figure 7-4, you can see an un-normalized sound.

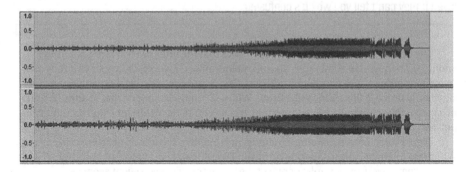

Figure 7-4. An un-normalized stereo sound

In contrast, Figure 7-5 shows one that is peak normalized, vertically filling the maximum range of the sample so that the noise occupies a smaller fraction of the total output.

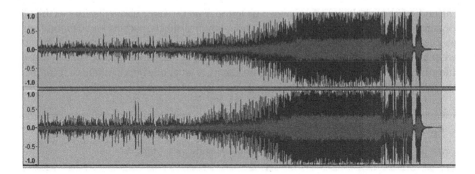

Figure 7-5. A peak normalized sound

The reason for doing this is so that the maximum extent of the sample can be used; that is, all 256 possible values of an 8-bit sample are used, or all 65536 of a 16-bit sample. This ensures that the largest dynamic range is used to represent the sound, and therefore it is of the highest quality and lowest noise.

When working with sound, the audio designer should ensure that each sample is created and edited at the highest possible resolution (usually 24- or 32-bit) and then normalized when exporting it as a 16-bit sample suitable for the game engine.

It is also possible to normalize any existing sample with free tools such as Audacity. To do this, simply select the entire sample and click Tools-Normalize. You won't increase the clarity of the sound, but it will be uniform with all other samples.

This process has one unfortunate side effect. That is, quiet sounds (like footsteps) now sound as intense as loud sounds (like explosions.) To compensate for this, you need to create a denormalization process suitable for the game engine. This will apply a volume to each sound, returning it back to its correct level.

Audio Groups

The first stage is to collate all the sounds into groups: bullets, ricochets, footsteps, explosions, and so on. Every group should be matched with other sounds in the sample category, and with approximately equivalent volumes. If the volumes vary by too much, create a separate group. That allows both "loud guns" and "quiet guns" to use the full bit range of the sample data.

Each group now contains a set of sounds where every sample within the group is relatively correct. The group itself is then given a denormalization factor, so that when the sound from within a group is played and mixed with others, it is at the correct relative volume. In code, this might appear as follows:

```
var audioGroups = {
  "guns_quiet" : {"factor": 0.4},
  "guns_loud" :  {"factor": 0.7},
  "explosions" : {"factor": 1.0}
};
```

With the code being parsed as follows:

```
var groups;
for(var groupName in audioGroups) {
  sgx.audio.Engine.get().assignNormalizationGroup(groupName,
  audioGroups[groupName].factor);
}
```

Naturally, this data could be loaded as a data-driven resource, instead of being included directly in the source code.

With the group normalization assigned, the samples are then defined.

```
var audioDataset = {
  "bullet1" : {"group": "guns_quiet" },
  "bullet2" : {"group": "guns_quiet" },
  "bullet3" : {"group": "guns_loud" },
  "explosion1" : {"group": "explosions" }
};
```

And assigned to each group.

```
var sample;
for(var sampleName in audioDataset) {
  sample = sgx.audio.Engine.get().registerGlobalSound(sampleName);
  sample.setNormalizationGroup(audioDataset[sampleName].group);
}
```

This idea could be extended by having a denormalization factor for every sample to handle cases where sounds need to be amplified or quieted slightly on a sample-by-sample basis. However, these cases are so limited in practice that they are not considered here. (And there is no reason why a separate group could not be created for such edge cases.)

You will see how these denormalization factors are applied in the game engine when I discuss the mixer.

Audio Metadata

Depending on the game and the needs of the audio component, you may have a set of metadata alongside each sample. This includes parameters about the sound that needs to be expressed to the game or audio engine. A typical example is the range of the sound, beyond which the sample is considered inaudible. (Given that all sounds are normalized, you need to explicitly set this information, because you can't rely on quiet sounds to be naturally buried under the louder ones, since there might not be any louder sounds playing at that time.)

Something we *don't* consider in the audio engine are parameters that affect other gameplay elements. A bullet ricochet sample, for example, shouldn't need to indicate that this is the sound for a *concrete* ricochet, and that the bullet-hole texture necessary is rendered as bullet_hole_concrete3.png, because that information should have been generated by the game when it detected that the bullet had hit concrete. The audio data should be thought of as a slave to the game, not the other way around.

Metadata, such as the audible outer range, is loaded and assigned in the same way as the normalization settings, through an external data file and applied to each sound. Some engines might like to use "range groups" akin to normalization groups.

In our game, we go beyond the standard "outer range" parameter to create a little more realism. (Although, to be honest, in a game of this scale it's unlikely whether anyone would notice it!) That is, we have two range parameters: inner and outer.

The inner range indicates the distance within which the sound will be equally as loud. A jet engine, for example, measures 140 decibels at a distance of 100 feet. It measures much the same at 200 feet. So there is an inner range at which we consider the volume to be identical. There is then a fall off between the inner range (at maximum) and the outer range (where its volume is 0) that is considered to be linear. This is represented in Figure 7-6.

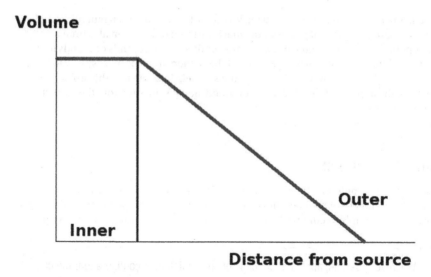

Figure 7-6. *Inner and outer ranges of audio falloff*

▓ **Tip** In the real world, volume decreases on a logarithmic scale, and not a linear one as suggested here. Most audio drivers handle this automatically, so it is an exercise for the reader to adapt this, if necessary.

Naturally, in order for this to work, all sounds must be given a position in the game world. Consequently, there must also be a "listener position" so that the audio engine can determine how loud or quiet each sound is relative to that listener.

```
sgx.audio.Engine.get().playSoundAt("explosion", positionExplosion);
...
sgx.audio.Engine.get().setListenerPosition(player.position);
sgx.audio.Engine.get().setListenerOrientation(player.direction);
```

Of course, UI sounds are not played with position information. They appear at the same volume, panned centrally to the speakers.

Multiple Files

As I've alluded to throughout this section, there is generally more than one sample attached to a single sound. A ricochet or gunshot may have three or four variations to stop the ear tiring of it, or from sounding like a stuck snare drum from a 1980s drum machine! It is usually the responsibility of the game code to determine how many variations of each sound are to be used, and how they are sourced. The two simplest ways to create variations are as follows:

- Have the audio engineer create them

- Tweak parameters in the audio engine for pitch and reverb

143

What is necessary, however, is knowing how to distinguish between multiple samples that play the same sound. Not just from the machine point of view, but also from a human's point of view. An engineer may create hundreds or thousands of sounds for a game, and if there is a problem with any one of them, there must be an easy way to fix it. A bug report such as "gunshot was too loud" doesn't help indicate that the problem lies with the fourth variation of the M16 gunshot sound, and it's missing from the correct normalization group.

That's where conventions come in!

Naming Convention

The one thread that pulls all others together is the naming convention. Without it, file names such as "bullet1" would be commonplace, impossible to understand, and prone to error with every sample needing to be assigned explicitly into a normalization group.

■ **Tip** Wherever possible, apply the principle of convention over configuration. You can eliminate metadata with judicial and effective use of file names.

My approach is as follows:

1. Categorize all sounds as general game, interface, or level specific.

2. Create directories for these.

3. Subcategorize each according to the object that emits the sound.

4. Create directories for these.

5. Determine the actions of the object and the sound that it makes. Name it accordingly.

6. Quantify the default normalization group and properties of these sounds.

7. Append a _01 to the file name for the first sound. A _02 for a second variation, and so on.

8. Add a meta file, if necessary, to override the defaults.

Let's look at some examples.

```
level/prison/bars_open_01
level/prison/bars_close_01
level/prison/bars_lock_01
level/prison/bars_unlock_01
```

Here you can see four sounds that only appear in the prison level of the game. They all belong to the "bars" object, because that's the word preceding the underscore. The bars have four actions (or properties) that cause them to make a sound: being opened, closed, locked, or unlocked. There is also one variation of each of these sounds, so we append a _01 on the end. When we want to trigger an "unlock" sound, for example, we *don't* do this:

```
playSound('level/prison/bars_unlock_01');
```

Instead, we would more likely have a member function on the object itself, and call it like this:

```
this.playLevelSound('unlock');
```

Assuming all game objects descend from a common base class (or have an injected method), they can use the common playLevelSound method. The playLevelSound method knows to which object it's attached (it'll be "this") and which level the game is at (either because it can ask the parent that spawned it or query the global game state), and can so generate the file name directly.

It is then a simple matter to see how many bars_unlock samples there are in the game and pick one at random. The code might appear like this

```
GameObject.prototype.playLevelSound = function(action) {
var name = 'levels/' + GameState.level.id + '/' + this.name + '_' + action;
var count = AudioEngine.getSamplesCalled(name);
var index = ('00' + Random(1, count)).slice(-2);

AudioEngine.play(name + '_' + index);
}
```

There is an extra bonus here. You can use the object name as the normalization group. Because it's part of the file name, it can be automatically assigned when the sound is first loaded.

■ **Tip**   In development mode, always report an error when a normalization group cannot be found, because it's a sign of missing data or a misnamed sample.

Another example might be the standard game sounds for a bullet ricocheting from a brick. That could be called

```
game/bullets/ricochet_brick_01
```

The approach is the same as the unlocking sound on the bars. In this case, however, in addition to including the normalization group in the file name (it's called ricochet in this case), the second parameter (brick) indicates on which surface the sound is applied, thereby eliminating that piece of metadata.

For the most part, it is simple to implement this type of audio system; as an extra special bonus, the approach makes it very difficult to make mistakes because any missing parameter can be highlighted early on by the tool chain.

However, depending on your game engine, you may need to do some extra work for the *game* code to know that the *audio* code has four samples for the ricochet.

■ **Caution**   Games built to work across the Web need extra work since HTTP does not allow you to enumerate files on a remote server. Instead, you need to include a manifest file, or similar, to indicate the sound names that exist, so that they can be downloaded and enumerated.

Playback

Having prepared all of our samples and being able to load them into the game, we have to consider how they will be heard by the player. This includes:

- Position of the listener relative to the sound sources

- The denormalization groups

- The user's audio volume settings

The metaphor we follow here is of a mixer in a recording studio.

The Mixer

The mixing desk is a formidable-looking piece of equipment, with hundreds of dials and switches that can affect every nuance of the sound. In reality, they're all quite simple as each track contains identical functionality to every other track. Furthermore, sets of tracks are grouped together so their collective volume can be varied in one action. We've seen an example of this already with the denormalization groups. However, there are other use cases, and by chaining these groups together, we have a fully flexible audio playback system.

To begin, each sound is assigned a mixing output that details the volume and pan information for the sound. Both ranges are stored as floating-point numbers: the volume between 0 and 1, and the pan between –1 (left) and +1 (right).

```
CMixOutput.prototype.reset = function() {
  this.fVolume  = 1.0;
  this.fPan     = 0;
}
```

At each mixing stage, the parameters are affected by the appropriate mix settings while, at the end, these parameters are then validated and applied to the sound itself.

```
CMixOutput.prototype.validate = function() {
  this.fVolume = sgxRange(this.fVolume, 0, 1.0);
  this.fPan = sgxRange(this.fPan, -1.0, 1.0);
}
```

Throughout the pipeline, each sound is on its own *logical* channel. This is distinct from a *physical* channel since, in many cases, the hardware may not have enough channels to playback audio from all requested sounds. In these cases, our audio engine must consider the importance and volume of each sound and make an informed decision as to which samples should be assigned to which physical channel.

Naturally, the volume mixer settings affect every logical channel because it is impossible to tell which samples may get culled should the audio engine become exhausted of physical channels.

The following are the stages of the mixing pipeline:

1. Gameplay logical

2. Gameplay control

3. Technology

4. User mixer

5. Device mixer

At each stage, the volume is multiplied by a factor to increase or decrease the volume, while a panning effect is added to (or subtracted from) the pan variable. Let's now consider the meaning and purpose of each stage.

Gameplay Logical Mixer

The gameplay logical mixer affects the parameters of the sound on a logical channel, according to the gameplay logic. So, if the sound is a beep emanating from a computer in the game, and the computer can be switched on or off, then the gameplay logic has the ability to affect its volume.

```
CLogicalChannel.prototype.updateLogicalMixer = function(time_elapsed) {
  this.pMixOutput.fVolume *= this.volume;
  if (this.muted) {
    this.pMixOutput.fVolume = 0;
  }
}
```

■ **Note** We continue to pass the time elapsed variable through to each mixer so that fades and other such audio effects can be easily processed.

Gameplay Control Mixer

The gameplay control mixer allows us to change the volume and pan based on elements within the game that can be controlled by something other than the game object emitting the sound. Most of the time, this refers to the distance between the player and the sound source. This requires us to set up and maintain three parameters:

- The sound source position

- The listener position

- The listener orientation

While all should be self-explanatory, splitting the listener into two parts may need further explanation. This is necessary to facilitate cases where the listener is split across two different concepts, as is the case in a third-person game. Here the listener position would be reflected by the character you are following since you'd only want to experience the sounds that they could hear. However, you'd want the orientation from the camera, so that objects emitting sounds, which appear on the left of the screen, would appear from the left speaker.

Calculating the volume is therefore a simple matter of considering both the inner and outer ranges where the sound is audible, and affecting the volume thus.

```
var fromPos = sgx.audio.Engine.get().getListenerPosition();
var distance = fromPos.getDistance(this.m_vPosition);
var inner = this.m_pAudioSource.getInnerRange();
var outer = this.m_pAudioSource.getOuterRange();

if (distance < inner) {
  // m_fVolume *= 1, which is a no operation
} else if (distance > outer) {
  this.m_pMixOutput.m_fVolume = 0;
} else {
  var volumeDistance = sgxRescaleExtern(distance, inner, outer, 1, 0);
  this.m_pMixOutput.m_fVolume *= volumeDistance;
}
```

A similar technique is used to determine the pan position within the stereo field. In this case, however, the mathematics is a little more involved.

```
var vectorOrientation = sgx.audio.Engine.get().getListenerOrientation();
var vectorTowardObj = new sgxVector3f(this.m_vPosition);
vectorTowardObj.sub(fromPos);

var cross = vectorOrientation.cross(vectorTowardObj);var dot =
vectorOrientation.dot(vectorTowardObj);
var angleBetween = sgxToDegrees(sgxAtan2(cross.getMagnitude(), dot));
```

```
var isObjectToRightOfListener = (vectorOrientation.y*vectorTowardObj.x >
                                 vectorOrientation.x*vectorTowardObj.y);
var pan = 0;
if (isObjectToRightOfListener) {
  if (angleBetween < 90) {        // in front and to the right
    pan = sgxRescaleExtern(angleBetween, 0, 90, 0, 1);
  } else {                        // behind, and to the right
    pan = sgxRescaleExtern(angleBetween, 90, 180, 1, 0);
  }
} else {
  if (angleBetween < 90) {        // in front and to the left
    pan = sgxRescaleExtern(angleBetween, 0, 90, 0, -1);
  } else {                        // behind, and to the left
    pan = sgxRescaleExtern(angleBetween, 90, 180, -1, 0);
  }
}
this.m_pMixOutput.m_fPan += pan;
```

The next part of the control mixer is to affect fades, either in or out. This is the first practical use of the time elapsed variable. Since it's rarely useful to have a sound fading in and fading out at the same time, you can reuse most of the variables.

```
CMixChannel.prototype.startFadeIn = function(durationSeconds) {
  this.bFadingIn = TRUE;
  this.fFadeTime = 0;
  this.fFadeDuration = durationSeconds;
  this.bFadeComplete = FALSE;
}
```

During each update cycle, the fFadeTime is amended by the time elapsed.

```
CMixChannel.prototype.update = function(time_elapsed) {
  if (this.bFadingIn || this.bFadingOut) {
    this.fFadeTime += time_elapsed;
  }
}
```

Finally, in this section, a new fractional factor is computed.

```
CMixChannel.prototype.applyMixer = function(pOutputMix) {

  if (this.bFadingIn) {
    this.m_fVolume = this.m_fFadeTime / this.m_fFadeDuration;

    if (this.m_fVolume > 1.0) {
      this.m_fVolume = 1;
      this.m_bFadingIn = FALSE;
```

```
        this.m_pCallbackHandler.onFadeInComplete(this);
    }
}

pOutputMix.fVolume *= this.m_fVolume;
}
```

Although the bFadeComplete parameter may appear superfluous, it is often useful to trigger a stop event once the fade has completed. Since fades are often used to provide a gentle end to levels or menu screens, this allows the game logic to continue with the next screen without repeatedly polling the audio engine.

■ **Tip** Use events and callbacks whenever possible to ensure that audio and visual actions are synchronized as closely as possible.

Technology Mixer

The technology mixer step is used to compensate for any technological issues in the system. Our primary concern here is the denormalization step to reduce the volume of the samples to their usual level, which means the code is simply.

```
var normalizationGroup = this.audioSource.getNormalizationGroup();
var level = sgx.audio.Engine.get().getNormalizationLevel(normalizationGroup);

this.pMixOutput.fVolume *= level;
```

User Mixer

The use of the user mixer is the first time the actions from the player have a direct effect on the volume of the sounds within the game. The number of mixer channels over which you give the player control is up to you and your game, but I consider five to be a good maximum.

- Music
- Sound effects
- Voices
- Cut scenes
- Master

The first four allow the player to vary the intensity of each sound group, to compensate for their hearing or personal preferences. They might decide to mute your music, so they can listen to their own, but still want to hear the effects that indicate how the game is progressing. Similarly, they might increase the voices because they often convey important game clues and can get lost among the music and sound effects.

The final mixer is the master, which affects all channels equally. Also, if the user has decided to mute the entire game, the volume is considered zero.

```
this.pMixOutput.fVolume *= sgx.audio.Engine.get().getMasterVolume();
if (sgx.audio.Engine.get().isMuted()) {
        this.pMixOutput.fVolume = 0;
}
```

■ **Tip**   Even if the volume gets set to zero, you should still pretend that the sound is playing, and don't simply mute it. A muted sample is unlikely to trigger a "sample has finished" event, whereas a playing sample at volume 0 will.

The Hardware Mixer

The hardware mixer is the unspoken sixth mixer. In almost all cases, audio APIs translate the 0–1 linear range used to control the audio, into a 0–1 logarithmic range that affects the real-world acoustics of an audio signal. After all, 0.5 on a linear scale is what most people expect "half as loud" to be. Whereas in reality, it's probably closer to 0.9. If you are unlucky enough to not have such an API, or you are writing low-level drivers for your game, then you can get the same scale by computing a log table with.

```
scale = 600; // number of "units" in a 6 dB drop
for(i=0;i<tableSize;++i) {
  fLog = log10( i / tableSize ) / log10(2.0);
  volumeTable[i] = sgxFloor(scale * fLog);
}
```

Some devices may also require you to commit these parameters via a deferred settings mechanism. That also happens here.

■ **Tip**   Default all volumes to 75%. In this way, the player can increase or decrease the volume of any component.

Summary

After a gentile beginning looking at the different types of audio present within a game, we uncovered the process by which this audio is spotted and cataloged with all in-game objects and screens having their own set of sound effects or music loops.

From here, we looked at the legalities of sourcing music and special effects from an external composer, including the legal minefield of Creative Commons licenses.

To end, we studied the implementation of the audio system, including how sounds should be normalized (and then denormalized), grouped, and replayed. This latter point included both the multistage mixing process necessary to allow the game objects full control over their sounds and the playback methodologies that reflect the physical workings of sound in the real world.

CHAPTER 8

Writing

Everyone thinks that they're a writer. Everyone. How often have you heard someone say that, one day, they will sit down and write their memoirs? Or that they wish they had the time to write a novel? It's almost as if writing is an inalienable ability bestowed upon the entire human race. While musicians might believe themselves to be at the bottom of a producer's "want list," writers can take small comfort in the knowledge that they've been on the bottom rung of this ladder since the ladder was invented. So much so that few teams have historically had a writer, even as a part-time or contract position, and that only recently has it become an acknowledged role within a professional games team. And since it's not an area that interests most developers, it'll often languish until the end of a project before it's done. If at all.

It is not unusual to find a producer (or occasionally an artist, or very occasionally a programmer) to believe that they are capable of writing the script necessary for the game. They might not have a piano at home. They may not be capable of playing the piano keys in the right order to make a pleasing sound. But they *do* have a computer keyboard and they do know how to press the keys. This, in their mind, gives them the right to call themselves a writer!

Apparently.

There's a truism in development that says that naming things is hard. It is no easier when it comes to choosing the right words for a script. Even a short paragraph of introductory text that explains the game's backstory can be hard work. Indeed, the following was once said by President Woodrow Wilson:

> *"If I am to speak ten minutes, I need a week for preparation; if fifteen minutes, three days; if half an hour, two days; if an hour, I am ready now".*

The length of time to write something is inversely proportional to its duration. Taken to its logical conclusion, finding a single word must take the longest. Any programmer that's spent hours trying to think of a better, more descriptive word than *object* will know this feeling well.

Furthermore, because everyone believes that they are capable of writing, this topic can be fraught with more arguments and opposing points of view. All equally valid. All perfectly suitable.

© Steven Goodwin 2016
S. Goodwin, *Polished Game Development*, DOI 10.1007/978-1-4842-2122-8_8

Even words like *player* and *score* are open for debate. They're both good words, if a little generic. But would a sports simulation, for say track and field, really consider *player* to be the best word available? Would *sportsperson* be better? Or *challenger*? Or *competitor*? Or *athlete*? A thesaurus can provide many replacements for the generic terms so often used, as alternatives better suited to the specifics of your genre.

Sometimes the thesaurus isn't enough. If the score is computed in terms of money, then maybe the in-game currency is a better word. Or in a beat-em-up game, perhaps it should read *victories*.

The best word might not be obvious at the planning stage of the game, but rest assured it is so important to find one that accurately describes the property being presented.

■ **Tip**   The more specific the word is, the better it is at describing the thing in question.

The Nomenclature

At the start of the game development process, you should create a document for the nomenclature.[1] This is one that covers every word, sentence, and term in the game and is part of the writer's bible for that game. It ensures a consistency in prose across the whole game so it's easier for the player to follow along. It also ensures that the words work well together. The former case is easy to get right, if the document exists at the start of the process. The latter is more difficult, as it requires a modicum of talent in choosing the correct names.

Consider a pirate game, for example, where all the pirate characters are tough blaggards that'd as soon as cut you from ear to ear as look at you. Now imagine having a pirate trait labeled as *health*. It might seem a reasonable (if obvious) word to use, but it is a rather clinical term and so doesn't fit with the rest of the language. A better word or term, which would be more in-keeping with the pirate theme, might therefore be *scurvy meter*[2] Other words, like *state* or *status* could have been used here, and even though alliteration is often deemed cheap writing, it is very effective with games and often encouraged. Words like *status* might even be suitable in some games, but in popular Internet culture, *status* is usually first thought of a politely worded sentence that you write on Facebook concerning your dinner. It is hardly something that the average games player immediately associates with a pirate's health!

■ **Tip**   Ask a friend who's not connected with your game, "What's the first thing you think of when I say...". If the word conjures up the same imagery in their head as yours, it's a good word.

---

[1]Derived from the Latin *nomen*, meaning "name," and *calare*, meaning "to call."
[2]To prove my earlier point, it took me longer to find two good replacement words for *health* than it did to write the rest of this page!

Since words create such an emotional evocation, you should use them as often as possible when you know it will create that connection. (This goes against the rule in UX where words should be used as little as possible. I trust you to resolve the conflict when it occurs!) So, alongside the parameter of "scurvy meter," instead of a simple number or percentage to indicate the amount of scurvy present, you should use words that relate to the term, such as

- Damaged but normal
- Toxic
- Ravaged
- Contagious
- Fatal

Notice here that the best term (i.e., when health = 100%) is labeled *damaged*. This is intentional and plays on the notion that the life of a pirate is, at best, awful! The words are creating a meaning and a picture in the mind of the player, without you having to state, *the life of a pirate is awful*. This is a common theme for all media. (But we also add *normal* so that the player starts looking for a health potion on their first play through.)

■ **Tip** Show, don't tell.

Creating a Nomenclature

While there are guidelines as to what should appear in the nomenclature, it is truly up to you as to the how and where the information is stored. It might be on an internal wiki, a shared document, or a text file somewhere in the version control system. The most important fact is that it's available to everyone in the team so that they can name the assets, variables, or on-screen text correctly. This ensures a common vocabulary between all members, leading to less miscommunication. Also, if you can eliminate the need to have data in two different places (e.g., a source code file for displaying on-screen and a spreadsheet for the writer), then so much the better.

My preference is to store such text in a JSON-formatted text file, held within a resources folder of the game itself. I chose JSON because it's free-form, allowing whitespace and comments to be added, and because almost every language and platform has a suitable library for parsing the structure. This file is loaded into the game at run-time and used throughout.

```
{
    "score"  : "Gold pieces",
    "health" : "Scurvy meter",
    "health0": "Damaged but normal",
    "health1": "Toxic",
    "health2": "Ravaged",
    "health3": "Contagious",
    "health4": "Fatal"
}
```

It is perfectly acceptable to have words and phrases in the file that are used solely as reminders to the development team. For example, you might decide to refer to all interactions on a phone screen as *touches, presses,* or *taps.* However, it is highly unlikely that you'll ever use the word in isolation, but having that line in the same file makes it easy to find. And, therefore, more likely to be used.

The nomenclature file starts with simple sections to describe the word used in-game for *score* or *missile*, and goes on to cover the interface actions, such as *swipe left* or *double tap.* There is nothing wrong with changing the word as the development process evolves (most people would be concerned if it didn't change), but having a single source of truth for these terms is necessary, as is making it easy to change them.

Although you might think it's unlikely that you'd change such a dictionary while the game is running, it is possible that a foreign language version will exist in the future. At this point, you would need the functionality to change words in real time. Later in the chapter, we look at some programmatic methods for doing this.

Let us now consider the categories for the required nomenclature.

Game Words

Game words are the basic words and phrases present in the game world. This includes the appropriate synonyms for:

- Player

- Score

- Lives

- Bullets

And so on.

When dealing with a fictional world, the races of characters also appear here, along with their plurals, and if appropriate, their gender. This is not the place to include the character allegiances or descriptions—just the correct spelling.

The game words dictionary is essentially that—a dictionary. It can also include game- and genre-specific words and phrases such as "Aaarrrrr!" from our make-believe pirate game. Although a simple case, having a different number of r's in each appearance of this exclamation is disconcerting at best and a sign of amateur hour, at worst.

The User Interface

As discussed, you also need to think of a consistent naming convention for the user actions such as *press* or *touch.* Similarly, you need to add a comment about how these words are used. Do you *press* the screen to *click* a button, for example? Or do you *touch* the screen *on* the button? The differences are slight, and for most purposes are less important since they are *in* the game and not essential in establishing mood. From a usability point of view, however, they are important. Furthermore, they are important from a uniformity standpoint, as an iPhone user that reads *The game will issue pop-ups outside of the game* is less understandable than the phrase *The game uses the Notification Center*, which is standard iPhone jargon.

Most proprietary platforms operate in a walled garden environment. This means that the creator of the platform can enforce rules on third-party developers as to which words are used to describe their device. Although they're not immune to change, it's less likely. That said, you should still add the words to your general nomenclature document so that consistency exists from the outset. All the current suite of games consoles are walled gardens, along with the Apple devices.

■ **Tip** When including external documents into your version control system, or copying sections of it into your data files, remember to add a URL back to the source material. If the document isn't publicly available on the Web, place the file on a team-shared server and include a path to it. You need to check this before submission. Finding the original source many months later can be a time-consuming/wasting experience.

In addition to the words, you'll also want to include the phrases for how the interface is used. As mentioned previously, the phrase *swipe left* might be considered in preference to *touch and drag your finger to the left*. In fact, the phrase *swipe left* is a perfect example of how two innocuous words are able to conjure such a concise description of an otherwise cumbersome action. It even makes an appearance in the urban dictionary, such that everyone knows what it is (as an action) and what the convention means (it's a bad or unattractive thing). In fact, if you were building your own Tinder-beater app, then you'd naturally use the phrase *swipe left* and assign it to the same action as the original. Why would you break the convention?

Abbreviations

For the most part, all words should be written out in full, so abbreviations are not necessary. There are two cases when this is not true.

First, when the word is traditionally written as an abbreviation, such as with the rank of military personnel. *Captain* might be written in full, but it is not uncommon to see it as *Capt.* without any explanation necessary. Similarly, words like *Lieutenant* are generally abbreviated to *Lt.*, which also helps avoid the confusion between *Lieutenant* and *Leftenant*.[3] (Although you should have that entry in the game words dictionary to avoid such confusion!)

The second case for when abbreviations become necessary is as part of the in-game user interface, especially in foreign language versions where the length of the replacement word was not considered when laying out the original screen.

---

[3]The difference being that *leftenant* is an old English way of spelling the more modern *lieutenant*. However, if your game is set in the 1700s, then it would be in keeping with the theme of the game to use *leftenant*.

■ **Tip**   Always include the word in full before using its abbreviation. If the abbreviation is needed in-game, then ensure that it is shown in the instructions or tutorial prior to the game.

It is recommended to adopt a basic convention and include both a full and an abbreviated version in the nomenclature file. For example, the textual ID of *health* has an equivalent of *health_abbr*. In this way, it's easy for the writer or programmer to find the approved abbreviation or to determine that one doesn't exist and needs to be created.

Beyond Words

Once the basic vocabulary has been considered, you can move on to the areas in which those words are combined. This is a meta level and breaks down simply into a style guide, prose style, and game bible.

Style Guide

The style guide is a formalization of rules that indicates the editorial nature, grammar, and structure of English that will be used within the game's writing. It includes things like *Do we use the Oxford comma?*, *Do we capitalize words like "A" or "The" in titles?*, or *Is it gametime, game-time, or game time?*

This is a document that generally does not need to be written, as most writers have a preferred style. This might be *The Chicago Manual of Style* (CMS), the *Associated Press Stylebook* (AP), or something entirely different. What's important is that it's referenced and adhered to within the project.

Although style guides are updated regularly to handle the ever-changing nature of language, you may still find it necessary to make amendments of your own. *Save game*, for example. These amendments may be phrases that appear in the game words section of the nomenclature, but also separately detailed in a more formal guide. Particularly, if there is more than one writer on the project.

Even a project with a single writer should adopt a style guide, because it's very easy to forget a rule or make up one on the spot and be unable to remember where you last used it, thereby making it impossible to refer back to.

Prose Style

While a single style guide might be used in many projects across a writer's career, the prose style will vary with each game. Or, if you're lucky, each franchise. This section of the document is for phrases that describe the hows (and whys) of particular speech patterns. I'm sure Tolkien would have had one when creating the various languages and spoken nuances in *Lord of the Rings*. Similarly, in *Star Trek: The Next Generation*, Lt. Cmdr. Data never uses contractions. (He always says "cannot" instead of "can't".)

Going back to our pirate game, a good example is how you would use a prose style guide to dictate the rules for how pirates address the captain, their crewmates, and so on. In doing so, you create a language (pun intended) that the player can adopt to fit in with the game. It can also be used to give clues to the player of changing relationships within the game. For example, a pirate who's required to tribute the captain with the phrase "Sir, yes sir," might only say "Sir." This could be a clue as to his disrespect and upcoming mutiny. Or two characters that start the game referring to each other by their full names, but by the end of it are comfortable using pet nicknames for each other, gives an emotional depth to the characters and shows the journey that they have come on together.

These elements are closely tied to the game bible. Speaking of which...

The Game Bible

The game bible is a document covering the backstory of all the characters and the game world itself. Granted, a simple puzzle game does not need such a document, but most others will. Start by asking the question *Why?*. *Why is the player trying to overcome this hurdle? Why are they motivated to do it?* Even a simple story like *Fly the space ship through an asteroid field* could have several different interpretations.

- Is the character escaping from something? An exploding planet? A ship?

- Is the character escaping from someone? Can this someone else follow the character into the asteroids?

- Are they trying to reach a certain place? Why?

- Are the asteroids artificial? Is the pilot testing the abilities of the ship? Why aren't there any safety features?

- What's the cargo? Could the cargo be jettisoned to clear a path?

All of these questions shape the game in some small but noticeable way.

■ **Tip** Even if the backstory is never directly used, it can ensure that the developers never add puzzles or situations into the game that would conflict with those pre-existent scenarios and cause an anachronism.

It is easy to see how anachronistic conflicts could occur without a game bible. If the purpose of traversing the asteroids is to deliver a message, then why don't they deliver it via space radio? (We have secure data transmissions on Earth— they'd certainly have it in space!) If the asteroids are from an exploding planet, then why is the pattern of rocks linear and not spherical? And so on.

Alongside the basic elements of the story, you want to create a history for the characters within the game. Who they are, where they come from, and their allegiances. Even in its most simplistic form, *Space Invaders* had three characters: the player, the invaders, and the mother ship. You knew the relationship between the mother ship and the invaders, and understood the importance of shooting it down, if possible. In *Die Hard: Vendetta* there are several scenarios where the mercenaries surrender without shooting if you captured their leader. This wasn't written in dialog, or as explicit instructions, but as part of the narrative and gameplay itself. Each scenario was written in such a way that it suggested which character was the leader (often the one giving orders or with the extra insignia on the uniform). Again—show, don't tell.

Getting Text into the Game

Best practice favors a data-driven approach in all forms of game asset. Text is no different. We therefore need a data file or files containing a series of name/value pairs that allow the appropriate text to be referenced given a suitable key. Let's first consider the storage of that text before moving on to the text file structure.

From General to Specific

Depending on the scope of the game, you may need to consider one or more of the following areas:

- Alternate languages (EFIGS: English, French, Italian, German, Spanish)

- Multiple platforms (PC, Web, Android, iPhone, etc.)

- Different devices (Samsung, HTC, etc.)

In 2014, it was reported[4] that there were 18,796 distinct Android devices. There are no doubt even more now. It is up to you which of these distinctions are important to you, given the development schedule.

So within the text resources folder there might a structure like the following:

```
en/main.json
en/credits.json
en/android/main.json
en/android/credits_for_porting.jsonen/android/samsung/4G.json
en/iphone/main.json
```

This would be mirrored by each of the supplied languages. For now, let's consider only English.

---

[4]See http://opensignal.com/reports/2014/android-fragmentation/

The code would work through and load the necessary files, from most generic first (en/main.json), to platform (iPhone or Android), and finally to the most specific, causing the more device-specific wording to overwrite the general. This would ensure that the most suitable instructions regarding the user interface and platform-specific nomenclature were present.

It is also possible—but stretching the point slightly—to have duplicate folders to handle additional cases, such as an American SKU, where the grammar and spelling changes slightly. Perhaps adding separate files:

```
en/lang/en-US/main.json
en/iphone/lang/en-US/main.json
```

This gives two places where American English text may be used, but is often limited to credits for the various regions.

■ **Tip**   Place the game text and credits text in different files and create a separate credits file for each platform. This is because there are likely to be more changes to the credits text than the game during the late stages (e.g., thanks to X for finding this show-stopping bug), and each platform often has its own publishing team of hangers-on that want credit.

Requirements of a Text System

Before considering the format of the text file, you should consider the necessary use cases. From an initial standpoint, you must have a way of retrieving a text string using a given ID. The data type for this ID is immaterial. In JavaScript, it's unnecessary due to the dynamic typing of the language, but in others, it may be important. Despite this fact, there is still a strong case for using text strings. Integers may seem to be a more obvious route, especially when working in C/C++, since code like this provides a very efficient run-time because the CPU needs to only perform a simple look-up:

```
#define STRING_SCORE    1
#define STRING_HEALTH   2

const char *szStringTable[] = {
"score",
"health",
...
}
```

This code has several problems, however. First, the definitions of each string are constant and not easily changed; you would need to set up a separate array and copy the pointers from here into szFrenchStringTable (for example) if you ever wanted to change language. Second, the IDs are static and generally require a recompile of the entire code base once any change is made.

Strings, on the other hand, are dynamic by their very nature and support a data-driven approach out of the box. Furthermore, the IDs look like genuine text. This second point is often overlooked. Consider code like this:

```
highscore = get_text_for("High score");
```

Now consider its fail case. If the textual ID is not found, the get_text_for method can return the input string ID as an output. This means that even without a textual data file, the game still functions perfectly. Sure, there may be some text that conflicts with the given nomenclature, but there will never be a blank area on the screen. Nor will it silently fail, rendering blank lines to the screen and the user wondering what to do next.

■ **Tip** Using strings as IDs also helps when it comes to translations, as someone playing the game in French, for example, can detect missing text by noting whenever an English string (i.e., the ID) appears. As a bonus, it's trivial to find the ID of the string required, because it's written on-screen!

The next use case to consider is that of plurals. Games that build strings in code often display something like this:

```
You have scored 1 points
```

Having a score of 1 and a plural word in the same sentence is a surefire way of detecting a lack of polish. The solution to this is to *not* write this:

```
write("You have scored " + score + " point");
if (score != 1) {
  write("s");
}
```

But to start thinking along the lines of this:

```
if (score == 1) {
  write("You have scored 1 point");
} else {
  write("You have scored " + score + " points");
}
```

This second approach ensures that you are thinking about words that are not pluralized by simply adding an "s"—such as *fly* and *flies*.

■ **Tip** Always create two strings for any text that incorporates a number in its midst. Not only does this ensure the correct plural, but it helps in foreign language versions, too.

From these two basic requirements (a string used for the data type and the preparation of pluralized text), we can create the first pass of our text system. It might not be the ultimate in text processing, but it will be a step up from the majority of games on the market—and it might be all that you need. Remember: MVP (minimal viable product)—create the smallest thing that you need to get going.

The File Format

With the use cases considered, you can look at the format. Our previous structure was a good start, but it was limited to a 1:1 relationship between ID and string. With the inclusion of plurals, we need a 1:2 mapping. It's possible to demonstrate this as a JSON literal in two primary ways:

```
'score': [ 'Gold piece', 'Gold pieces']
```

or

```
'score': { s: 'Gold piece', p:'Gold pieces'}
```

The first uses an array and a convention to say *write the singular case first*. The second uses an explicit identifier, s or p, to reference the singular and plural versions of the string. Either approach is valid. Since most strings have only a singular version, the former is quicker to write (and less error prone, if creating it by hand), but it's not worth arguing over.

Since we're concerned with JavaScript here, we support both variations because JSON handles both methods in the same file. Once the JSON is loaded into memory, we can process the data by copying it into a hash (also known as an *associative array*) of our own design, thus:

```
sgx.text.processTextData = function(textData) {

  for(var id in textData) {
    var text = textData[id];
     if (text instanceof Array) {
       this.data[id] = { s: text[0], p:text[1] };
     } else if (text instanceof Object) {
       this.data[id] = { s: text['s'], p: text['p'] };
     } else {
       this.data[id] = { s: text, p: text };
     }
  }
}
```

Note that we process the Array variation first, since (in JavaScript) an array is also an object. We also accept the case of a 1:1 mapping, as a final case.

■ **Tip** When reading data from an external source in JavaScript, it's always a good idea to use text['s'] instead of text.s since an obfuscator might rewrite text.s and make the file unreadable.

With this approach, switching in an alternate language is as simple as loading a new text file and calling sgx.text.processTextData again. Of course, it does not need to be a different language. Having a debug menu that allows a tester to reload the language assets means that they can make pseudo-live edits to the text, which ensures that everything fits correctly on-screen, or amend and abbreviate the text when it doesn't.

Processing Code

With the data loaded and in-place, it's a simple matter to retrieve it with the following:

```
sgx.text.getText = function(id) {
  if (typeof this.data[id] === 'undefined') {
    return id;
  }
  return this.data[id]['s'];
}
```

To handle the cases where it might contain a plural, we need the number passed into the method. We use this:

```
sgx.text.getTextN = function(id, value) {
  if (typeof this.data[id] === 'undefined') {
    return id;
  }
  return this.isSingular(value) ? this.data[id]['s'] : this.data[id]['p'];
}
```

The method for isSingular is as obvious as you think, with 0, 2, 3, and so on considered a plural, and 1 the sole singular value. However, this has been split into its own method to handle the case for other languages where 1 might use the plural form and 0 uses the singular.

We return to this module in Chapter 11, when we go further into foreign language territory.

Workflow

The text IDs are written directly into the source during development, with the programmer checking each ID for duplicates. This isn't strictly necessary, as dupes can be eliminated later, but it ensures that the consistency demanded from the nomenclature is followed at all stages of the development process. The code is simply this:

```
render_health = sgx.text.getText('health');
```

For those strings that incorporate a number, we use this:

```
render_score = sgx.text.getTextN("score", score);
```

This variant returns a string containing a placeholder variable, such as %d, indicating which part of the string is to be replaced with the number. You can process this with something as simple as this:

```
render_score = render_score.replace('%d', score);
```

If there are likely to be multiple placeholder variables within a string (and most games do), then it would normally be tricky to distinguish between the first %d and the second %d, should the word order change.[5] For this reason, I prefer %1, %2, and so on, which can be implemented thus:

```
function simpleSprintf(s) {
  var result = s;

  for(var i=1;i<arguments.length;++i) {
    result = result.replace('%'+i, arguments[i]);
  }

  return result;
}
```

When working in C/C++, use %1d to indicate the type, along with the position. There are various homespun implementations of sprintf available on the Web for you to try.

When all the text is handled through the getText and getTextN methods, you can run a simple script over the source code to see if there are any text strings present that are *not* wrapped by either of these methods. One such script in Perl would read as follows:

```
perl -n -e
  'print "$. : $1$2\n" while /(n?getText(?:N)?\()?\"(.*?)\"\)?/g;'
  -- filename.js |
  grep -v gettext
```

Finally, you might want to create variations in the text to provide some extra interest, especially for simple and repetitive phrases like "Yes, sir." The recommendation here is to add it specifically as a library method:

```
sgx.text.getTextVar = function(id_list) {
  return this.getText(id_list[Math.floor(Math.random()*id_list.length)]);
}
```

You would then add each variation from a file, which appears as follows:

```
'yes1' : ['Yes, sir'],
'yes2' : ['Sir, yes, sir'],
'yes3' : ['Right away sir'],
```

---

[5]This could happen if the writer decides to change "The %d pirates share %d gold pieces" to "The %d gold pieces were shared among the %d pirates"

And request the string with this:

```
yes_sir = sgx.text.getTextVar(['yes1', 'yes2', 'yes3']);
```

With a little extra effort, you could enforce a convention whereby a string labeled yes0 would indicate the number of possible variations, and then adapt getTextVar to pick one of them at random, thereby eliminating the passing of an array.

In this way, it is you, the caller, that decides to pick a random text string and not the getText library. To realize the problem in doing the latter, imagine that you had a cut-scene or were displaying subtitles to a voice on-screen. If the audio played the words "Yes, sir," but the subtitle read "Yeah," then the difference between the sentences might be nuanced enough to change the meaning. (Consider the case covered earlier about how an interpersonal relationship changes based on the name used.) Therefore, the caller must be in control, so the cut-scene and subtitle code would call the traditional getText method, while the rest could use the adaptation presented as getTextVar.

Not an English Lesson

At the very start of the chapter, I mentioned that everyone thinks they're a writer. Now, at the end, I'll show you how to become one! Or rather, I'll cover a few brief guidelines on how to stop you from making the more obvious mistakes that prove that you're *not* a writer. While this section won't help you create beautiful and engaging prose, it will hopefully give you some hints on how to improve what you have already written.

Avoiding Typos

When text is written into a machine-readable form, like JSON, it is very difficult to determine which text is misspelled, because the spell-checker highlights almost every line due to the formatting or the non-English identifiers, such as health1 and ply_death_tally.

You can eliminate this by creating a small program to dump the text into a single document that can be loaded into your least unfavorite word processor and spell-checked manually.

```
sgx.text.getTextDump = function(id) {
  var s = '';

  for(var id in this.data) {
    s += id + " : " + this.data[id]['s'] + ", " + this.data[id]['p'] + ".";
  }

  s = s.replace(/\%[^\s]*/, '');

  return s;
}
```

This code also removes all variable placeholder strings that might cause issue with a spell-checker.

■ **Tip** Linux users can make use of command-line tools like ispell to automate this process.

If your game has a lot of text, you can include the line number of each piece of text into the output to make it easier to find any given typo, like so:

```
Line 12 : identifier of "health3": "Contagious"
```

Genre titles may wish to create a custom dictionary for words like *blaggards* and *Aaarrrrr*, along with character names and other fictional pronouns.

Avoiding Grammos

Grammatical errors are often the hardest to spot, since bad habits get engrained very early on, especially concerning the rules governing use of the apostrophe or whether to use *that* or *which*, so a second pair of eyes is always recommended. Many software-based spell-checkers also check grammar, and so are often an acceptable first step. Alas, they are also used as a panacea such that sentences "in the passive voice" are blindly reworked by the novice writer to remove the warning without any real reason as to why, along with any personality behind the words.

For any small game, a professional proofreader should be able to work through your text in a very short space of time—and would cost less than a programmer to do so! The Society for Editors and Proofreaders,[6] for example, recommends an hourly rate of £22.50 (about $35), which covers about 10 pages and should be within reach of an indie developer.

Words that Sound Similar

It is very common to mix up words like *access* and *excess*, or *alleviate* and *elevate*, so always ask another person to read through the text. It is easy to become word-blind to your own prose, and so miss some rather obvious errors. It's also less time-consuming than having to check every word in the dictionary to ensure its meaning is what you intended.

Some of the most commonly confused words can be found in Table 8-1 or one of many sites online.[7]

---

[6]www.sfep.org.uk
[7]Such as http://www.alphadictionary.com/articles/confused_words_english.html

Table 8-1. _Words that May Be Confused_

Word	Confused with	Word	Confused with
accede	exceed	accept	except
advice	advise	affect	effect
all ways	always	among	between
appraise	apprise	ascent	assent
ensure	insure	bare	bear
censor	censure	each	every
elicit	illicit	farther	further
fewer	less	i.e.	e.g.
imminent	eminent	lay	lie
like	as	precede	proceed
raise	raze	stationary	stationery

There are also many homophones (words that are pronounced the same as one another, but have a different meaning) and heterographs (sound the same, but with different meaning and spelling) to confuse the unwary.

Another tip in this area is to use a thesaurus, which provides an alternate to the word you've just written. If the alternate word doesn't make sense in the context you intended, then you've used the wrong word!

Basic Style Hints

While there is no substitute for a thorough knowledge of a formal style guide, such as _CMS_ or _APS_, this section attempts to provide a shortcut by highlighting some of the most common style elements.

- Include a space after each comma or period.

- Writer numbers in full for one through nine, and as digits for 10 and above. Ages always use digits.

- Only abbreviate months when used in a full date.

- Maintain consistency when using single or double quotes.

- Place punctuation inside the quotes. (Although this differs in the United Kingdom and the United States.)

But, as before, adopt a style and stick to it. If there's any such thing as a golden rule in writing (and I doubt there is), then this is it.

Summary

We started by looking at our nomenclature and discussing the precision of words and how specific words can add depth to the game world. We then looked at how those words are combined into prose to define a style guide and a game bible to ensure that the conventions are always followed.

Once we had some text to display, we looked at how that text is stored, loaded, and drawn in-game. This included the handling of multiple languages and devices. We extended this to discuss how plurals need to be handled to avoid displaying *You scored 1 points*.

With the increase in code necessary to facilitate the written word, the next chapter examines code in detail and explains how it can be effectively written.

CHAPTER 9

Coding Practices

Good code is felt but never seen. Its impact permeates the whole game in both the audio and visuals. Unless you're writing a game for a university project, you might think that your code—as in the quality of your code—is unlikely to come under much scrutiny once it's working. That, alas, is a fallacious argument.

Throughout the development cycle, you likely have to revisit your code many times. Even the low-level engine components that "just work" may need to be fixed for obtuse edge cases, refactored to incorporate new functionality, or optimized for performance. Each time you have to delve into the code, you risk breaking existing functionality. Each time you have to delve into the code you need to understand your thought processes from the time before; which may be last week, month, or even year. Each time you have to delve into the code you are expected to leave it in a better than which you found it.

Tip The worst critic of your code will be you. In six months' time. When all the logic of today has been lost to the mist of yesterday.

Furthermore, if your game is a success, then you'll want to make a sequel. And a sequel should be something that you can build quickly. At least, it should be quick, compared to the trials and tribulations of the first version. After all, the gameplay is tuned, the graphics are clean, the engine is optimized, and you have a complete breakdown of all the assets needed for a game of this type. Chances are that the idea of returning to year-old code is anything but pleasant. If that is true for your current project, then it's likely the code isn't as clean as it should be. Games development is one of the few creative industries where the sequel is as good, or usually better, than the original. Very few films manage it. But games can take advantage of faster processors for highly involved effects or AI, larger displays, longer and more extensive user testing, and a vast reusable code base. The latter being important since none of the paying public can spot a reused code base. Therefore, keeping the code clean allows you to pay forward the benefit of preparing for a sequel.

© Steven Goodwin 2016

S. Goodwin, *Polished Game Development*, DOI 10.1007/978-1-4842-2122-8_9

■ **Note** Sequels can follow the "second album" syndrome. You have years to write your original game, but only months to write the sequel. So you must strike while the proverbial iron is hot.

And what about online games? Very few products are finished when they're realized. We're not just referring to the "zero-day patches" either.[1] Any game deployed to a website is downloaded to the local machine so that the user may play it. This gives the developer a chance to create updates for large or small features or bugs on an almost daily basis. If a bug is announced on the game's forum, you can usually have a fix ready within the hour. Push it through testing. And get it ready for deployment before lunch. No other medium has this ability to react so quickly to end-user testing. So use it!

Furthermore, most (if not all) online games are updated regularly to keep their players actively involved, so you'll want to implement incremental data structures for saved games, achievements won, and objects bought so that the player doesn't lose any of *their* items when *you* need to upgrade your database.

Let us look, then, at the elements that constitute a solid coding environment.

Preparing the Development Environment

Before we can start animating the lead character, or adding an Easter egg on level 12 (i.e., doing the interesting bits!), we should prepare an environment that all team members can use which pre-answers basic questions like *Where do I put this asset?* or *Where is XYZ stored?*

Ideally, all team members should be able to run an up-to-date version of the game on their local machine, make their changes, and see how they have improved upon it. This should be the goal of the preparation stage. Sometimes this is not practical, as artists are likely to be unable (or more likely, unwillingly) to administer local MySQL databases on their machines,[2] or have copies of whatever esoteric programming tools the coders have deemed necessary for this particular project. Therefore, alternatives must be found. In the example of databases, maybe install an office-wide local database that holds the necessary information. Perhaps instead, the programmers will provide a special "local-only" build of the game, or even a custom tool, which allows them to see their animations at work as if it were in the game. The precise means by which this happens isn't important—the fact that everyone can review their work, is.

---

[1]The first day of release requires the player to download a 100MB (or larger) update to the game they've just bought. This increasingly worrying trend is increasingly frustrating for all players. Eliminating this ensures that the first thing in your game review won't be a complaint about downloads!

[2]These applications are typically installed under Unix-like operating systems, while art tools are generally developed first for Windows. This alone necessitates a little configuration creativity.

■ **Tip** Consider using a virtual machine with prebuilt images so that you can instantly set up a development environment.

Application Structure

The source code of a project is generally considered the most hidden part of any game. Even HTML5 games—written in JavaScript and downloaded to the player's web browser—are not shipped with the source code. Instead, the source files are munged into an amorphous blob and minified into an unreadable form! We need to build a directory structure with this in mind.

The elements of the source tree start at its parent, since that directory should contain both the original source code (and art assets) and the built and minified version suitable for public deployment.

■ **Note** At this time, let's consider the development on a single platform. Later on, we'll examine the complications of cross-platform development, where the game needs to work on both PlayStation and Xbox, for example.

So let's consider the following directory structure:

- game
- game/app/source
- game/app/resources
- game/build
- game/config
- game/thirdparty
- game/tools
- game/copy
- game/target

These directories break down as follows.

Application

The app directory contains both the raw source code and resources for the game. Depending on the platform and scope of the game, this could contain any structure within it.

An HTML5 game, for example, is likely to mirror the code shape necessary to run on the server; it includes the following:

- `index.html`, which is the surrounding file that loads the JavaScript and so forth

- CSS files for styling

- JavaScript game files

- JavaScript library files, like jQuery, stored locally so that development can continue in the event of a network outage

- `robots.txt`

- `favicon.ico` to appear in the browser's address bar

If your game team is separated such that artists are not allowed to modify files under the game/app/source directory tree, then you may need to place `favicon.ico` elsewhere, and accept that it will be missing in the local development build.

■ **Note** In HTML5 games, you should be able to load the game and all of its assets from a local web server pointing its root to the app directory. This is so that you can instantly turn around changes during development.

In most native games, where source must be compiled before use, it usually contains only further subdirectories for each section of the game.

In both cases, the source code is likely to run many hundreds of files, especially if you adopt the "one file per class" rule, in which case time is spent considering how the subdirectories are broken down and the code is organized for each section of the game; for example, menu, online, levels, engine, and so on. Build a full directory structure at the start, even if each contains only one file.

The main point of contention is likely to be whether an in-house game engine appears under the source hierarchy (where it is implied that game devs have the right to modify it), or an external directory (implying a "do not touch," as would be prevalent with a third-party engine.) This can be a complicated issue and can only be resolved by considering the specifics of your company and your game.

- Is the engine maintained by a separate team?

- How are the engine updates handled from that team?

- Who checks that new engine updates don't break your game?

- If your game team find bugs in the engine, can they fix them without being reliant on an external team?

- How do these bugs find their way back upstream into the main engine?

- What is the turnaround time for that to happen?

- When you need a new version that fixes an old bug, but also includes unwanted new features and potential bugs, how do you reconcile these two issues to prevent new engine bugs from affecting your existing code?

In truth, the same questions should be asked for a third-party game engine, too. But with an internal team (where communications and unobfuscated source code may flow more freely), the dividing line can become quite hazy. Let's look at potential solutions when covering the workflow issues.

Application Resources

The same questions that are asked of source code must now be asked of the art assets and other resources. How will 1,000+ art assets be separated across a directory structure that makes them easy to find and organize in a way that eliminates the chance of two identically named assets (such as the icon for the gun pickup and the sound heard when it is picked up) appearing within the same directory? (And without forcing the file names to be unwittingly long.)

It is quite common to split resources by type rather than by team divisions, since it's likely that the game or engine code has different processes for loading a texture compared to an animation. Thus, the resources folder could break down into the following categories:

- animations

- backgrounds

- fonts

- loading screens

- menus and user interface

- static sprites

- title screens (and publisher banners)

- audio

Within each of these categories, there may be subcategories, as you saw in the chapters on audio and graphics.

Build

The build directory contains all the necessary scripts and build-specific tools for taking the source code and resources to build into a game-ready format. It doesn't need to include the compiler (since that's often installed to a specific location and shared among many projects) but a game-specific make file would live here.

The build directory is also the place where all the custom art tools live, such those to unify the resolution or file format. They take the raw asset files, such as a texture and its metadata, and combine them into a single file for the game engine, as appropriate. They should also validate the metadata to ensure that it's suitable. On many consoles and PC graphics cards, all textures should be square and use dimensions that are a power of two; this process should check for that. Or the tools can check that the textures are not overly sized for purpose, with a 1024×1024 texture used only on meshes that appear on small objects in the game world.

■ **Tip** If your engine only supports a few different file formats, then the art tools here can warn against bad files and other problems before they get into the game for real. As always, the sooner a problem can be detected, the sooner it can get fixed, and the fewer systems it has the chance to disrupt. Most image formats, for example, support myriad options, such as compression, bit depth, and so on. If the development platform supports more options than the target platform, then a lot of head scratching will begin when a single texture appears corrupted in the game.

There are essentially two parts to the build process. The first processes the files individually, compiling and/or optimizing them as appropriate for the environment, such as debug or release. This is followed by a process that considers the file system as a whole, combining several files into one, ignoring those that are unnecessary for this build, and including others. You'll see more on the build process in Chapter 11.

Configuration

During the development, all games exist in at least two versions: debug and release. A debug build contains a lot of internal information (perhaps checks for array bounds), safety code (which defaults all variables to zero), and a symbol table to help programmers and their tools determine the line number and variables referenced by the binary. Release builds are streamlined to run much faster and contain none of this. The configuration directory contains all the necessary files and parameters that you need to switch between them. This is distinct from the files in build, since the build type determines how the compilation process occurs; whereas config indicates how that build reacts at run-time.

It might contain the location of the database server (or a reference to the fact that none exists), the obfuscation methods required, which compiler optimizations are to be applied, how errors are to be logged and reported, and so on.

For online games, it's also likely to include API keys to third-party services, such as Facebook or Twitter.

It can also include configuration information about the art assets; for example, the size of the assets to be used—small, medium, or large—because it might be used to switch between an HTML5 game on a desktop and an equivalent build on mobile.

The primary purpose of these files is to remove magic numbers and magic strings from the source code, and then move them into an easily tweakable location. In this way, tests can be performed by simulating real-world scenarios like a broken database (by putting erroneous information in the database fields) or missing content.

Since each configuration is customized by each developer, according to the area on which they're working, the configuration file should not be added (known as a commit in the vernacular) to source control. So, instead of adding `config/database.conf` you should instead create a `config/database.conf.example` file, which includes stubs for each configuration parameter, an example of the format accepted, and a description of its purpose. A JSON-oriented file might mean that `config/database.example.conf` looks like this:

```
{
  "main":{
    "host":"INSERT_DATA_HERE",
    "port":INSERT_DATA_HERE,
    "database":"INSERT_DATA_HERE",
    "adapter":"INSERT_DATA_HERE",
    "username":"INSERT_DATA_HERE",
    "password":"INSERT_DATA_HERE"
  },
  "assets":{
    "host":"INSERT_DATA_HERE",
    "port":INSERT_DATA_HERE,
    "database":"INSERT_DATA_HERE",
    "adapter":"INSERT_DATA_HERE",
    "username":"INSERT_DATA_HERE",
    "password":"INSERT_DATA_HERE"
  }
}
```

Each developer then copies that to `config/database.conf` and amends it to something akin to this:

```
{
  "main":{
    "host":"192.168.0.110",
    "port":3306,
    "database":"bounce_game_main",
    "adapter":"rest",
    "username":"steev",
    "password":"somesecret"
  },
  "assets":{
    "host":"192.168.0.111",
    "port":3306,
    "database":"bounce_game_assets",
    "adapter":"rest",
    "username":"team_data",
    "password":"some_other_secret"
  }
}
```

The developer then modifies the file locally, so there is no fear that they will mess up another person's configuration, or vice versa.

■ **Caution** Online games rely a lot on API keys and secrets. Putting them into source control widens the perimeter of possible security incursions; therefore, it is important to not include these types of files in source control. There have been several incidents in the past.

Third Party

The thirdparty directory holds all the necessary files (art and code) for any game-reliant technology that is not developed by the game team. It primarily stores the current working versions of any third-party engine and similar libraries. As noted earlier, even a game engine developed within the same company (but by a different team) may be stored here, since the purpose is the same; that being to isolate upstream changes by those third-party vendors until they can be properly tested within the game.

■ **Tip** Any code added here should include its URL, place of purchase, and any additional license agreements.

Depending on the number of games under active development and the variety of platforms, you may decide to create a separate directory hierarchy outside of the game folder so that all the necessary third-party tools can be shared.[3]

Tools

The tools directory stores all the code and resources necessary to build the internal tools used within the team. They might facilitate UI layout, animation playback, or audio mixing. Most of the time this code references the game code (in the app/source directory) and the game engine (in whatever location you decided upon earlier) so that an identical in-game experience can be had without the turnaround time or distractions of having to load the entire game, and play through it up until the point where a problem occurs. (Jumping to specific parts of the game, or making specific characters or objects available, might require a lot of time to play-through until that point, or need a programmer to add specific hacks into the game.)

In many cases, the internal tools have a duplicate structure with source, resources, config, build, and so on.

---

[3]Mine is called *devlib* and contains known good versions of Fmod, OpenGL, Freetype, and so on, which were approved by the team and shown to work with our game.

Copy

If there are resources that are not needed to develop the game, but are provided to the end user, they live in the copy directory. It's typical for manuals, README files, and icons to live here. No process occurs on these files, although there is no reason why the build scripts couldn't be improved to permit it; for example, to build the PDF manual from separate files.

Target

The target directory stores the resultant game, fully built, for each platform and each environment. It includes the compiled, copied, or obfuscated versions of the code. It includes the built version of the art assets. And it includes a copy of any extra resources that are necessary, such as manuals or icons.

Generally speaking, the target folder is never committed to source control, since its contents can (and should!) always be regenerated from the source folders.

A typical structure within target might include each platform:

- target/ios
- target/online
- target/pc

Each of these has a debug and release folder inside. The contents of these folders are later deployed to a web server or burned onto a disc for physical distribution. This is often a manual process, although given time, this can improved via automation, as I'll cover in Chapter 11.

Cross-Platform Considerations

When you are building for multiple platforms, the complexity of the development increases exponentially. Someone could write an entire book on the problems and necessary processes to cope with it.[4] For completeness, however, we should briefly cover the complexities that you'll experience.

Code

The source code will vary significantly between platforms; it may even be in a different programming language! In these cases, you have to either accept the duplication of effort or use a scripting language (such as Lua) that can be used on each platform for the majority of game-specific tasks. You rely on the platform-specific game engine to do all the main work.

---

[4]At the risk of sounding like an advertisement, my first book, *Cross-Platform Game Programming* (Charles River Media, 2005), covers this area fully.

> ■ **Note** This is how the SGX game engine works. There is a natively developed engine for C++, JavaScript, and ActionScript. Each engine has identical method names and nearly identical signatures, so writing custom code on each platform is as simple as possible. Additionally, there is a scripting engine on top (which calls these identically named methods) so that game code can be written using an abstracted language, if desired.

Even those reliant on a cross-platform game engine have to ensure that the endian-ness of their data is maintained, that storage solutions are abstracted, and that the limitations of each platform are considered.

Environment

You often need different compilers and tools to build each platform. While this isn't a technical problem, per se, it does mean that you need to ensure clear delineation between each platform, and good code reviews to ensure that platform-specific bugs or features of the language are not accidentally used. For example, the qsort method in C/C++ does not implement a quick sort. The standard only requires a *sort* algorithm to be implemented. Therefore, if you build for two different platforms, it's very likely that two different sorting algorithms implementations are used, which consequently means that any list (with duplicate keys) is sorted into a subtly different order on each platform.[5]

> ■ **Tip** Ignore as many standard libraries as you can and use cross-platform equivalents where possible, as these have been pre-tested to a greater extent than your internal equivalents.

From a management point of view, when developing on multiple consoles, you need an NDA from each of the manufacturers. If the team does not have suitable paperwork (such as when part of the work is being done by a third-party developer), then you need to ensure that all console-specific code is placed in a console-specific directory and that the source control software is set up to deny specific developers from those parts of the source tree.

Assets

Once the problems of individual assets—such as graphics and sounds—has been solved, there is then the problem of asset management and the generation of an asset pipeline, as the complexity grows exponentially with cross-platform development. You will have several instances to deal with.

---

[5]Writing this line brings back (bad) memories of a bug that occurred only on the GameCube, but not the PC, many, many, years ago!

First, there is a set of common generic assets. These are used across all versions of the game, such as the developer logo or the game title. They may be autoconverted by the asset pipeline into platform-specific ones to match the screen resolution, but the content remains the same.

To complicate matters, these generic versions may also get replaced by custom versions, such as when the PlayStation version differs from the Xbox versions. (And Microsoft won't like you if you accidentally include a Sony banner in your game!) Being able to switch assets in the asset pipeline eliminates one more potential problem from the code side, and frees up one more coder to fix code-specific bugs.

Sometimes these assets are complex, such as video clips. In some cases, your tool chain is able to convert a video effectively between 25 and 30 frames per second (fps) (to handle the differences between PAL and NTSC, respectively) or between MP4 and AVI (to handle platform codec differences); but other times, you need a completely new replacement file (such as for high definition, widescreen, or letterbox variants). Often it won't be an en masse replacement, because some files need custom movie clips (such as when a cut-scene is rendered with the in-game graphics engine); whereas others can use an automatically converted version and no one will be any the wiser. Thus, the metadata for every file needs to be expanded to cover the processing method that is used.

Assets might also be replaced according to country. Obviously, this includes text files for the in-game text and subtitles for the cut-scenes, but less obviously, it might include a green blood texture for shipping to countries that do not allow red blood in games.[6]

■ **Tip** Avoid placing text into image files, if possible, since that necessitates new art assets (and a custom element in the asset pipeline) to ensure correct localization.

Finally, consider the necessary SKU, or stock keeping unit. You might have a game for the UK market that includes only the English text files and videos, and a separate one for Germany (with German text, videos, and green blood patches), and a separate one for Europe with the basic language configuration of English, French, Italian, German, and Spanish (also known as EFIGS) and all the associated language assets. This introduces an extra step in the game build process, as well as code configuration changes to trigger a *Select your language* screen at the beginning of the game.

If your game includes voice acting, then an EFIGS build contains five complete banks of audio data. In terms disk space volume, this might get loud! So the tool chain needs to support extra metadata to reduce the resolution of the Spanish textures (for example) so that everything can fit within the necessary size limits.

■ **Tip** Match your hierarchy according to the business structure. Often this is platform-sku-environment, in that order. A different platform is more likely to be handled by a separate part of the business; the SKU is only likely to change with the localization teams; and the build environment is typically under the developer's jurisdiction.

---

[6]Germany is the most common example.

In short, your target folder will grow to the point where it won't be uncommon to have file names that read like this:

```
game/target/ios/debug/sku_uk/resources/audio/lang/en/welcome.wav
```

As you can see, it can get messy! But that's par for the course when precision is both necessary and expected.

Using Databases

As more and more games use databases to hold content, statistics, localization text, and game balancing information, so it becomes more complex to prepare a basic development machine. There are three basic methods to simplify this.

The first is to maintain an internal development database that all team members can use by simply configuring a file in `config/database.conf`, for example. Each team member may have their own account, to restrict their access rights to read-only, or to limit changes to a specific part of the DB. All modern DBs allow for fine-grain control like this.

The DB itself is maintained by a responsible admin, who may also write or download a custom front-end to allow the necessary content developers to amend the data. Often you work with two different databases: one used by the developers and one for the content team. This is because it is very easy to make mistakes in content curation. And it's likely that the database as a whole will be inconsistent while the changes occur, which may also introduce many transient and non-reproducible errors. It also gives everyone a chance to find and fix old bugs reliant on the old data before it is lost with the new content. We'll consider this idea again in Chapter 11, when deploying these databases to live production servers.

Second, you can export the necessary data into a file and incorporate it directly into the game via a CSV or similar flat file. Note that this is not a general solution, but in many cases, it is suitable.

Finally, you can set up a database on each local developer's machine. MySQL, SQLite, and similar open source databases are easy to set up on most development platforms nowadays. (Linux is still optimal due to its lineage with servers.) In this case, you need to ensure that the following are update to date:

- The *schema*, which initializes the database structures

- The *fixture or seed file*, which places the initial data within those structures

- The *migration plan*, so that changes can be made incrementally to the database structure, without needing to rebuild all the data

The last point is the important one when it comes to live production data running a game in the real world, since that database contains records of all of your players, their purchases, and their achievements. You do not want to lose that data! Fortunately for us, such details are reserved for server-side developers and so we do not need to consider it here.

The Development Process

Even a solo project needs a process— a place to store code, resources, notes, ideas, bugs, and so on. Furthermore, every team needs to refine the process to improve. It's a never-ending process that evolves to fit the needs of the specific developers on the team, rather than being something that can be prescribed.

The Prototype

Before beginning on the real game, you should build a rough prototype to test the basic game mechanics and ideas. It can be in any language or platform you like—the prototype might be thrown away entirely at the end of the process. You don't even need to worry about having proper animations or graphics. Your focus should be to test the most difficult areas of the game, either to play or to build, and to test the area with the most uncertainty.

If your game is about the creatures that swarm and multiply in a drop of water, then create prototypes to see if it's possible to render 1,000 microorganisms on the screen at once, as that's likely to be your choke point. Similarly, if you're building a sandbox game with an outdoors terrain, see if the draw distance is acceptable given a sample environment.

When prototyping the gameplay for a puzzle game, build the basic idea to determine if it's possible to succeed. Or does your design have a subtle flaw or feature that makes it impossible to win in some circumstances?[7] If you can't reason mathematically about the game theory behind the puzzle, there's nothing wrong with building a small AI system to try to solve 1,000 randomly generated puzzles.

If the game (without audio or graphics) is still fun to play, then you can consider the prototype a success and move on to a formal build.

Designing the Flow

The first part of the process is to take the design document and compose a formal design and walkthrough. This makes sure that all parts of the game are accounted for. Drawing the screens on paper can help because it ensures that none of the "obvious" things are omitted. A typical game might follow this pattern:

- Publisher title screen(s)

- Developer title screen(s)

- Licensed software title screen(s)

- Language selection screen

- Main menu

---

[7]The Gem Puzzle (a.k.a. the 15-puzzle) is a deceptively simple puzzle that can be rendered impossible by transposing two pieces.

- Instructions page

- Credits page

- Options page

- Load a previously saved game, or memory card slot selection, screen

- Game intro screen or cut-scene

- Main game

- In-game menu

- In-game, save state dialog

- In-game, options dialog (to mirror the options page)

- End level screen, or cut-scene, when level or game won

- End level screen, or cut-scene, when level or game failed

- High-score screen

- Achievements screen

Each step should be broken down further to include any features necessary to fulfill the platform's technical requirements for being ready for development. These steps can in turn be broken down further with paper outlines, so that each feature is formally declared. For example, the options page must indicate which options are to be shown, such as music volume, screen resolution, and graphics quality. This reveals whether they need to have an entire screen or a dialog box, or if they can be incorporated elsewhere.

■ **Tip**   Leave the game design breakdown until last. It's the most fun (and the reason most of us got into the industry!) part to work on, so leaving it as a reward ensures that the other components get done and to a reasonable standard.

When these steps are known, you can create the first build.

Implementation

To build the game, each of the designed areas has to be broken down into tasks for development. Each task has a priority based on its importance in the game, and a series of dependent tasks that must be finished before this can start. In the beginning, a small amount of every task must be completed. After all, it *is* possible to release a game with a visually poor menu screen, but it's very difficult to release a game without a menu at all.

Often we adopt an agile approach (as opposed to a waterfall approach), enabling us to execute on the management structure of an MVP approach (minimal viable product) to negotiate features in smaller batches, thereby reducing risk. Furthermore, by adopting MVP and building the smallest amount necessary of each section, we can progress to other areas faster. Consequently, every feature is broken down into categories: necessary, important, and nice-to-have. In this way, there is always something available to play, even if the quality is lacking. Once each area of the game has been developed to MVP standard, each developer can look to the least developed area to raise its level of quality above that of its nearest neighbor. Then rinse and repeat.

■ **Tip**   Always ask the question, "What's the most important thing I can do today?" and work to fix that.

There are many different methodologies available, such as TDD,[8] agile,[9] and waterfall.[10] A prominent approach is *agile* software development, such as the Scrum[11] or Kanban[12] practices.

Scrum, for example, works on two-week blocks of work called *sprints*. Before each sprint, the most useful tasks are moved from the total list of tasks (called a *backlog*) and placed into the working area or current sprint board. This is often Post-it notes on a window, but there are also digital online versions, such as Trello. Estimates are then made on the time required for each task; priorities are reassigned, if necessary. Developers take the next task in the list to work on.

At the end of each sprint, the game is demoed to the team to show progress. A retrospective compares the actual times with the estimates to help improve the team in the next sprint. And the process begins again.

Testing

Although often considered as the last thing involved in the development cycle, testing should be the first, if only to instill a sense of professionalism in the team. There are many bug-reporting and issue-tracker tools available,[13] although it's the process that we're concerned with here.

At the basic level, all bugs can be placed into categories of severity. The number and grading of the categories is up to you, but the following is a typical breakdown:

A.   Showstopping bugs that prevent the game from being played or completed.

B.   Important elements of the game are missing or broken, but you can still complete it.

C.   Elements are noticeably missing or broken.

D.   Elements are missing or broken, but unless you knew where to look, you wouldn't notice.

E.   Features that are nice to have.

---

[8]See https://en.wikipedia.org/wiki/Test-driven_development
[9]See https://en.wikipedia.org/wiki/Agile_software_development
[10]See https://en.wikipedia.org/wiki/Waterfall_model
[11]See https://en.wikipedia.org/wiki/Scrum_(software_development)
[12]See https://en.wikipedia.org/wiki/Kanban_(development)
[13]Mantis, Sifter, Lighthouse, 16bugs, Jira, etc. (Google is your friend)

Having a formal classification ensures that all bugs are treated according to their merits, and not the whim of the team. Naturally, over time, the classification will grow to accommodate the specifics of the game.

Alongside the category, you also need to write a formal bug report. This doesn't need to be an essay, a series of bullets points is best, but it should detail as many points as possible, including the following:

- Your name

- The build version of the game

- Full details of the machine, including OS, memory, hard disk, screen size, and so on (there are tools that can capture this information for you)

- The smallest reproducible use case, with a step-by-step guide on how to reproduce the problem

- A save-game file, if possible, from just before the bug occurs

- A screen capture of the game in action (using a tool like Camtasia)

Ideally, you should be able to reproduce the bug yourself by following your own instructions. In doing so, you'll be able to demonstrate it for the programmer while under the debugger, and ensure that you have documented the problem completely. You should also try to reproduce the steps on a newer or an older version of the game to help determine when the bug was introduced.

Someone on your team should be the QA manager. Or if you're a small team, the project manager or someone non-technical should be assigned the role of QA manager, since they are more likely to describe the symptoms of the problem, rather than what they think is causing it. Their job is to ensure that the bugs are cataloged, that duplicates are removed, and that the reporting is correct. Along with the producer, the QA manager ensures that the severity category is correct. Once a bug has been claimed fixed, it is also the QA manager's responsibility to check that it truly has been.

■ **Tip** The QA manager should also ensure that old issues don't clog up the bug database.

Bugs are generally tackled in order, starting at A. However, this means that a lot of important features may never get done. It also means that the game will never be properly polished. This is because the real polish occurs when those features and bugs in the C–E range are fixed. There is a school of thought that says you should periodically fix these issues ahead of the showstopping bugs. Although a producer is happy to ship a less-than-polished game, they will never ship a game with a showstopping bug!

■ **Tip** Near the end of development, introduce "anything goes Friday," where developers are allowed to fix any bug on the list. Since developers like the fun stuff, this ensures that the "fun" and "polished" items get resolved, even if there are still A-grade bugs to fix.

Regression testing should also take place. This process ensures that new functionality hasn't reanimated old bugs. Most of the time, new bugs show themselves readily. But since you have a bug database detailing many deviously obscure little critters, it makes sense to retry them on the later versions of the code.

Version Control

The purpose of a version control tool, such as Git or Subversion, is to store each change made to a set of files during their lifetime so that you can review those changes at a later date. Whereas a naïve solution might simply copy the files to a new directory and add a timestamp, version control stores only what parts have changed since last time, producing a more lean solution. You can also switch between parallel versions to help determine at what point a bug was introduced.

All the files within that project, as stored in the tool, are collectively known as a *repository*. Each time a new feature is written, or a bug is fixed, the set of changes that constitutes that improvement[14] is committed to the repository. The change set also includes metadata such as the time, date, and the person who changed it, and a comment from that person indicating why. Every time a change happens, the repository updates its internal revision number. The revision number is always used in preference to a date, since there can often be many change sets committed on a single day, or within a single hour—or even a second.

The version control tool performs all operations with these revisions numbers in mind. It enables you to review the code from a particular revision, compared to the current version, to see what's changed or what's gone wrong. It can mark a revision as a "gold master," or "fixed that stupid bright-green rendering bug," and so on.

Once your basic game framework is running, you should start to employ version control, for both source code and assets. Even if the game comprises of only a blank screen and a placeholder background of "coder art" and a trivial build script, commit it as soon as possible to version control so that others can start work. It is not necessary to wait until the build process works perfectly. Start small and iterate.

■ **Tip** If you're building a cross-platform game, then there will always be a lead development platform. Add the code into source control once this lead platform is working so that everyone else can start work on that lead platform. Once your development processes have been ironed out, you can create a build structure for the second platform with more insight into the problems.

It is unimportant which source control tool you use, provided you use one and have a formal process for using it. Git is the most popular today, with Subversion and Perforce still holding ground in a few development studios.

---

[14]Called a change set, funnily enough.

Some teams prefer to split version control into source control and asset control, with separate repositories for each. The history of this decision originates from a time when *source* control applications were used to store *assets*. Since the text in a source file changes very little, the algorithms behind source control needed to store very little data to indicate that a change has been made; for example, "add .normalize() after the 7th character on line 20." These same algorithms could not cope so well with binary data. Consequently, an entire copy of the binary files was often stored, leading to large version control repositories that slowed down access for everyone.

Since then, this has been less of an issue, because there are often options to store only the last N revisions of a file; or to regularly prune old revisions in a given directory path; or because file systems can routinely handle multigigabyte repositories without issue. In adopting the MVP approach, one should use the smallest, simplest, thing to begin work and upgrade as and when necessary. In most cases, you'll be able to build a polished game with only one Git or Subversion server.

Our primary concerns are with the process of how we handle the two lynchpins of externals and branches.

The Basics of Version Control

If you have never used version control before, then you must start now. There is no way of developing product, of quality or otherwise, without it. For a solo developer coming onto a new team, having to share work (and by extension, mistakes) with a bunch of strangers is terrifying. If the team is unaware of this anxiety, then the developer is more likely to develop in private and release only large amorphous blobs of code that cannot be easily understood. This, in turn, leads to even lower overall code quality.

Even the solo developer on a one-person project benefits from version control. Not least because it shows the thought process of each feature being built, especially if the developer adds good comments to each commit, fully explaining the problem and its solution.

▦ **Note** The worst programmer you will ever meet is yourself from six months ago. Write comments as if you are explaining and apologizing to your future self in six months, covering all necessary context. Using an in-joke that referenced a film that you saw is likely to bemuse you later. So, if you don't think the future you would understand it, then rewrite both the code and the comments.

In a team environment, make use of other developers to help write effective comments. Before every commit, ask another programmer (junior or senior) to review the code that you changed and ask them if the comments make sense. We'll look at the purposes and goals of such a code review later, when discussing process.

Using External Repositories

Externals are a way of creating a link between one source control project and another. Instead of copying the entire source tree (of, say, the game engine) into your project, you can use a URL to the other repository and reference it directly in your project.

In Subversion, this is called *externals*. It is set up by using the properties feature. Whenever you update the main repository, all of its externals are updated too. This means that if you do not have control over the commits that happen in the external repository, you might get new and/or broken code. To prevent this, you should use the -r option, which ties the external to a specific revision of the remote code.

In Git, there are two options. The first are subtree merges, which act like Subversion's externals and ensure that all clones and checkouts also pull data from the external project. Since this automatically pulls data from the remote repository, you might be concerned about new library code breaking old game code. Consequently, you can fork the existing project into your repository, and let it reside in a quarantined area of third-party elements. The lead is then in charge of pulling new code down once appropriate tests have been performed and measures have been taken.

The second method involves Git submodules, which are tied to a specific revision of external code, but requires the users to manually checkout or clone them.

Using Branches

Branches are the way source control keeps old stable releases and brand-new features separate. Each branch contains a copy of the entire source and asset tree, and keeps a history of one single feature or bug fix. In the beginning, there is usually a branch called trunk, from which all branches emanate. The manner in which developers use branches, however, differs between companies. And even teams within companies. I outline two popular strategies, although most teams find their best approach lies somewhere between the two.

The first strategy is "trunk-heavy,"[15] as shown in Figure 9-1. Here, all developers work on features on the main trunk of the project. They don't branch from it (i.e., they don't make their own copy.) Instead, they work directly on the files they need to and when the code is ready and tested, commit it back to the trunk. This works well for teams that need to iterate fast and don't want to spend time merging changes between lots of developers. Git facilitates this workflow well, since each developer can commit many changes to the local copy of their repository without pushing it back to the other developers. In this way, a full history of the changes it kept without the possibility of the changes breaking the whole game (which, by the way, is the major disadvantage of this approach). Small teams often like this method.

---

[15]Also known as trunk-based or mainline development.

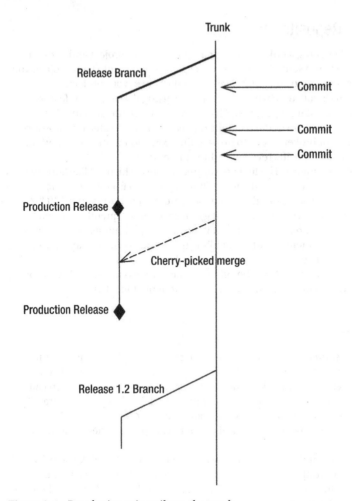

Figure 9-1. *Developing primarily on the trunk*

In order to create a release build, the developers create a new branch from the trunk and call it *release*. It is tested and fixed as appropriate, before being tagged with a release version (so that bugs can be retested on old versions) and deployed.

Fixes can be made to the release branch in one of two ways. Either they are made in the release branch itself and then cherry-picked back into the main trunk, or they are made in the trunk and cherry-picked into release. Either approach works. The conceptual difference is that in the case of the latter no changes are ever made to the release branch, therefore the only way to affect a release is with a cherry-picked merge.

The second method is to create a develop branch from the trunk (which is often considered the master) and branch again from develop for each feature and fix you make. The feature branches are then built and tested before being merged back into the develop branch.

Releases are created in a similar way to the trunk-heavy version; a branch is taken from the current working version (in this case, called develop) where is it checked to ensure that the previous features haven't conflicted to produce a broken build. This release branch is fixed as necessary before being merged into the master (or trunk) *and* the develop branch.

Fixes are made identically to the trunk-heavy version. In many cases, a separate "hot-fix" branch is created from the master and merged back, instead of working on the master directly, as shown in Figure 9-2.

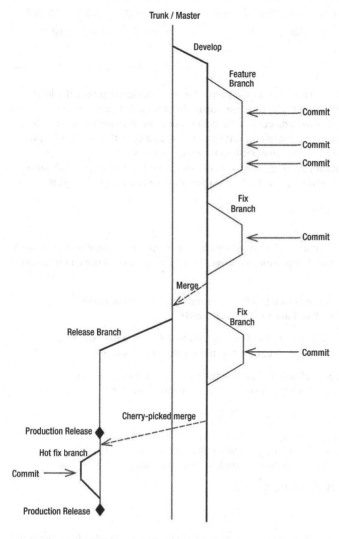

Figure 9-2. *Developing with feature branches*

This approach has the advantage of there being less chance of the develop branch breaking, and greater chance of it containing all the necessary up-to-date features. It is often favored by larger teams. The stability of the develop branch makes it more suitable to those sharing code with non-programmers.

There is a lot merging between the branches, however, which can cost a lot of time, and has the potential for a developer to miss another's changes. (The trunk-heavy approach doesn't have this, since every developer has the full ready-to-release code on their machine all the time, and so are more likely to spot conflicts and problems.)

■ **Tip** Always delete feature branches after they have been merged, since they are not typically useful, and the existence of too many branches can cause performance issues in products like GitLab.

The merge process also has human elements. You may decide that only the lead developer is permitted to merge a feature into the main branch. When reviewing a feature with another developer (as we'll discuss in the next section on code reviews), it might be a good idea to require the *reviewer* to commit the code, rather than the original author, thereby making the reviewer an active participant in the process.

To recap, any branching strategy can work, provided the team is diligent in testing each merge and feature, and there is always a stable branch from which to deploy.

Code Reviews

The purpose and goal of a code review is for another developer to sanity check your work, which, in turn, ensures that the product improves as a consequence of the change. This can mean many things.

- Does it fulfill the design brief? Were there any implicit or explicit requirements that have not been covered?

- Are the inputs to the method clearly defined? Can you pass 0 into the method? Can you trust the input to be non-malicious?

- Are the outputs clearly defined? If the method is finding objects, but none exist, does it return a NULL or an empty array?[16]

- Does it return an error code? Throw an exception?

- Have the edge cases been considered (such as when there is a chance of a divide by zero, or code will process a NULL or empty list)? Is it possible to become stuck in an infinite loop?

- Is there a set of tests for the code?

---

[16]An empty array is typically better, since it prevents the calling code from needing to explicitly test for NULL as a standard enumerator will handle the case normally.

- If this is a bug fix, does it accidentally introduce any new ones?

- Does it conform to the project guidelines regarding naming conventions, use of comments, and so on? There may be automated tools that you can use for this stage.

We'll consider the implementation when looking at testing in the next chapter. Since there is a lot to consider in each code review, it is better to commit a lot of small changes (and perform a number of small code reviews) than to make very few large ones. With that in mind, let's consider what's necessary to facilitate a good review between the original author of the code and a reviewer. There are many more ideas than what is presented here, obviously, but this should give you a good grounding in the basics.[17]

Before beginning a code review, *the author* should always read the differences between the working code and the revision in version control. This helps refresh their memory as to what all the changes were and gives them a chance to remove any debugging or temporary code that they may have added and since forgotten about. This time can also be used to insert additional comments to the source.

Before beginning a code review, *the reviewer* should think about the feature or bug fix they're being asked to review. This gives them the opportunity to think about how *they* would solve the problem, where the issues could occur, and what systems are likely to be affected.

When they finally see the code under review, they can use this knowledge of the problem domain to ensure that all angles have been considered effectively. Votta[18] argues that more defects are found in reading code, than by holding a meeting about it, so it is an approach to consider.

Review only a small number of lines in a single sitting—often quoted as between 200 and 400. Beyond this, and the ratio of times compared to code studied changes dramatically because a Pandora's box of potential problems can emerge. Furthermore, it is a sign that the feature you're trying to commit is too big and/or complex for a single change set.

Timebox each review to never exceed 60 minutes. This should allow you to be fully immersed in the minutia of the code, without wasting time. It also encourages the change set to remain small, since any large code block could not be understood within that time frame.

Timebox each review to be at least 5 minutes. Even a simple one-line change has the potential to affect multiple systems. Even fixing a spelling mistake could cause the text to overrun on some, hitherto unconsidered, screen. Or if the word now contains an accented character, is that letter in all the fonts that might be used to render it? Similar possibilities exist for cases where objects are moved on-screen by a single pixel.

Review the code in the editor and the debugger. This allows assumptions to be tested. For example, if the author claims "this function can never be passed 0," it gives the reviewer a chance to verify that claim, either by playing the game in a peculiar way or by amending some code further up the call stack to simulate the use case.

---

[17]You might also want to search on the terms *peer review* and *code inspection*.
[18]Lawrence G. Votta, Jr., "Does every inspection need a meeting?," Proceedings of the 1st ACM SIGSOFT Symposium on Foundations of Software Engineering, p.107-114, December 8–10, 1993, Los Angeles, CA.

Follow review checklists (such as this) to ensure that a systematic approach is taken to the review and that conventions are followed. For example, does all display text go through the localization routines? Does the deploy process need updating because of this change? Use the checklists as a start to hone your own process that is molded to the shape and size of your team.

Always ask, "Why?" This forces all parties to question the underlying components of the code and verify their assumptions. It is also good for finding omissions, like edge cases that have not been considered or coded, which are often the hardest issues to detect.

Review other methods of best practice to determine which apply. Software engineering is awash with acronyms such as SOLID[19] and DRY,[20] and while it's an ongoing battle to recall them all, introducing a new one each week can raise the standard of each individual programmer, which in turn improves the whole team.

If your team is large enough, ask a third person to attend as moderator. By being more hands-off, they have the capacity to ensure that checklists are followed since they're not as deep into the internal specifics of the code. That is, they're able to look at the wood, and not the proverbial trees, to ensure that the goal of the review is achieved. Being a third person, they can also function as a tiebreaker.

Once the review is complete, the code can be fixed, if necessary. You may then decide to have another full code review process discussing those fixes (if they are large or fundamental) or simply perform a five-minute review that checks that the author has made the changes discussed in the first meeting. As long as a follow-up review happens every time an issue is found, you can be happier that your code is of a higher quality at the end of the review than it was at the start of the review.

The final words in the review process are simple: review it. First, determine the hard data surrounding the process: count the lines of code reviewed, the time taken, the number of defects found, and so on. After each review, consider what could be done better or more effectively to catch more problems earlier. Keep a record of them and you'll soon find that specific issues are endemic to you and your team. Amend your checklists and processes to adapt to these discoveries, so you can focus on the more productive areas; that is, those more likely to be problematic in the future.

A Typical Review Checklist

There is no such thing as a "complete" checklist because you won't know everything that can go wrong until it has already gone wrong. At least once. Instead, it is a working document that covers each area that can potentially cause problems. Don't worry about creating a long checklist. It won't take as much time as you think to work through a long checklist since, by working through it repeatedly, you no longer create the bugs that the checklist includes, which makes each point very quick and easy to answer. (Since you asked yourself the same questions during the code design and development stage.)

---

[19]See https://en.wikipedia.org/wiki/SOLID_(object-oriented_design)
[20]See https://en.wikipedia.org/wiki/Don%27t_repeat_yourself

Documentation

Document the code and the updates to the design; the latter is generally used to write the manual or tutorial text. Consider the following questions when writing your documentation:

- Are the method names sensible and descriptive?

- Are the input and output parameters described in terms of the types they'll accept and the range of permissible values? If it describes a unit (e.g., length) is the unit (e.g., meters) documented?

- If there is a complex algorithm or idea, is it explained? Does it link to an explanation? Is it on Wikipedia? Is it a private site that will likely disappear eventually?

- If the code borrows from elsewhere, is the license and reference included in the comments?

- Are all external influences, dependencies, and impacts mentioned?

- Does any code need a TODO comment for future maintainers?

For documenting methods in code, there are tools like Doxygen and TwinText,[21] which allow you to write specially formatted comments directly into the code, which are then processed into an API manual.

Testing

We'll formally look at testing in the next chapter, but by way of an introduction, consider the following.

- Does the code have or need unit tests?

- Are there any new code paths that necessitate a change to an existing test?

- Are all code paths tested or considered in the code review? Does the algorithm have a set of known issues?

- Could there be null references or pointers that need checking? Do dependent methods return null reference or empty arrays if results are not found?

- Is it possible for the code to extend beyond the bounds of an array?

---

[21]See https://en.wikipedia.org/wiki/Comparison_of_documentation_generators

- Is the new code already available in another (pre-tested) library? Does this code belong in a library?

- Does the bug fix actually fix the bug in all cases, or just the one that was initially discovered?

Handling Errors

There are several ways that code responds to errors. The specifics of your game and team indicate which is suitable for you. What's important is that you understand from where the errors occur and that *something* is done to handle them. You will notice a strong resemblance to the documentation checklist here, leading to the truism that if the code differs from the documentation, then both are wrong.

- Are the input parameters validated?

- Are the return values from this method checked?

- Are the return values from any methods that this one calls checked?

- Are all resources released in the case of an error? (Most notably in C++ when dynamically allocated memory is not freed after an exception is thrown; but there are many others, including opened file handles and still-captured mutexes.)

Using Threads

The complexity of thread programming is far beyond the scope of this book. Just to say it's a necessary evil to maximize the CPU cycles of PC and console titles, and therefore necessary to push the hardware as far as it can go.

- Ensure that globals are protected and locked.

- Can these objects be accessed by other threads? Is there a locking procedure in place?

- Is it known whether these objects are being used for read, write, or read-write purposes? Does this affect your locking strategy?

- Does every lock have a corresponding unlock?

- If multiple locks are used within a method, are they handled in the right order?

- Are threads synchronized? Or are there busy-wait loops?

- What causes deadlock?

- What causes livelock (or similar resource starvation issues)?

Allowing multiply elements of the game to have access to a single resource (i.e., the game state) is fraught with trouble, so a thorough understanding of concurrent[22] programming is recommended if you intend to take this route.

Performance

It is generally not enough to ask, "Does it work?" or "Does it work on my machine?" Instead, the question needs to ask if it *will* work fast enough when things change.

"Make it work, make it right, make it fast".

—Kent Beck

While it's true that CPU speeds increase, the size of data also increases—and it usually outpaces processor speed. If your game has any form of dynamic content, user-generated content, or external input, then those parts of the code that deal with it need to consider CPU speed and data size.

- Is the algorithm suitable? For now? For later? How long does it take to add your name to the high-score table when there are only 10 entries, compared to 10,000?

- Is the algorithm suitable in this use case? For example, if you want to sort a list that only has one or two entries out of place (such as in the high-score table), then consider an insertion sort instead of the pre-built quick sort, because it scales linearly for larger values (see Table 9-1).

Table 9-1. Sorting Algorithms

Algorithm	Worst Case	Average Case	Best Case
Bubble sort	O(n^2)	O(n^2)	O(n^2)
Heap sort	O(n*log(n))	O(n*log(n))	O(n*log(n))
Insertion sort	O(n^2)	O(n^2)	O(n)
Merge sort	O(n*log(n))	O(n*log(n))	O(n*log(n))
Quick sort	O(n^2)	O(n*log(n))	O(n*log(n))
Selection sort	O(n^2)	O(n^2)	O(n^2)

- By increasing the performance, you are decreasing the time taken for parts of the game to work. Are you decreasing the time of the code running, the data loading, or of the memory accesses? While heavy memory use often leads to more processing, the reverse can also be true (as is the case with most caches.)

---

[22]See https://en.wikipedia.org/wiki/Concurrent_computing

- Do you have scaffolding or mocks to create a large data set that might highlight a problematic use case with non-scalable code?

- If the code has been optimized for speed, is the original implementation still visible? You might want to run both concurrently as part of a testing procedure, or to use the original as a teaching tool.

- Does the profiler show this code to be on the critical path? If not, it doesn't need optimizing.

- Are objects (re-)constructed too often? Can constant references and pointers be used to help the compiler/interpreter execute the code more effectively?

- Is a cache a possibility to improve the speed?

- Is a cache necessary to improve the speed?

- Do you really need to use assembly? A better algorithm achieves a better speed, regardless of language.

A polished game consistently runs at 60fps. Any weak algorithm or implementation that causes this to drop to 30fps is a sign of a non-polished game. Even if you only aim for 30fps, aim for it consistently.

▪ **Tip** The best way to ensure that your game runs at 60fps is to never introduce any code or data that causes it to drop below that. If something does, then either optimize the code or data at that time, and do not continue with other work until it's back to a consistent 60.

Summary

Throughout this chapter, we looked at the many ways in which good code is felt, but never seen. Starting with the development environment, we ensured that all team members could work with the most recent build of the game and that all assets were properly structured in appropriately named directories. This covered source code files, art assets, sound files, and additional meta files, such as the README and icons.

We then covered the basics of the build process, so that the game assets could be combined into a single target folder, ready to be played, with one target for each platform and environment for those cases where the game needs to work across multiple platforms.

Continuing, we discussed the development process and how to build a prototype (or MVP) to ensure that all features are implemented and tested. We also discussed along with the methods for version control and code review to ensure that the process is smooth and introduces as few errors as possible.

We extend this idea in the next chapter by looking at other ways that the game can be tested and any other errors preempted.

CHAPTER 10

Testing

Working Right, All the Time

To most developers, the concept of testing comes with dread and postponement. In reality, it should do neither. It should be a welcome addition to the programmers' arsenal, because it gives a confidence and peace of mind that little else can. It is something that should be part of the entire development process, and not just tacked on at the end.

In this chapter, we'll look at several solutions to turn bug-ridden games into polished gems. But we start with the other side of that coin—how to stop the bugs getting in there in the first place!

Prevention

For some reason, there's always a lack of surprise on the face of a developer when they are told, "There's a bug in your code." Why? If they are unsurprised then surely the only reason for there being bugs in the code is if they added them in, purposefully! Consequently, the best cure is in the prevention, so alongside a code review (see Chapter 9) we should look to other tools and techniques to eliminate bugs.

Static Code Analysis

Starting with the source itself, there are several exploratory tools that you can use before the code is ever executed. Depending on the language and platform, the name of these tools will vary, but a variation of Lint is available for most platforms and is the primary weapon.

Lint scans the source code to look for suspicious code constructs, which are elements that are syntactically correct but likely to be wrong, based on the experience of the tool authors. This might include variables being used before being initialized, ignored return values, and expressions and conditions that are actually constant. It can be thought of as a very strict compiler. Indeed, many compilers have incorporated many of Lint's features over the years, but in the same vein that having two virus checkers is always a good idea, having a second Lint checker is a similarly good step.

© Steven Goodwin 2016

S. Goodwin, *Polished Game Development*, DOI 10.1007/978-1-4842-2122-8_10

CHAPTER 10 ■ TESTING

■ **Tip** Non-compiled languages don't have this benefit and so should always feature a Lint'ing step.

For C/C++ programmers, there are many Lint variations available, including Splint and PC-Lint; whereas JavaScript developers look toward JSLint. All can be configured as part of the build process so that it runs automatically.

Defensive Code, or Otherwise

There are generally two ways of failing: loudly, and quietly. All software features a combination of both. During development, all errors should be loud, wherein the code should fail hard and fast. That is, the game stops and you can't continue playing the game, in any form, until the error is fixed. This error might include missing assets, out-of-range world coordinates, missing or inconsistent metadata, and so on. This "fail early, fail hard" philosophy ensures that problems don't remain in the code base for very long, since you are forced to fix them immediately.

However, once the game is in production, you want a quieter, more defensive, approach so that the methods can fail, but not cause any long-standing after effects. One simple example might be with the in-game menu. Under normal circumstances, the in-game menu can only be opened from the game screen; therefore, the openInGameMenu method makes various assumptions about the code's state and how it is called. However, a defensive programmer will often write the following method:

```
function openInGameMenu() {
  if (isInGameMenuOpen) {
    return false;
  }
  // Code as normal...
```

Similarly, we always expect there to be a valid state and a draw method attached to it. But it is extremely common to see code that protects against both, because it's simpler to be protective in the first instance, than defensive later on.

```
if (currentState && currentState.draw) {
  return currentState.draw(surface);
}
```

This code doesn't noticeably affect the performance since the CPU cycles spent handling the draw method far exceeds the two comparisons. However, including such validation checks in low-level math and animations libraries would be a performance killer. Instead, place such defensive tests higher up in the call stack.

One approach to argument validation is with assertions. Often these are simple macros that check that the function inputs are within a known range.

```
function calculateFactorial(number) {
    sgxAssert(number >= 0, 0);
    ...
}
```

The code for such a development-stage assertion is likely to be as follows:

```
#define sgxAssert(expr, unused) (((expr) ||  \
    ((sgxTrace(SGX_ERR_ERROR,__FILE__,__LINE__,#expr)) )))
```

This banal example would normally write a warning message to the player's console or screen, but attempt to execute the code anyway—most likely causing a hard crash via an infinite loop or an exhausted call stack. In production, however, this could change to the following:

```
#define sgxAssert(expr, retv) do { if (!(expr)) {       \
    sgxTrace(SGX_ERR_ERROR,__FILE__,__LINE__,#expr);  \
    sgxBreak(); return retv; }                         \
    } while(!(expr))
```

This second version returns a predetermined value in the case of failure that the programmer of the calling function has determined is sensible. Alternatively, you may wish instead to throw an exception so it can be caught higher up the call stack.

■ **Note**   It is not necessary to load every method with such checks, as that is likely to make the whole game run too slow to be playable.

Dynamic Code Analysis

Turing et al have taught us via the halting problem,[1] that finding all errors via static analysis is undecidable. Also, it is an undecidable problem to find them during run-time. We can, however, utilize various tools to indicate when a problem is occurring so that its side effects do not impact other areas of the code base at a later time.

■ **Tip**   It is inevitable that bugs will exist, no matter what you do. So try and minimize their impact as much as possible.

While not every tool is available, or applicable, to every language, knowing the types of problems that software in general is able to experience means you should be able to reason an equivalent solution for your specific game.

---

[1]See https://en.wikipedia.org/wiki/Halting_problem

Buffer Overruns

The most common example of this is in C/C++ software when string buffers overrun or memory corruption errors occur. This rarely has any effect on the code being executed, except maybe an incorrect answer, but because the computer has written arbitrary data into memory, it doesn't own another subsystem will use this data (thinking it's still valid) and break the integrity of that other subsystem. Tools like BoundsChecker, Intel Parallel Inspector, and Purify can help here.

Memory Leaks

For every allocation, there must be an equal and opposite deallocation. This applies to all languages, not just those with explicit memory management functions, like C/C++. Memory blocks that are not freed cause leaks, and freeing a block twice can imply a hidden bug somewhere else in the code. Naturally, there are tools to help you here, such as Dmalloc, Parasoft Insure++, Purify, and Valgrind.

Alternatively, you can wrapper all your memory allocation methods with your own and write something yourself. This is often too much trouble than its worth, and doesn't help you prove that the leak is happening in a third-party library to which you have limited access.

■ **Note** Because the methods used to detect memory leaks have close ties with buffer overruns and memory corruption, it is not usual for one tool to provide a solution to both problems.

Coverage Testing

A coverage tool, like Gcov, lets you run the game as normal, and once it's ended, review the number of lines that were actually executed. This helps you prove that your tests are truly testing the whole code base.

Data Testing

Within the game and tool chain, there are several places where the data can be checked automatically, thereby eliminating errors (or at least providing warnings about them) ahead of time.

As you read in Chapter 7, subtle audio bugs occur when sounds don't play, because the QA team is unaware that there is a sound that's meant to play. There are several reasons why that sound might not play.

- The sound name requested doesn't exist.

- The sound name requested has been misspelled.

- The sound name hasn't been preloaded before playing.

Fortunately, there are a couple of helper solutions to this problem.

The first method occurs at build time and is a custom tool that processes the source code to generate a list of each sound resourced and played. You can simply eliminate the duplicates and order them alphabetically to determine which files have not been correctly requested. You can then manually review the lists to determine if any have been misspelled.

It is also a simple addition to extend this process by asking it to scan the disc to look for the specific file, and then to report if it's missing.

Since this type of check is likely to produce false negatives, especially for sound files whose names are computed algorithmically, we need to include a second check at run-time. For example, we could store an in-memory sample of an annoying sound. (Maybe some white noise, fingernails on a chalkboard, or Justin Bieber!) Then, whenever a sound can't be found, this temporary sound is played instead.

▓ **Tip**   Make this sound part of the binary, since it could introduce a false negative if the annoying sound doesn't exist on disc and therefore is never heard to indicate an error.

To ensure that these sounds are audible, you should make two (temporary) alterations to the audio library. First, rescale all positioning code so that the active sounds always play at a higher audible level than normal. This modifies a distant sound from 0 to 0.5, for example, which allows the tester to hear otherwise (almost) inaudible sounds. If there are effects that are only truly audible by going up close and personal to specific walls and doors in the level, this rescaling allows them to be heard in a more casual and non-exhaustive walk-through of the level, thereby saving time. Second, you need to trigger all alternate sounds, regardless of gameplay logic. This one is harder since it often requires additional game code. A case like this:

```
if (sgxRand() > 0.5) {
    playSound('monster_roar');
}
```

needs to become this:

```
if (true) {
    playSound('monster_roar');
}
```

Furthermore, any randomization needs to be amended, as follows:

```
roar = sgxRand(4);
sound_file = 'monster_roar_' + roar;
playSound(sound_file);
```

To something much more complex to ensure that each possible code path (and therefore, sound) was played. The most surefire way of ensuring that all variations were played is to trigger all variations, one after the other, on the first invocation of the code, since you couldn't guarantee that the code would be run enough times for you to hear all variations of the sound.

■ **Tip** The audio engine has its own play random sound method. Through a precise naming convention, the audio engine is able to know how many variations of each sample exist. It then picks one at random in such a way that if one is missing, that one is never chosen for playback. So although it might only ever play three of a possible four sounds, there will never be a gap. (Although the console and trace logs still report the missing file, so it can be fixed.)

There are similar techniques for graphics. A typical example is to initialize all textures to a checkerboard with squares in black and bright-green colors (0,255,0 or 0x00ff00) before attempting to load them. In this way, the texture loading code can still report an error for those that read the console logs, but this fluorescent checkerboard is then rendered in the world with such an obviously garish image that it is fixed quickly. A check pattern is used in preference to a solid color, since the latter might be part of legitimately blank textures.

These same techniques can be adopted for other asset types, like meshes and animations, although in practice, they are normally very obvious when they are not present. Indeed, many assets have codependencies such that the omission of one will generally cause a NULL pointer exception in the other, alerting you to the problem much earlier.

Input Sanitation

Whenever the user is given the chance to input data, there is a chance that the data will be broken in some fashion. Consequently, there is the requirement that it is sanitized before use.

■ **Caution** The more paranoid among you will realize that any data from the client cannot be trusted. So even if you are downloading assets from an online server, or loading them from a machine's (unencrypted) hard disc, they exist in the system's memory before being processed, and are therefore open to modification. In reality, this has a very low chance of ever happening, so is rarely worth the trouble.[2]

Validating input data should work on one very simple premise: describe a white list of what data or format is acceptable, instead of rejecting anything that isn't. Why this way around? For a start, it's normally a shorter list, and therefore simpler to implement. But more importantly, it stops currently unknown issues and techniques from breaking your game in the future.

---

[2]Conversely, this attitude is why it is possible to soft mod an Xbox using the *James Bond 007: Agent under Fire!* game. A few modified bytes on the memory card caused the game to execute unsanitized code, which allowed an installation of Linux.

Length Checks

In many cases, the player will be asked to enter their name or their team's name. Check the locations where this will be displayed to make sure that the name doesn't overrun the string buffers (if you're using C/C++ without a suitable string library) or the screen space allotted to it. It isn't enough to simply limit the string to 16 characters, or some other arbitrary number, since the display routines generally use typefaces that aren't monospace. Therefore, the five-letter name *Iliad* will consume significantly less screen real estate than the name *WWWWW*. Of course, no one other than a tester or an erstwhile hacker is likely to use such a name, so it is up to the producer and the development schedule whether you test for this or not.

Remember that when checking for string length, as well as screen width, there may be several places in which the text appears, each with a different maximum length based on either the position of the text or the typeface used. Start by determining the maximum screen width possible, and either limit the text string accordingly or crop it to this width. Noting, of course, that if you crop the text, there's nothing to stop repressed players using the team name "Scunthorpe" knowing that only five letters will be displayed, therefore bypassing any profanity filters you might have.

Range and Type Checks

Through good interface design, you can make it impossible for a player to enter a value outside of an accepted range. However, when that's not possible (such as in a text adventure, or when text entry boxes are an expected norm), you need to ensure validation.

■ **Tip** Defensive coding suggests you should always include validation, regardless of the interface.

If your player is trying to buy an in-game item, for example, then the range should be one or greater, and the type should be integral. While obvious, if the validation test is not done, then the player could buy -1 bullets. The following code would unintentionally increase the player's financial position!

```
money -= quantity * purchase_price;
```

Whenever an input field is shown, it is expected that the tester will type anything except the expected input, so be prepared.

> *"QA Engineer walks into a bar. Orders a beer. Orders 0 beers. Orders 999999999 beers. Orders a lizard. Orders -1 beers. Orders a sfdeljknesv."*
>
> —Bill Sempf

Type checking can be more complex if it's not a built-in type, like integers or floating points. Ensuring a distance is valid, for example, requires an understanding of units and conversion to know that both 1.5m and 150cm represent the same thing. Similarly, depending on the programming language used, an entry of 040 could be understood as 40 (in base 10), and not the octal number 40 (equivalent to 32 in decimal.)

Regular expressions (also known as *regexes* or *regexps*) are often touted as the savior of most arbitrary data parsing issues. For the most part, this is true. They are quick, expressive, and make it easy to process very complex data patterns. Unfortunately, they are also difficult to write well and likely to introduce false positives when specific edge cases are missed. Anyone who has experienced web development and needed to validate an email address will report writing regexps such as this:

```
\A(?:[a-z0-9!#$%&'*+/=?^_`{|}~-]+(?:\.[a-z0-9!#$%&'*+/=?^_`{|}~-]+)*
|"(?:[\x01-\x08\x0b\x0c\x0e-\x1f\x21\x23-\x5b\x5d-\x7f]
|\\[\x01-\x09\x0b\x0c\x0e-\x7f])*")@(?:(?:[a-z0-9](?:[a-z0-9-]*
[a-z0-9])?\.)+[a-z0-9](?:[a-z0-9-]*[a-z0-9])?
|\[(?:(?:25[0-5]|2[0-4][0-9]|[01]?[0-9][0-9]?)\.){3}
(?:25[0-5]|2[0-4][0-9]|[01]?[0-9][0-9]?|[a-z0-9-]*[a-z0-9]:
(?:[\x01-\x08\x0b\x0c\x0e-\x1f\x21-\x5a\x53-\x7f]
|\\[\x01-\x09\x0b\x0c\x0e-\x7f])+)
\])\z
```

This is most compact regex to correctly handle the official standard RFC 5322 of an email address!

Again, prevention is better than cure since the preferred method of data input is an interface that only allows you to enter the data in the format you require, rather than code to validate and sanitize it later. If you need a length, then the UI should suggest the units and the player works with that. If the units are variable, then introduce a drop-list, and so on.

Integrity Checks

I left the best for last because integrity checks are game-specific and often introduce many problems of their own. An *integrity check* is one where the game looks at the data being presented to it and determines if the information is reasonably correct. In single-player games, on locked-down hardware, this answer is usually that it can always be trusted to be correct. In online games with multiple players, the answer is usually that it can never be!

■ **Caution**   If working online, be sure to handle validation on both the client side (for speed and clarity of UX) and on the server side (to prevent the game from breaking.)

Take the example of the sprint race in a track and field game. The player bashes the buttons as fast as possible to make their character run 400 meters around the track. They do so in 46.5 seconds. Does that sound reasonable to you?[3] Should your game

---

[3]The world record, at time of writing, is 43.18s, so the answer is "Yes."

logic examine the two parameters—distance and time—and deduce that this player was cheating and therefore ignore the score? What if they ran the first 390 meters in 46.0 seconds, and the final 10 meters in 0.5 seconds?

What about a javelin throw of 103 meters?[4]

The point is that without the context of history, it is impossible to know what is humanly possible and what is not. A fictional computer game is no different. Even if QA cannot manage to score more than 100 points on a particular level, it doesn't mean that a talented player with many more months of obsessive playing time won't be able to do so at some point in the future; so, rejecting scores because they appear unreasonable to you may not be the best option.

Most of the time, you can compute the highest theoretical score by adding all the bonuses and awards possible within a level, and assuming the time bonus is scored at its maximum extent. However, even this can be misleading, since some elements of the game will be mutually exclusive so that it is possible to collect either the gold sword or the gold dagger, but not both. Consequently, knowing this information gives you a way of detecting and blocking cheats based on their data.

Ultimately, integrity checks are only possible with an explicit understanding of your entire game and every possible route through it.[5] But even then, it may be difficult to quantify *every* possible route. For example, in one game that I wrote, hackers were running software to slow the internal clock of the Flash player, while keeping the input handler running at normal speed, making it possible to collect a lot more objects that should have ever been possible. In this situation, however, since the internal clock still reported 10 seconds, it didn't look as if anything was wrong. Furthermore, blocking players that fall foul of these ranges comes with the risk of annoying very good players when they start reaching your predetermined upper boundary levels.

Bug Reporting

As I've said, it is inevitable that there will be bugs; so since it's inevitable, there's no reason why one shouldn't have a process for reporting, reproducing, and fixing bugs. There are many tools on the market to help here, even if you don't wish to spend a bean: Bugzilla, Jira, Mantis, Trac, and Lean Testing, to name just five! Whichever you choose is immaterial. What's important is that you use it and use it well. And you must have a known process—that the whole team is prepared to follow—for handling the life cycle of each bug.

The Team

The testing team, as ever, will be as large or small as you can afford. The people holding the roles may share the duty with their day job; for example, the deputy artist may also lead this team. More correctly, the testing team is called *QA*, since their role is of quality

---

[4]Again, the world record is 104.8m, so it's possible, although new specifications were introduced in 1986 meaning this record may never be broken.
[5]Including speed runs, if they apply to your genre.

assurance, and not testing. Since everyone should be focused on producing a quality product, no one in the company is too important to partake in testing. Conversely, everyone should understand that their opinion carries no more weight than anyone else's, and that the QA team lead is in charge.

The QA lead prepares a test plan for the game in conjunction with the rest of the leadership team. It details every area that needs to be tested before the game can be considered complete. It includes the legal compliance (e.g., size of company logos, duration of title screen), technical requirements of the console manufacturer, spelling and grammar throughout, and notes on every feature of every level and how they interconnect. The last part (although the most extensive) is the simplest to execute if there is an up-to-date design document available. (Even more reason to maintain such a document.)

When new features are added to the game in any form, or the requirements change, then the test plan needs to be updated accordingly and the QA team tasked with verifying that the new features are good and that old features haven't turned bad as a consequence.

There are many facets to how the game should be tested. A large part is to simply play the areas in question and be creative about finding ways of breaking the code. Can you buy -1 bullets (to use our previous example)? Push every limit. Hammer every button. This part of testing isn't pretty, but it's essential.

The Bug Life Cycle

In the first instance, a bug is reported by a test engineer (the posh term for "someone that finds a bug") into the bug tracking software of choice. Every bug is the result of a single problem—something that the programmer assumed was true actually wasn't! Consequently, this report should enable the programmer to see the code falling apart in front of them in such a way that it demonstrates that their assumption was false.

Writing the Bug Report

Begin with a detailed breakdown of both the hardware and software in use. Consoles have their own devkits, for which you'll need to know the firmware version and other such information. For browser-based games, you want full details of the browser—it's version, resolution, and so on. Sites like http://supportdetails.com can help provide this. Bug reports for native games include similar parameters (like screen resolution, OS version) but may also benefit from a list of software and drivers installed on the machine. Most of this can be automated.

Then indicate the version of code that exhibits the bug. This part involves cooperation with the programmers, since they need to update the version number each time and present it as part of the build. One popular method is to use the date and time of the build as the version number and display it on the title screen.

Next, you need to write a detailed description of the bug itself. This should start with a brief description of what the bug actually is. Here, as in all parts of the bug report, differentiate clearly what is a fact that happened and what is an opinion.

Then explain what you did to cause the bug to happen. This is usually presented in the form of a story and involves a step-by-step process of the actions you took, weapons collected or dropped, and so on, until you get to that point in the game where the error occurs. Be specific here. You may have found a rare and intermittent bug, so you might not have the chance to go through the game again to reproduce it, so make the best notes that you can when the bug is first witnessed. (Olden-day scientists drew their microscopic discoveries in a sketchbook, but they never made a rough copy. Their first version was invariably their first release.)

Each part of the description should be highly specific, which is where good communication skills come to the fore. Stating that you "started the game" might not be enough. Did you click the button? Did you use the key shortcut? Did you use the cheat screen? Did you go into another screen first, realize it was a mistake, exit, and then start the game? Again, be specific. Everyone has a particular quirk in how they navigate around the features of a game; the bug might be a consequence of those quirks.

Finally, if you can reproduce the bug in a shorter fashion, then include those steps too. Since the primary purpose of the bug report is to get the developer to see the problem as quickly as possible, giving them a shorter route is always welcome. (Maybe heading to that other screen wasn't the cause of the bug. Maybe the same problem is exhibited if you start the game with a button click, key shortcut, or cheat screen.) Take the time to explore a few avenues yourself in order to reproduce the bug in the most minimal way possible. Ideally, you'll want to be able to reproduce it upon request should the programmer find that they are unable to do so.

■ **Tip** Reproducibility is the key. If you can't work through the explanation yourself to reproduce the problem, then it is unlikely that the developer will. This normally happens when you have omitted parts of the story that you consider to be "ordinary" or "unimportant." Take no shortcuts! Even typing a shorter player name to get through to the game quicker might render the problem unable to reproduce, since it might be the cause of the problem.

Also, use your intuition to think, *If there's a problem with X, I wonder if it also happens with Y?* I've seen cases where the bug report referenced the letter A not working on the *Enter your name* dialog box, only to find out that the A key was broken on the tester's keyboard! Conversely, I've seen multiple bugs filed for the letter A didn't work, the letter B didn't work, the letter C didn't work, and so on! Share all of these notes with the developers in as succinct a manner as possible, because this helps get the bug fixed more quickly. The following is how a sample report might appear:

- *Product*: Space Bounce

- *Version*: 1.0a (build 300773)

- *Platform*: Windows 10, Chrome browser (49) at 1600×1200, 32-bit color

- *Reporter*: Steev

- *Found on*: 2016-04-21

- *Overview*: Character overlaps the right-hand wall

- *Reproduction*: Enter the game via any means. Jump to the right-hand wall by clicking or touching the main game area. After the swing animation has played, notice the whole body overlaps the wall; whereas when on the left-hand side, only the arm overlaps.

- *Expected result*: The right-hand visuals should mirror those on the left.

- *Keywords*: graphics, character, wall

- *Bug number*: 35

- *Severity*: B

- *Status*: Open

- *Assigned to*: Steev

Providing Helpful Resources

In addition to the textual bug report, there are many things that you can provide to help the developers solve the problem more quickly. (But not at the expense of providing text reports, as these are the easiest things to search.)

The primary medium is of screenshots or movie clips of the bug happening. Disc space is so cheap that it is truly easy to run screen-capture software (like Camtasia) on all testing sessions, and then edit and upload any videos depicting bugs onto a shared office server. If you don't have the facility to edit the video down to the bare minimum, then include timestamps for the developers so that they don't need to sit through an hour of gameplay to watch a ten-second clip.

If you don't periodically save your game during a session, then get into the habit of doing so, because this allows you to provide a saved game from just before the bug occurring, so that the developer can replay the game from this point to see it in action. Depending on the specifics of the bug, it may be impossible to reproduce from a saved file (particularly in cases where the problem was due to a temporary state variable that is not saved), but provide it if you can. It can also be useful to supply a saved game from a point immediately following the bug.

■ **Tip**   Provide access to the save-game functionality at all points in the level, for development purposes, even if the final game provides it only at specific waypoints.

Finally, ensure that the programmers have added a debug trace, call stack, and log to the development build of the game so that they can comb through it if useful.

Report Review

Once the report has been submitted, the QA lead reviews it. This is to ensure that it is not a duplicate or extension of an existing bug, and that all fields have been adequately filled in.

The QA lead's next step is to grade the bug according to its severity. Everyone has their own ideas about the number of grades and the precise meaning of each. As long as there is a fixed grading system to avoid confusion or arguments, the precise distinction is up to you. The following are mine.

- *Showstopper*. Prevents the game from being played or completed.

- *Severe*. Prevents the game from being played or completed, although a work-around may exist. Something happens to make the game look or play amateurish.

- *Major*. Causes the player unreasonable inconvenience. Something happens to make the game look or play poorly.

- *Minor*. Causes the player some inconvenience.

- *Time permitting*. Offers tweaks and fixes that only a die-hard fan would notice.

There is one further level—legal, which trumps all others. During development, legal issues appear as grade-A bugs. Afterward, they take on a higher priority insomuch as they must be fixed and deployed before any other changes are made or deployed.

Bug Fixing and Regression

At this stage, the developers can take the bug report and fix the problem as necessary. Once this is done, they mark the bug as fixed (along with the version in which the fix will appear) and continue with other work.

"When debugging, novices insert corrective code; experts remove defective code".

—Richard Pattis

The test engineers later review these bugs to ensure that they truly are fixed, and then apply their insight to ensure that any similar areas of the game have not broken as a consequence of this change. This is a form of regression testing (ensuring the game still works after other changes), which should also include a test on previously closed bugs to check for old issues that may have been reopened as a consequence of this new code. If everything is working, then the bug may be formally closed.

Change Requests

Is it extremely common for bugs that aren't actually bugs to be submitted. A bug implies something that exists but doesn't work correctly. In many cases, what is submitted is a change request; something that doesn't exist but should. Or a suggestion that the way it was designed could be improved. There are usually a lot of these and it requires the skill (both technical and personal) of the QA team lead to separate the two and assign them accordingly.

All requests for features generally follow the same pattern as for bugs, except that the priorities range from 2 to 5, instead of 1 to 5.

Reproducibility

The first phase of debugging starts with the developer being able to reproduce the bug under their development environment. The more difficult the bug is to reproduce, the more frustrating it is. I now present some methods by which bugs and game situations can be more easily reproduced. Additionally, by its nature, this also means that we can place the game in a state that is difficult to achieve under normal play conditions. This lowers the bar for those wanting to polish or improve such areas.

The Cheat Screen

The cheat screen has been a staple of all games since, er... well... forever. It is a simple dialog box or screen that allows the development team to give themselves more lives, resources, scores and so on. It also allows them to skip through to points in the game between designated save points. All of these reduce the time the QA team needs to spend progressing to a particular part of the game to check that it's working as designed. A cheat screen is not difficult to implement, and so should be included in the development schedule of all games. Just remember to remove it before the final release.

Seeding Random

Many games, by their nature, utilize random numbers in some way. Even games of pure skill, such as chess, may use a random number to pick one of three equally good moves, as the unpredictability adds a human element to the play. Therefore, the random number generator should not be random!

Luckily, all random number generators that exist in software are technically known as *pseudo-random number generators* (PRNGs), since it is impossible to generate a random result from a fixed and known algorithm.[6] Therefore, at the start of your game, you should seed the PRNG with a value that is identical for each execution of the game, which ensures that the same random numbers are generated each time.

In C/C++, the two calls in the random library are *srand* and *rand*, which sets the randomization seed and requests a new (pseudo-)random number, respectively. Your language of choice will likely have equivalents. JavaScript, notably, doesn't have such a method, so we are required to implement something equivalent.

```
var gRnd_w;
var gRnd_z;
var gRnd_mask;

function sgxSetRandSeed(seed) {
    gRnd_w = seed;
```

---

[6]Even the seemingly chaotic results present in chaos theory are known; they're just unexpected.

```
    gRnd_z  = 987654321;
    gRnd_mask = 0xffffffff;
}

function sgxRandom() {
    gRnd_z = (36969 * (gRnd_z & 65535) + (gRnd_z >> 16)) & gRnd_mask;
    gRnd_w = (18000 * (gRnd_w & 65535) + (gRnd_w >> 16)) & gRnd_mask;

    var result = ((gRnd_z << 16) + gRnd_w) & gRnd_mask;
    result /= 4294967296;

    return result + 0.5;
}

sgxSetRandSeed(0);   // never forget to seed the PRNG
```

▓ **Caution**   Make sure that you understand the guidelines in Chapter 5, so that the number of times that the random method is called remains identical between successive run-throughs too.

Input Logging

The most useful, and unfortunately most complex, method to help reproduce bugs is by logging all the input from a play session and replaying it at a later time. It is, however, not just the logging code that is complex, but the gameplay logic itself, because it all needs to be deterministic. We have seen one such example through the random seeding of a PRNG. Others exist when timings and inputs are taken directly from devices such that they cannot be faked by the logger itself. In essence, you must consider the inputs (as a whole) to any part of the game (as a whole.) This is quite a wide footprint and includes keyboards, mice, network traffic, and disc loads, because even a slight variation in timing can affect what happens in the update loop.

▓ **Tip**   You can also use the input logger to replay pre-programmed game examples to work as an attract or demonstration mode to highlight your game in action while no one is playing it. Or it can be used as the basis for an instructional guide. Both add polish.

To develop an input logger, first modify your input library to take its data from an independent source and not the input device it would under normal circumstances.

```
sgx.input.Engine.prototype.applyMousePosition = function(x, y)
{
    this.mouseX = sgxFloor(x);
    this.mouseY = sgxFloor(y);
```

```
  if (this.logger) {
    this.logger.submitEvent('mouseposition', x, y);
  }
}
```

Notice that the input library isn't pulling data from anywhere; the data is being pushed to it with code such as this:

```
canvas.onmousemove = function(e) {
  var x = e.offsetX;
  var y = e.offsetY;

  sgx.input.Engine.applyMousePosition(x, y);
}
```

In this way, the game can continue as normal, but it is the input logger that feeds the applyMousePosition method to simulate the device in the same way that the input from the onmousemove event does.

Logger events can be stored in any manner that you desire, but storing the difference in time between events, rather than an absolute from the nearest epoch, means it's easier to handle the case where you wish to pause the logger playback code.

```
sgx.input.Logger.prototype.submitEvent = function(msg, params)
{
  if (this.running) {
    var t = this.getMilli();
    var dt = t - this.lastTime;

    this.recording.push({'delta':dt, 'message':msg, 'params': arguments});
    this.lastTime = t;
  }
}
```

The next element of the logger is the replay logic, which processes the game logic according to its own rules. That is, it invokes the update and draw loop by force-feeding the input library with the mouse and key input. In our first implementation, this might begin as follows:

```
sgx.input.Logger.prototype.replay = function() {
  this.replayTimer = this.getMilli();
  this.replayIndex = 0;
  this.replayNext.call(this);
}
```

With a basic update loop appearing as thus:

```
sgx.input.Logger.prototype.replayNext = function() {
  var timeSinceLast = this.getMilli() - this.replayTimer;
  var ended = false;
  var input = sgx.input.Engine.get();
```

214

```
  timeSinceLast  -=  this.recording[this.replayIndex].delta;
  while(!ended  &&  timeSinceLast  >=  0)  {
    var  r  =  this.recording[this.replayIndex];

    switch(r.message)  {
      case  'mouseposition':
      input.applyMousePosition(r.params[1],  r.params[2]);
      break;
      case  'mousebutton':
      input.applyMouseButton(r.params[1],  r.params[2]);
      break;
      case  'keyaction':
      if  (r.params[2])  {
        input.applyKeyboardKeyDown(r.params[1]);
      }  else  {
        input.applyKeyboardKeyUp(r.params[1]);
      }
      break;
    }

    timeSinceLast  -=  r.delta;
    this.replayTimer  +=  r.delta;

    if  (++this.replayIndex  >=  this.recording.length)  {
      ended  =  true;
    }
  }

  if  (!ended)  {
    var  self  =  this;
    setTimeout(function()  {  self.replayNext();  },  1);
  }
}
```

While this works well enough for many cases, there are still issues from those external elements that are variable, such as the loading times and network traffic. Consider the following sequence of events:

- 0:00 Loading starts

- 0:05 Loading ends

- 0:06 Player presses button; it is stored in the logger

Nothing unusual there. Now consider the case where the loading takes a little longer. It's perfectly reasonable to expect this to happen on PC and console games due to the nature of the hardware. It's almost guaranteed when it comes to networked games.

- 0:00 Loading starts

- 0:06 Player presses button, as replayed by the logger

- 0:07 Loading ends

The logger's events are triggered normally and correctly, but because the game hasn't finished loading yet, the logic ignores the button press at 0:06 and nothing else happens. To solve this, all external inputs (not just the joypad/mouse/buttons) should be logged so that they can be checked and replayed correctly.

In essence, there are three types of events:

- Human input devices

- System mark

- Trigger methods

System marks are points in the code where the game must wait for part of the system to reach before allowing the game to continue. The loading sequence mentioned previously is one such case, since the problem disappears entirely if the loading methods instigate a mark:

```
this.logger.submitEvent('loading', 'filename');
```

This is paired with a corresponding block of replay code that stops executing input events until that mark has happened. Notice that the input event ("player presses a button") now happens 1ms after the load event has completed (which is correct), instead of 6ms after the load event has begun (which is wrong.)

Trigger methods are simply indications that the replay engine should call an arbitrary method. Most of the time, this is used to instigate the update method, with an identical time_elapsed variable to the original recording. But it is also used for calling the sgxSetRandSeed method at the start of the game.

■ **Note**   The draw methods must not change any state within the system (including random numbers) and so could be called any number of times, and in any order, without side effects.

While you should be proud of this technological marvel you've created, be aware that input playback isn't a silver bullet for fully automated testing. If you created an input log file of the character traversing a level, then there are many things that would prevent you from using the replay engine in all future tests. It might work in the first instance but it would break if you changed the level design, or the collision boxes or logic, the physics code, or the dimensions or animation of any mesh within the world. For a fully automated playback system, you'd need to place explicit waypoints in the level and move the camera between them, which is another chunk of work!

Network Abstractions

When writing online games, the biggest headache is invariably caused by instances of a broken network. But the real problem is testing on a reliably broken network. That is, one that breaks in the same way every time.

To effectively test this scenario and others, you need to create your own virtual network by wrapping the real network code into a separate module. This includes all the file downloading and directory enumeration code, as well as API calls to various services. This module is able to carry out the usual functions of the network layer, but have the additional functionality so that its success can be controlled by the test suite to return failure codes to reflect missing files, lost network, corrupt data packets, slow file downloads, and so on.

Summary

Throughout this chapter, you saw that bugs can come from anywhere, but also that they can be prevented and cured from as many places. From static source checkers that perform a machine-oriented code reviews on the game before it's run, to run-time checkers that look for memory corruption during the game, and to input replay loggers that let you reflect on the actions after the game has completed to reproduce problems so that they are found (and fixed) more quickly.

You also saw that bugs can come from outside the code, such as in user data or game assets, but that through good tooling and human intervention, there are rules and processes that can help track them down too. So much so that testing is a truly accessible field where everyone in the company can help polish the game, such that it is no longer a task that should be dreaded.

CHAPTER 11

■ ■ ■

Final Thoughts

Never Too Much

There is no such thing as an "easy" day in game development. At the start of the project, there's the air of anticipation and the dream of an ambition in creating the greatest ever game as we plan, brainstorm, and work frantically to give our baby the best possible start we can in its digital life.

During the mid-game, we're working hard to implement each new feature without breaking the old ones, and to ensure coherence in vision and consistency in design.

At the end, we hit crunch.[1] Every hour that the universe sends is swallowed whole into the development cycle to ensure that every ambition is realized and that every ounce of polish we perceive is applied to the game.

But that's also not to say that there is such a thing as "too much" polish. There is always *something* to improve upon. It could be an increase in quantity through more art, more animations, or more levels. In quality, more animation frames, improved textures, or additional effects. Sometimes there are improvements to be made behind the scenes, with better tool-chain pipelines, or more structured and maintainable code.

By way of a short finale, this chapter is for those who think that there's nothing else that they could possibly add; here are a selection of possible ideas.

More Design

Too often we're focused on building our game to work cross-platform,[2] that we often forget there are platform specifics that always help improve the final product.

When working on mobile there are simple features that need implementing like the pausing of the game (and all associated audio) when the phone rings. And the obligatory functionality to restart the game once the call has ended. This is a simple case of watching for the "call happening" event, and triggering a screen with a single Restart Game button. Plus some code for correctly pausing all the elements in the game. And probably a mock version to test on the PC.

---

[1]Even those of us that no longer crunch are consciously aware of taking shorter breaks near the end of the schedule, just because we want to.
[2]Almost all games are cross-platform to some extent.

S. Goodwin, *Polished Game Development*, DOI 10.1007/978-1-4842-2122-8_11

Furthermore, phones, tablets, and controllers often have the ability to issue vibrations or force feedback effects. The scope of the effect can range from a mildly annoying shake, to a fully directional effect that could accurately mimic an M16. Again, more work. And more mocking required on a development PC that might be lacking in such devices. (Remember to turn the vibration off when a phone call comes in!)

Looking further at phones and tablets, most devices now support (at least) one camera that can be used to take a photo of the player that they can use as their avatar; or, coupled with QR code–reading software, use as an in-game bonus item if they scan the code on the website.

Easter Eggs

These are hidden elements within game that are not advertised or promoted, but let the player discover an inside joke or give them a feeling of camaraderie with the developers.

There are two main elements to an Easter egg, the method of triggering it, and the action itself. In many cases there may be no trigger, it might just be a message or reference that you'll spot while playing the game (if you're observant or understanding). Or it could be triggered by any combination of logical (and not so logical) actions.

■ **Note** Not all eggs need to be explicit, such as the phase of the moon example in Chapter 6.

There have been many examples of Easter eggs over the years, such as Warren Robinett's inclusion of his name in the Atari version of *Adventure*[3] or the entirety of *Maniac Mansion* within *Day of the Tentacle*. Unfortunately, many larger companies frown on such activities because the development time is unaccounted for and considered frivolous in light of whatever bugs are still present. Furthermore, with lawyers being ever keener to verify that no content is untoward in their games,[4] all Easter eggs need to be disclosed to them—meaning they become documented features rather than secrets.

But for the rest of us, there is still the scope to include some pleasant surprises for our more ardent players.

Secret Messages

By far, secret messages are the most innocuous egg is within the text. The names of the developers and friends within the game are probably the oldest Easter eggs known. Any game with named characters probably intentionally shares their name with at least one developer.[5] Or perhaps your friends are immortalized as the name of a weapon, building, or room within the game.

---

[3]I added a similar feature in my own ZX Adventure for the Sinclair Vega!

[4]Such as sex and violence unsuitable for the age range claimed, as well as trademarked characters from other franchises.

[5]In Grand Prix Manager, most of the reserved drivers where named after the band members of whatever album I was listening to while writing it.

Often the trick with eggs is to make them non-trivial to find, so perhaps include them in textures so they can only be read if you walk very close to a specific wall. Or affect the design of wooden crates so that if specific ones are pushed together they spell out a name. The more inventive and difficult they are to find, the more your players will love them.

And the more Internet-based forum action you're likely to receive.

Special Resources

If you play certain games at certain times of the year, you may notice that Halloween masks or Santa hats have become available within the game. They may function identically to the usual graphic, or might give way to even more Easter eggs.

For those working with non-trivial game engines, you can affect the existing graphics without acquiring new resources through effects like vertex coloring or shaders. In 3D games, rendering the player heads at double size is a popular effect, as is applying a special effect, like lightning, to all textures in the model.

Sound files can be a similarly fun thing to switch. Instead of the serious game you intended, a magical key combination could switch all the gun sounds to fart noises, for example.

Unsecret In-Jokes

Believe it or not, it is usually easier to hide jokes in plain sight! Using game and pop-culture references is standard fare for developers. One such case appears in the game *Dead Rising*, where there's a shop called Jill's Sandwiches; a reference to that horrendously cheesy line in *Resident Evil*.

Hidden Rooms and Levels

Hidden rooms and levels are probably the second-most common egg to introduce. There are many ways to hide these—from invisible doors to timed jumps, the typing of special keywords, shooting a special place in the level, waiting for unreasonably long time in the same spot, or purposefully dying when your score hits a specific value.

Mini Games

Mini games are generally restricted to the larger development teams. It's increasingly common to see entire games replicated within another. *Call of Duty: Black Op II* had several Atari games that could be played if you carried out a specific action quickly enough. Even with a large number of open source games available, the time taken to integrate them seamlessly with an existing product isn't normally worth the effort, unless you're spending thousands of person-hours on the project.

Extra Bonuses

If you lack the time to create extra levels or graphical content, then there is nothing wrong with awarding a few extra points for doing something arbitrarily weird with three unconnected items and pressing the action button. This extends to infinite lives, ammo, or money.

In *Aladdin on the Genesis* you get an extra life for positioning Aladdin underneath (the not so secret graphic of) a pair of Mickey Mouse ears.

These have the advantage that they can be left in the game for testers to use, without necessitating a brand-new "release-only" build, which may be harder for them to complete, and therefore effectively test. Being able to access such features through an Easter egg, rather than a "testers-only" dialog box, is preferable since it gives the player the feeling of accomplishment when they manage to achieve the trigger,[6] and it doesn't expose all of your secrets at once like a cheat screen would.

Foreshadowing

Foreshadowing is a writer's technique for dropping hints about the story arc that is yet to come. In *Dead Space*, the initial letters of the chapter titles spell out a message that reveals the main plot twist.

More Money

In Chapter 3, I mentioned the additional localization issues that occur when dealing with money. Specifically, the game world that surrounds the currency itself needs to fix the context. That is, even if your game is written in English, for an English-speaking audience, but the game is set in Japan, then the game currency is better dictated as yen. Similarly, if you are building a game set in a non-real world, then ensure that the unit of currency fits your setting. Games set in space, with trading between planets, can use terms like "intergalactic credits" or "space tokens" to distance themselves from the realism inferred by terms such as dollars, pounds, or euro. For fantasy games, it is common to use gold, silver, and bronze coins, as there's an obvious real-world counterpoint, and it's only a matter of inventing the relative ratios to determine how many silver coins match a gold coin, and so on.

Since the trilogy of gold-silver-bronze is fairly common, a good step is to invent a word for the currency units that reflect the game world (or universe), such as Leddrak, for example. The better step is to look at the game's backstory and pick something with a historical meaning to your setting. For example, if the game world is set to the backdrop of the Intergalactic Space Federation, then which planet or planets founded it? It's highly likely that they'd pick a name to reflect the union of both their worlds. If it was founded from the desires of a tyrannical empire, then an evil-sounding word would be in keeping.

---

[6]Your testers, having played the game for months, should be able to activate the trigger on the first attempt. New players will take a little longer.

If your game is rooted in the real world, and you are a brave soul, then you can include a strong element of localization by providing the option of playing the game with different currencies like yen, dinars, or krone. Like the introduction of foreign languages, allowing the player to use their local currency provides a significant element of realism and makes it much easier for them to connect directly to the game, because it's more natural for them to relate to buying a new car for 5400 złoty than it is 1300 euro. (And this is before considering the difference in purchasing power between various countries.)

In *Powerhouse*,[7] for example, we added an option to play in yen, dollars, or pounds sterling. To avoid any complications, our exchange rate between the units was one to one: 1 yen = 1 dollar and 1 dollar = 1 pound. The implementation was as cheap as it sounds—we simply changed the symbol! Since the game involved buying and selling nuclear power stations, we probably got away with it, because no one in the halcyon pre-Wikipedia days knew how much they cost.[8] But to do it properly, you need to consider some realistic exchange rates, purchasing power, and representative context given the range of the numbers. That is, when talking about a multibillion-dollar power station, the finances would be expressed as $8BN, $8.2BN, or maybe $8.21BN, but rarely with any more precision than that; whereas in a game where the player is running a primary school snack shop, money units would be processed according to the penny.

Like our representation of scores back in Chapter 6, this highlights the two elements that describe the cost of an in-game item.

- The cost of the item, as stored in memory

- The cost of the item, as displayed on screen

The former is chosen at the start of the item's lifetime (maybe via a currency conversion process) and maintained. The latter is affected according to the needs of the display or a specific screen. A running total might be rounded to the nearest billion or 100 billion, depending on the value itself, and might only render to one or two decimal places; whereas a profit-and-loss report details the numbers to the exact dollar. Again, you can vary the precision depending on the value itself, so once your cash stockpile drops into the millions, you can describe it as $10M, instead of $0.01B.

■ **Caution**   The American billion is 1,000 million, whereas the British is 1,000,000 million. Which billion you are using needs to be obvious to the player. There are edge cases to consider too, such as when a British player would choose $ (because it's a world currency) but expects (through cultural upbringing) to use the British billion.

Writing code for context-sensitive precision is not difficult, but it is often game-specific and deserves your full attention.

---

[7]My first PC game, released back in 1995, for Sierra/Impressions. Now largely forgotten.
[8]The cost varies, but it's around $8BN, if you're interested.

Increasing Assets

From a programming perspective, one of the easiest ways to improve a game is to increase the quantity of art resources in the system. This might be to increase the number of animation frames from 3 to 15 so that it looks smoother. Or it could be to take a graphic that didn't animate and make it so. (Remembering, of course, that you might have a core design motif that indicates that static objects are dangerous to the touch.)

You can also increase the assets themselves, by adding a moon to the sky as you saw in Chapter 6, or adding animating backgrounds behind the menu and title screens. Replay the game to look for the situations that are mostly static, and add some sparkles (figuratively or literally.) Then repeat, but stop just before the result would look gaudy or you run out of time.

Additionally, look to adding special effects in more situations in your game. Look for every instance of one object affecting another and reason what effect could be applied. If you don't have time to build a brand-new effect, maybe you can repurpose an existing one. Perhaps a gray smoke effect could be drawn in brown to look like a dust cloud, for example.

Moving from visual arts to auditory, we can repeat the same ideas by adding more Foley sounds (and more variety of sounds) throughout the game. That's not to say, "Just add more sounds for the sake of it," but to consider the environments in which the sounds are likely to play. A footstep will have several variations according to the surface on which the character is walking, concrete, wood, or grass. This can be extended to include the location in which those surfaces are present: a hall, a cathedral, or an office. Each locale has a specific set of acoustics.

You might be able to make use of some platform-specific features of the sound card to implement this very cheaply. But on smaller platforms, it is not generally possible to use the audio engine to add echo or reverberation in real time. Consequently, the solution is to take it offline. You can add the effect in your sample editor of choice, save the file with a new name, add the metadata to the level data, and then update the code to switch between versions. Naturally, this is the thin edge of the proverbial wedge, as by having a level in a cathedral with a lot of reverb on the footsteps, you'd naturally expect to hear a lot of reverb on the all other sounds that play inside the cathedral. To make matters more complex, remember that some objects may have been carried in from outside the cathedral, or from outside the current level.

More Writing

Once you have polished and repolished the language used within the game, and checked (and rechecked) the nomenclature, there isn't much more to do. Maybe you could add a variety of replies to an NPC's word bank, but otherwise, you are only adding quantity to the game, not quality.

Except if you decide to translate it!

Naturally, in all cases, it's only worth adding these extra languages if you know that you're getting traction that outstrips the budget required to translate the text, add the support code, and improve the tool chain to handle these languages. Alas, it's not always a clear-cut proposition.

Despite popular opinion, English is not the most prevalent language in the world. That award goes to Chinese (and its dialects.) And while the double-byte encoding of Chinese text strings is problematic in some programming languages, it needn't cause issues with Spanish, the second-most popular spoken language.

> ■ **Tip**   If your game can be taught and played without text, then that is better all-round. Although communicating in this way requires a very particular set of skills—skills often acquired over a very long career, so it's simpler to write text.

First, decide on a second language into which you'll translate the game, and then consider the rest, since the complexity of adding a second language is moderate, but then every language after that is trivial due to the framework you built for the second. Most games ultimately end up with EFIGS (English, French, Italian, German, and Spanish), with some adding Portuguese to the roll call, if they intend to attack the South American markets.

The best choice for the second language is highly dependent on the game's subject matter. If your game is about the Anglo-French War along the Mohawk River in 1757, then there's a natural demographic of people who may consider a game written natively in French, especially if they are not traditional game players. After this, look at the market size of traditional gamers for this genre of game.

Once the decision is made, however, there are the considerations to ensure that the French version looks as good as the English version.

Selecting a Language

Thinking about the flow sequentially, at what point does the player get to choose their language? Is it before the publisher's logo? After it? From the in-game menu? Somewhere else? The simplest place is to select it as soon as legally possible. That is, after any compulsory publisher or *Licensed by …* screens have appeared. You can then load the correct text data file, and forget about it.

If you need to also support the ability to change language mid-game, then consider that extra effort will be necessary to change all text strings present within the game's memory. In the SGX engine, for example, all text is translated via sgx.text.getText when loading the UI designs, so these need to be reloaded if the language changes, in order for the new translation strings to be applied.

> ■ **Tip**   If you are supporting the ability to change language mid-game, switch between languages from different language families (e.g., from German to Italian) during testing. This is because if the Spanish text was missing a couple of IDs, the game would most likely display the text strings from the previous language. If that previous language was Portuguese, it might be difficult to tell that no new text had been loaded.

Alas, introducing an alternate language is not just about adding a new text file—there is a lot of new code to write too.

Word Order

It is a natural, but unfortunate, fact that natural languages aren't something that fit well-defined patterns. The rules for grammar vary between languages, but also in and of itself. There are always exceptions. Consequently, it won't be long before a phrase such as, "There are 12 bullets in the gun," needs to be translated as the phrase, "The gun has 12 bullets in it." So let's say that your inventory uses this codified form:

```
There are [bullet count] bullets in the [weapon name]
```

You need to adapt your getText translation routines so that meta-variables can be used to replace the correct term in sequence, so the string can become:

```
There are %1 bullets in the %2
```

The JavaScript code for this need be nothing more complex than this:

```
var message = string_id;

if (languageTextData[string_id]) {
    message = languageTextData[string_id];
}

for(var i=1;i<args.length;++i) {
    message = message.replace("%"+i, args[i]);
}
```

Other languages, of course (like C++), may be more difficult and require a fuller parser.

The Case of 0, 1, and 2

All languages have the concept of plurals, and all of them are easy to code. The case that needs extra attention is when multiple languages are used. This requires additional logic of what constitutes a single or plural in each language, and a reference to the language in question.

Our getText code might then become this:

```
sgx.text.getTextN = function(id, value) {
    if (typeof this.data[id] === 'undefined') {
        return id;
    }
    return this.isSingular() ? this.data[id]['s'] : this.data[id]['p'];
}
```

The code for isSingular is an obvious as you think, with 1 being singular and everything else considered plural. However, this is only true for English. Indeed, some languages consider 0 as a singular entity.

Further complications occur when branching beyond EFIGS. A number of Slavic languages, for example, have the concept of dual grammatical numbers[9] when referencing two elements. That is, there is a version of the word for singular, another for the specific case of two, and another for all other plurals. This requires us to extend not only our getTextN code, but our text loader to handle these cases.

The Definite Article

Most of the words that appear in our games are definite articles: *the* gun, *the* bullets, *the* shield. This leads to output like "You have collected the [item]" when collecting it, and inventory text like "The [item]." This tends us to create a single list of all items within the game, so the preceding strings can be built with meta-variables, as you saw.

```
You have collected the %1
```

Wrong.

In many languages, there is more than one word for *the*. This varies according to whether the noun is masculine, feminine, neuter, or plural. (Or possibly some other less frequently used variant.) This is the correct text:

```
You have collected %1
```

Therefore, it becomes necessary to compile and translate one set of item text for each place it's used. In this example, there is a list of objects entitled "used when they are collected" and another for objects "to be displayed alone in a list."

It is possible that you might have to deal with definite articles and pluralized strings in the same phrase. Luckily, there aren't many sentences that read, "You have the 2 guns," that can't be rewritten to avoid the problem altogether. Instead, you can revert to the single/plural distinction that our code already supports, and another list of objects "for use alone in pluralized text."

■ **Caution**   Never try to build sentences in code through concatenation or similar means. You will end up trying to put natural language rules into the code. The time spent will outweigh any cost of having a second set of words translated.

Improved Code

Of all the elements to generally *not* get any extra love is the code! Most games start with the programmers putting a framework together, and end with them trying to find those last elusive bugs. For those rare exceptions when there's a coder available for work, consider the following.

---

[9]See https://en.wikipedia.org/wiki/Dual_(grammatical_number)

Preloaders

While a loading bar is a necessity in any project, on any platform, writing something a little more dynamic cannot hurt. It could be a simple set of instructions, with the lead character running through their idle animation. Perhaps it could play out the backstory. Or it could include a few missiles flying around the screen to match the in-game gameplay.

If the platform supports it, you can go interactive and have small mini-games for the player to enjoy while the load happens. Ideally, these involve the characters from the main game to give cohesion. Something as simple as a whack-a-mole would be enough, because the game is very easy to start and very easy to leave once the game has loaded. Although game's consoles have technical requirements that require games load in a specifically short time frame, anything dynamic on the loading screen makes the wait *appear* shorter for the rest of us, leading to a better experience.

Dynamically loading the game content is an alternative to preloaders that also gives an apparently shorter waiting time. This requires more metadata to describe which areas of the game or data should be loaded first and what to do if particular data is not ready yet. The first problem requires that the game state is loaded first and processed to produce a set of the required assets in the chronological order in which they'll be needed.

Custom Cursors

Replacing the standard operating system cursors (such as the arrow or hand) are commonplace in all games and expected as part of the standard polish. This is true in most games, except those on the Web where the browser actively tries to prevent you from changing the cursor. But it does allow you to hide it. Therefore, any game that uses the HTML5 canvas object can render a custom cursor as part of the canvas bitmap to create the same effect.

Optimization

All code is happy to receive the care and attention of a developer who loves optimization. This task should be a continuous and ongoing process of profile the code, find the slowest part, optimize it, and repeat. In this manner, you really can ship any day, with the benefit that every improvement made means the game can run on a slightly lower spec machine, opening the game up to their users.

The final element of code improvements is to have it clean. Very clean. Consider your current game. If you had to re-skin it, change some of the basic logic, scoring systems, and so on, how much of the core code would you need to change? How many hacks would you need to remove, or abstract away, in order to change the size of the main character? Are the levels truly data-driven? Are the scripts loosely coupled with the rest of the system? Or are there lines of specific code in the game engine to handle the edge cases? Until you can honestly answer that, everything is clean enough to sell or license as a separate engine, there is still polish to be made within the code base.

Applying Code Conventions

Throughout the development process, our writers and designers maintain a nomenclature for all the words and phrases that appear on the various game screens. But there is no reason why these conventions shouldn't be carried over to the development process itself.

Primary Code Entry Points

With so many independent elements to the code, it is prudent to have a set of naming conventions that all programmers can infuse into all the code to ensure a common vernacular. This should include common names and parameter lists for all the expected entry (and exit) points in the code. If your language supports inheritance (especially multiple inheritance), then enforcing this can be done at the compiler level. Otherwise, it requires discipline.

In Space Bounce, there are the following rules:

- `constructor`. Creates a valid object. Loads any required assets. Called once when the game is loaded. If the object is created mid-game, then another object must load the assets on its behalf. (This stops memory fragmentation and limits mid-game slowdown due to allocation and/or garbage collection.)

- `startGame`. Called once when the player begins a new game.

- `startLevel`. Called once at every level. Also called after `startGame` to initiate the first level. Levels start at 0.

- `draw`. Handles all rendering without changing the state of any local member variables.

- `postDraw`. Second pass rendering once the rest of the screen has been drawn; for example, used for filters and basic depth sorting. Must not change the state of any local member variable.

- `update`. Accepts a `time_elapsed` parameter to indicate the time passed since the previous call to update. Must handle 0 seconds elapsed. Must perform the same if passed 0.2 seconds or two calls of 0.1 seconds.

Secondary Code Elements

In addition to the methods that may be visible in the code as a whole, you should also adopt conventions in the day-to-day code that you write. This includes the following:

- Source control commit comments

- Comments

- Variable names

- Function and method names

- Animation names

Doing this has no effect on the game, naturally, but since the code is read more times than it is written, using bounce_left (instead of jump_left) makes more sense to the incoming developers because it matches the rest of the game.

■ **Note** If you change the notion during the game development (such as changing the name from "Space Bounce" to "Space Jump"), then you should feel obliged to refactor and change all the references so that your team isn't confusing the two (identical) terms and mentally translating the word "jump" to "bounce" the whole time!

This extends to the higher-level concepts. In Space Bounce, we have two audio buttons: music and sound effects. In the interface, the music icon appears first (the Apollo capsule, on the left) and the sound effects icon is second (on the right). This ordering is consistent wherever they're used in the interface. The code mirrors that with code such as this:

```
gui.refreshWidgetMusic(interfaceIGM.getWidgetOfUserData(0x0201));
gui.refreshWidgetSFX(interfaceIGM.getWidgetOfUserData(0x0301));
```

This helps us developers get into a pattern that ensures that we remember everything, as if we're working through a shopping list. Note also that the user data identifiers (0x0201 and 0x0301) are identical wherever the widgets are referenced (even on different screens) to conform to convention and cement the association in our minds.

Refactor for Consistency

Over the course of any project, you are bound to learn some new programming tricks or techniques as your understanding of the language and the problem domain increases. Refactoring is the process of shuffling and modifying existing code into a pattern than matches the current needs of the project, without changing or reducing the way the functionality. The longer the project duration, the greater the understanding of underlying problem and the more coding techniques will you develop. The more techniques, the more refactoring it takes to bring everything in line.

But for a clean internal code base, it is something to consider. In my first JavaScript code, the constructor for a class would have been originally written like this:

```
function GamePlayer() {
  var lots_of_class_variables_here;

  // constructor code
  m_pAnimState = sgx.graphics.AnimationManager.get().createState();

  function first_method() { ... }
```

Before long, I got bored of writing a pointless comment for the constructor indicating the floating block of code, so I created it as a method.

```
function GamePlayer() {
  ctor();
  function ctor() {
  // ... normal code ...
  }
```

I used the abbreviation to avoid name clashes, which then evolved into this:

```
function GamePlayer() {

  (function ctor() {
  // ... normal code ...
  })();
```

While this might look strange to non-JavaScript natives, it is a clean method to implement a self-describing constructor, with access to local scope like any other method. After discovering this technique, I went through my entire project converting all the other constructors to use this approach. Although it's not necessarily the best construction metaphor available, they at least all look the same. After all, if 90% of the constructors use one method and 10% use a different one, the first question a developer should ask is *Why?* Why is this one not like the others? What is special here? It will take longer to explain your tardiness and that they are all functionally identical, compared to the time it would take to refactor the code, that you might as well do it.

Better Build Systems

There is an exponential relationship between the size of a game when it is shipped out to customers vs. the size of the original resources. Indeed, it is not uncommon for a 10MB game to have 200MB in original PSD files alone. It is important to keep the source assets for all media in the highest quality possible. This is to help facilitate magazine screenshots (as we'll see later) and provide a quicker route to shipping a new HD version a couple of months later!

With the scale of the assets involved, we should consider writing an automated build system to take the original 100MB of data (called the *raw assets*) and convert them into the 10MB of cooked data.[10]

The Build Process

The primary rule here is that *everything* will be built—in some way, in some form, at some point.

---

[10]If you've ever wondered about the etymology of the terms, look at a burger before and after it's cooked.

■ **Tip** No file format will ever do everything you want from it. (If it does, then it's probably so bulky and complicated that you'll never have time left over to make a game!) Therefore, expect to supplement all assets with a metadata file.

At the bare minimum, you should prepare build scripts for the primary platform to work in debug and release modes. Taking the example of our HTML5 game, our first build script could be as simple as this:

```
#!/bin/bash
TARGET=target/html5/$1
mkdir -p $TARGET
cp -a src/*   $TARGET
cp -a copy/*  $TARGET
cp -a resources  $TARGET
```

The following are the important elements of a build script:

- It works

- Everything is done in a single step

- It can be run from the command line, meaning it can be scripted and run automatically

Believe or not, that's all that's necessary for the minimal version.

■ **Tip** Release a minimal working version to the team early. It doesn't matter that you'd never release this version to the public, since that milestone is many months away. Release early. Improve later, when and if it's needed.

As your project grows, you will want to expand on this, which I now demonstrate.

The Asset Pipeline

In the HTML5 version of the SGX engine, all assets are comprised of two files: the data itself (e.g., halite.dat.png) and an associated metadata file (such as halite.dat.json.) The format of the metadata file changes according to the type of asset it is. Textures, for example, have metadata describing each subarea of the texture (called *regions*, as we saw in Chapter 6). In our case, they are JSON files and edited by hand or any JSON-friendly editor, and so there is a goodly amount of whitespace, making them easy to read. For example:

```json
{
    "texture":[
        {
           "attributes":{
           }
        },
        {
           "stdregion":[
                {
                    "attributes":{
                        "count":"16",
                        "width":"32",
                        "height":"32",
                        "units":"pixels"
                    }
                }
            ]
        }
    ]
}
```

In the deployed version, however, we would not want to waste our bandwidth (or that of the user) by downloading all of those blank spaces thousands of times each day, in each of a 100 different files. Therefore, the asset pipeline for our sprites might be as simple as pruning all whitespace from the file. We could alternatively convert the text into a binary format and write a specific binary loading routine into the game engine code, instead. Indeed, we could extend the build script to combine both image data and metadata into a single file, and upgrade the engine code accordingly. The amount of time spent here depends on what you gain by doing so (improved loading times, data obfuscation, etc.) compared to what you lose (time that could be spent on better features and bug fixing.)

Pruning whitespace with PHP is simple, and looks like this:

```php
$jsonText = file_get_contents($argv[1]);
file_put_contents($argv[2],
json_encode(json_decode($jsonText)));
```

And produces the following:

```json
{"texture":[{"attributes":{}},{"stdregion":[{"attributes":{"count":"16",
"width":"32","height":"32","units":"pixels"}}]}]}
```

We can then upgrade our build script to handle the sprites differently from other objects and generate JSON data in debug mode differently to release mode. However, in doing so, you notice that a lot of our original code needs to change; we can no longer copy the entire resources directory and hope it works, because each subfolder needs special consideration. Also, we quickly run into the problems of Bash scripting as a suitable tool, since file and directory enumeration isn't the nicest-looking code.

■ Tip   If you have to write the build scripts yourself, pick a language that you're really comfortable with. You'll spend longer than you expect working in it.

As well as optimizing the metadata, you may also choose to repeat the process with the images themselves. Almost all file formats have the ability to include metadata *within* them. You might have noticed this when looking at the JPGs from a digital camera that seems to know the aperture and settings of the shot. This information takes up space that is not useful to the game engine, and so you could run it through tools (such as pngcrunch) to reduce the file size. You could also use ImageMagick to convert the size of the images for particular platforms or include validation code to ensure that they are of an appropriate size, such as being a power-of-two for better performance, or not being larger than 128×128 for certain mobile builds.

This build process can also improve the game by adding metadata where none previously existed. The SGX engine, for example, is able to load textures without an accompanying JSON metadata file. This ensures a faster development turnaround, at the expense of seeing lots of warning messages in the console reading, "file not found." You can therefore use the tool chain to generate compatible files to eliminate this.

■ Tip   Even benign warning messages can be problematic if they obscure more important warnings.

Highly complex games might use this process to automatically generate mipmaps for their textures, or restructure 3D mesh data to match the specific version of the engine in use.

■ Tip   If you're developing natively, there is a common problem with endian-ness that necessitates the swapping of all binary data before it can be processed by the machine. Moving this swap process into the tool chain ensures that the game will load much quicker, and that the data is more human-readable during the debugging phase.

After processing the individual files, we may need to aggregate them in a particular fashion. Consider the case of different SKUs—maybe one for desktop (with large images) and a second one with smaller, more mobile-friendly, graphics. In this case, we need to write our target file first to a temporary folder before writing a script that performs a second pass to pick the appropriate assets from that temporary folder to combine them.

We also need to consider whether it is the tool chain or the game, which flattens the directory hierarchy. Consider the case where we have an image to load into the game; it is called:

```
sprites/common/icon.png
```

Now, in the German language version of the game, we might need a special version, which we've called:

```
sprites/lang/de/icon.png
```

If the game can only support one language, then it is possible to write the tool chain such that it copies that file as follows, so that the game can use it directly.

```
sprites/icon.png
```

However, in all other cases, you have to write special code into the game that loads the common version, unless a language-specific version is available.

Some platforms use a start-up folder that holds a block of assets loaded immediately upon booting the machine. In doing so, they might be loaded by the operating system from a solid-state drive, instead of a (slower) magnetic disc. Normally, you wouldn't want to duplicate such useful files in two locations. However, with a suitable asset pipeline, this process can be automated, ensuring the best of both worlds.

Ultimately, even fewer people will understand or appreciate the complexity in your tool chain. Even fewer than that will understand the code. However, having a tool chain is the only way to ensure that you can release early and release often, and push new versions out very quickly, without the fear that some small file has been forgotten.

The Code-Processing Pipeline

All software has a code-processing pipeline, even though it's rarely called that. For native applications it's called compiling, and has been around since before most of us were born! Nowadays we can compile in various modes, such as debug, profiling, and release. Each resultant executable finds its way into a specific directory.

Interpreted languages may also have a processing step, where debug-only pieces of functionality are added or removed (such as cheat menus), or static code analysis tools (like Lint, from Chapter 10) are run.

During development, we have a copy of the SGX game engine in our application directly. This lets us debug and modify the engine, if necessary, at the same time as we're working on the game. Upon release, however, licensing agreements prevent us from distributing the engine in this form, and so we need to switch the following original lines:

```
<script type="text/javascript" src="sgx/sgx/bootstrap.js"></script>
<script type="text/javascript">
SGXSystem.include('sgx/sgx.js', function() {
  startGame();
});
</script>
```

With this:

```
<script src="//sgxengine.com/code/sgx/sgx-3.1.14.min.js"></script>
<script type="text/javascript">
$(document).ready(function() {
```

```
  startGame();
});
</script>
```

To do this, we could create separate index.htm files for each build, or add comments in the file to indicate which components should be added or removed with each build. We will adopt the latter approach.

The first problem is to exclude code from each build. This can be done with comments like this:

```
<!-- BUILD:ENVIRONMENT:START:local -->
// Local only code goes here
<!-- BUILD:ENVIRONMENT:END:local -->
```

Since we have no build environment called local, this block of code is always ignored when index.html is copied across to the target folder.

We then have to add specific code for the release builds. This requires an additional instruction,

```
<!-- ADD:ENVIRONMENT:sgx:release -->
```

This incorporates the sgx.inc file into the source file at this point. Alas, we cannot use the start-end blocks we saw previously, since they will be included in local build, since no code processing generally occurs there.[11]

We can extend this idea down to the source code level, where comments are removed and variable names are shortened because this (in many interpreted languages) will improve the run-time speed. This step is called *minimizing*. However, it is possible to go further.

In HTML5 games, the JavaScript code needs to be provided to the browser in order for it to work, which makes it very easy for the end user to discover how the game works by simply viewing the source. This results in most game developers post-processing their source code so that it is unreadable to everything except the machine trying to process it—even if you managed to change the variables back to their original names. That process is called *obfuscation*.

The first step to achieving obfuscation is to remove all comments and rewrite all the methods and variable names to something shorter. With more obtuse names, the meanings are obscured. The following is the result of one such method:

```
(u=o,o=c,z=x.V,e=x.ca,v=-1,B=f<j?f:j,M=f>j?f:j,c=b<d?b:d,j=b>d?b:d);
```

Without knowing what the original variables were, the structure called v is, or what the conditionals are, it's very unlikely anyone (including me, the author of the original non-obfuscated version) could decipher it!

Furthermore, a good obfuscator uses syntactic sours[12] to further hide the meaning of the code.

---

[11]If you have a server-side language in your armory, such as PHP or Ruby, then you can use this to dynamically switch code blocks in and out.

[12]The opposite of syntactic sugar; it performs the same thing, but makes it unpalatable.

In order to introduce such abominations into your own JavaScript, Google provides the Closure Compiler (at http://closure-compiler.appspot.com).

■ **Tip** Always use an automated means of obfuscating your code. The code processing stage happens a lot during development (especially in the latter days, when time is at a premium), and so it would be a time sink if this needed to be done manually. Furthermore, although it might be fun to rename your constants for TRUE and FALSE to 0 and 1, respectively, or call the x coordinate y in the source, it is a waste of time. There are always better ways to use your creativity.

Since the online version of the Closure Compiler can't be scripted, there are programming libraries that you can use to include it as part of the build process such as the one at https://github.com/dpup/php-closure/. You use it as follows:

```
include("php-closure.php");

$c = new PhpClosure();
$c->add("game.js")
  ->add("menus.js")
  ->add("title_screen.js")
  ->advancedMode()
  ->write();
```

Although this example uses advancedMode, there are actually three available modes. *Whitespace* and *simple* are straightforward and generally work without issue. The third, *advanced*, needs a little more coaxing.

Consider the case where you change the method called calculateScores to cs. As long as you change all references of calculateScores to cs, everything will work fine. Now consider the case where the Closure Compiler does this automatically. Every time you run the compiler, you are likely to get a different name for calculateScores. This means that if you call calculateScore outside of the obfuscated code, you need to (manually) update those methods.

■ **Caution** Anything that goes into, or comes out of, obfuscated code needs to be explicitly described so that the Closure Compiler doesn't rename it. This process uses externals.

One way around this problem is to create externals. This is a trick whereby you write hints to the compiler, telling it that, "this symbol is used outside of the obfuscated code, so please leave it as it is."

```
window['calculateScores'] = calculateScores;
```

Consequently, you can now access `calculateScores` as normal via the global variable window. You need to do this for each entry and exit point between the normal HTML5/JavaScript and the obfuscated code.

You also need to reference JSON literals with this notation:

```
json['key']
```

Instead of this:

```
json.key
```

In the case of the latter the closure compiler will rename the key member since it is not in quotes.

■ **Tip**   Regularly test your code with obfuscation turned on. It only takes one error to make the entire data set unreadable, and therefore the entire game unplayable.

API Keys

For those working with online components, such as Facebook or Twitter integration, you need to incorporate an API key (and usually an API secret) in order for your app to be able to talk to their servers. As discussed in Chapter 9, having this information in your source control tool is dangerous because it widens the security perimeter of your development process. Instead, you should apply those keys directly in the deployment process from a separate secure source. For example, a directory on the main server that it is only accessible by the administrator. (The web server usually runs with suitable privileges to read this information, whereas normal users can't see it.) In the staging and development environments, you can set up a completely separate developer-only app on Facebook and Twitter and use these, different, keys to test the game.

Manifest Files

Some platforms cannot enumerate a directory structure. Most notably, this is true of the Web. Unless the webpage tells you there is a file called `halite.dat.png`, there is no general-purpose way of asking the web server for a list of the files it can provide. Normally, this is of no issue. However, when your game is trying to determine whether it needs to load a SKU-, platform-, or language-specific file, or a common generic one, this becomes problematic.

It is not difficult to imagine a solution; you simply ask for files, ignoring any "file not found" errors, and keep doing so until the web server sends you one back. However, this is immensely wasteful on all sides. Therefore, you may wish to create a manifest file, which describes the games entire directory structure, along with file sizes and CRC checks, which can be loaded into the game's file system code so that it can then make an intelligent decision of which to load.

■ **Tip**   Always attempt to load the most specific resource first, and fall back to the next least common until an asset is found.

The advantage of including the file size in the manifest file is that it allows you to write a better loading bar or progress counter. The CRC check lets you validate the file to ensure that it hasn't been corrupted or compromised en route.

When data is stored in the cloud, it is rare but not unheard of to hit the physical limits of hardware error checking! A hard drive, for example, verifies all data written to it. However, the magnetic head has physical limits meaning it may return inaccurate data once every few hundred billion reads. Normally, a consumer disk isn't likely to hit these limits within its operating lifetime. But if your data is spread across many disks in a cloud, it could happen as often as once a week for a popular game on busy servers.[13]

Only the largest developers have cause to worry about such hardware limits, but since a CRC can also check for compromised (i.e., hacked) data, it is a worthwhile investment for professional developers of any size.

The . Problem

When writing a build script, you may notice a number of . (dot) files or directories. Such files are normally hidden from the standard directory view by virtue of them beginning with a period, and include files generated by your source control application of choice. Subversion uses .svn and Git uses .git, for example. These are files you don't want to export into the target directly. Not least because there maybe privileged information hidden within them.

If you use Subversion, you can remove them by exporting the directory from its source-controled location.

```
svn export source target/debug/source
```

Git is simpler, since the .git folder appears only at the root, so you can copy the contents of all other folders without worrying.

■ **Tip**   It is always better to use the export feature over a copy, since it will only replicate files that have been previously committed to source control. In this way, any files the current user has forgotten to commit will not be copied, thereby showing the error on their machine before it can affect anyone else.

If you have a manual build process, then you can get the same effective result by simply ignoring any file beginning with .git or .svn. (Or, since all dot files are hidden and generally not used by developers, any file beginning with a dot.)

---

[13]I experienced this first hand when architecting systems for Playfish back in 2009. It has a low risk, but high impact.

Targets: The Web Exception

Beginners to the web development field often cite the low barrier to entry as something that got them started in programming. That's a good thing. However, loading an HTML file into a web browser only works for so long. This is because that while the browser happily interprets an HTML file (along with all the attached JavaScript and images), it does not support many of the more dynamic features of HTML5. If you want to load an image via a method that isn't `<img src='player.png'>`, then it won't work. (And most games only want to load a restricted asset set at the start to reflect the needs of the first level.)

If you want to load arbitrary data, which isn't hard-coded into the source, then you can't do it. And so on.

Therefore, a web server (such as Apache or nginx) needs to be installed on all development machines so that the full HTML5 feature set can work. This delays the start of work (by a few hours), but it is absolutely essential (and in retrospect, obvious) for any real work to take place. After installation, point the "root directory" to your game folder, and work can continue as normal.

Furthermore, when dealing with fully interpreted platforms like HTML5, there is an important consideration in regard to external components. For example, imagine your game uses a third-party engine that has its own set of source files. Generally, you have three choices:

- Place the necessary files into a folder, called game_engine, under the root directory of your game; either a copy or external source control

- Configure the web server to direct localhost/game_engine to the folder containing the original resources

- Prepare a second web server to serve the game_engine files

All methods can be made to work equally well. What is important is the process that governs how, if, and by whom, changes to the game engine can occur. Is there a specialist core-technology team? Does the engine come from a third-party vendor? Are they only ones able to make changes? Do you trust updates to happen automatically from the vendor? If not, who's in charge of checking those updates and pushing them to the rest of the team? How is versioning handled?

■ **Caution**   If loading resources from different domains, ensure that you have learned about cross-origin resource sharing (CORS) because it causes confusion for a novice.

At this stage, the important element of the process is to ensure that the primary development environment matches the source code under test, without any form of post-processing, such as obfuscation. The reason for this is simple: if you find a bug while working on post-processed code, you have to remember to change the original code, re-run the process scripts, and retest. If you're only making changes to a local, post-processed version, then a lot of time is spent (wasted?) merging those changes back into the master.

■ **Tip** Always ensure that your source code–processing pipeline is as quick as possible, because a slow pipeline discourages people from using it and therefore they are more likely to work directly on the post-processed files, which is to be discouraged. The quickest post process is the one that doesn't happen.

As so often happens, there is one final complication when working in HTML5. As a developer, you generally prefer to have 1,000 files, each 100 lines long, than 1 file that is 100,000 lines long.[14] However, a single combined file is preferably in the final release build since it's quicker to load and process. Since you should only ever work with individual files, this leads to three build types.

- *Development.* With a direct one-to-one relationship with the files you edit, debug, and commit to source control.

- *Debug.* All source files are combined into a single file, with whitespace and comments maintained so any bugs can be found easily.

- *Release.* All source files are combined into a single file, but obfuscated so that prying eyes have more difficulty discerning your secrets.

Despite giving a reasonable amount of attention to obfuscation here, it is not something indies and smaller developers should spend much time perfecting. It's unlikely you will have discovered anything so fantastic that half the development community haven't already worked out. And obfuscation doesn't stop anyone from learning your secrets if they are prepared to spend some time doing so.

In a larger company, it is likely that management (who have neither read, nor understood the previous paragraph!) will require you to obfuscate in some manner, so you should do it.

As a bonus, though, obfuscated code generally runs faster so the effort isn't totally wasted!

Deployment

Once you have a version of the game that works on your machine in a satisfactory state, it is necessary to get that exact same version onto another machine. That may be a remote web server, in the case of online games, or a customer's mobile phone, or a hard disk in another computer. This process is called *deployment*. Depending on the medium, you may deploy once a week, once a month, or once a lifetime.

---

[14]For reasons for maintenance, as if you didn't know!

Game Consoles

Each console manufacturer has their own methods for doing this, and, unfortunately for us, non-disclosure agreements (NDAs) prevent me from discussing the details. Generally speaking, however, all involve a fairly manual process of taking the trunk assets from the source control and running them through the provided tools. Always take the assets from the source control, and whenever possible, get a different member of the team to create the build each time you need one. This not only increases the knowledge of the team as a whole, and therefore eliminates any bottlenecks or choke points in the deployment process, but it also encourages a clean build process since all the necessary files *must* exist on all machines. And therefore in the source control. It is certainly a more effective method than having a single machine on which all builds are done, because that also creates a critical point in the process. What happens if that machine develops a problem? How quickly could you prepare a second machine to build the game? Are you confident that all the necessary files are in source control? What about trying to create two builds simultaneously to determine a better approach? Or run two builds side by side?

All console manufacturers have technical requirements for their games to which you, as a developer, are expected to adhere. Failure to conform to anything on the checklist means that your game will not be released. It checks, among other things, that logos and branding marks are the right size and are displayed for the appropriate length of time, and that the nomenclature[15] is adhered to, and so on. Naturally, the turnaround time for your work to be checked, failed, fixed, and resubmitted can be quite long, so if you or your team is not used to this process, start with a pre-submission three to four months before you need to.

Stand-alone PC

The stand-alone PC has many similarities to console games, with the exception that you generally need to use an installer. There are many prebuilt installer packages on the market. Most streaming and app store services provide their own for you to use. Unlike a console game, you often have a lot of control over this installation process. So you can exercise this control to customize the experience, drawing the player in before the game has even installed. At the very least, it would use the game livery and styling. To go further, it could include a slideshow of preproduction images, starting with the basic wireframes and working up to the final graphics as the progress bar approaches 100%.

WixEdit,[16] for example, is a free tool to create MSI installers for Windows. At the basic level, an installer merely copies the files to a specific directory, checks and installs any dependencies (such as triggering Windows Update to download the latest version of DirectX), and prepares the registry.

---

[15]The correct names to be used in reference to the controllers, buttons, console, and other such ephemera. An incorrect name (even incorrect capitalization) is a failing offense.
[16]See http://sourceforge.net/projects/wixedit

However, underneath there is an important difference—the settings of each end-user PC may be significantly different from yours. Therefore, it is recommended you test the installer as a fresh install on as many different Windows machines as possible. VirtualBox, VMWare, and other virtualization technologies make it easy to create such machines. Simply create a virtual image and install a copy of Windows onto it. Then make a backup copy of this virtual image and install your game to the original image. Try different versions on each dependency that you're aware of; and don't forget to try this:

- Installing it on a D: partition

- Installing in a directory with spaces in the name

- Set the Windows color scheme to Brick, or something similarly non-standard, which lets you see if there's any latent Windows-isms left in the code that cause visual issues; for example, calls to native widgets, MessageBox, or dialogs

Each user may feel that their machine is "normal." So trying to clarify a bug report by asking the user if there's anything *un*usual about their machine is unlikely to help!

Mobile and Tablet

During development, the IDE includes the necessary functionality to connect to your device and upload the game to it. Once you're ready for the build to find its way into your app store of choice, there will be similar functionality to export that build into a suitable file that can be uploaded. As with console games, this is a manual process. But, since it should be a rare occurrence, there is little need to optimize it. (Nor is there often the possibility.)

Online

The problem with online games isn't so much that they're online, but that by being online, there is the expectation that the game will be updated. Regularly. It is not uncommon for online games, especially in the field of casual and social games, to have new updates every two weeks. This means that there must be more effort spent on automating the deployment strategy.

The technicality behind an automated deployment system is no more difficult than the build system you saw earlier. It's a script that copies files from one place to another, occasionally modifying them. In fact, the first part of most online deployment tools is to build the release version of the JavaScript so that it lives in a single obfuscated file.

The next step is to deploy any server-side components to the server. These might be an API to handle an online high-score table, or the player's in-game purchases. This breaks down further into two halves: deploying suitable code and maintaining existing data. After all, there is very little point to the player building up a large collection of in-game items if they get deleted upon each new version. This leads me to introduce the three phases of online deployment.

The first is the *staging* phase, where the latest code release is used alongside a development database for the purpose of development-focused testing.

The second is the UAT, or *user acceptance testing*, phase. It follows staging but replaces the development database with a modified copied of the live database. This is for user-focused testing to ensure that the code can scale to the full user base, that purchased items are still owned by the correct users, and that any file format changes are applied correctly. The key words here are "modified copy," since users' full names, purchase information, and email addresses are either removed or modified so that notifications are not accidentally to them.

■ **Tip**   If you amend the emails in the UAT database to read as *mygamename+original_ email@gmail.com*, then you can take advantage of Gmail's use of + to have all the user's email from UAT interactions delivered to the *mygamename@gmail.com* address.

Finally, there is *production* phase, in which the original database is married to the new code for the first time.

Moving Online

Everything has moved online, especially games. Our games consoles all have online leaderboards and achievements, so there is no reason that even a single-player web game couldn't benefit from a few similar online features. To discuss the implementation of each of these would be a book in itself. Instead, I focus on what needs to be done rather than how to do it.

The Client Problem

All online games feature two halves: a client and a server. The client is the part that you, the player, uses to experience the game. It could be Xbox One, PlayStation, or the web browser. It sends the game results, progress, and achievements to the server. The server is the computer, often in the cloud, that stores all of this information so that it can be displayed to other players.

Can you see the problem?

The client is telling the server its score! There is very little to stop the player from hacking the client to send a false score value. The consoles limit this risk by using closed, cryptographically signed, binary executables that (in theory) cannot be hacked and modified to send false data, and end-to-end encryption (hidden within this closed binary) to prevent a "man in the middle" (MITM) attack. In short, a MITM attack is an eavesdropping technique that occurs when a device sits between the client and the server and is able to monitor and modify the communications between them. An MITM machine could increase the score whenever it saw the correct data packet passing through its network.

Web games have the same problem but with an easier attack vector, since the code is held without encryption and in plain text within the web browser. Even Flash games can be decompiled and rebuilt with minimal effort.

■ **Caution** Everything that runs on a client computer is vulnerable to hacks. Its data can never be truly trusted.

Since there is currently no practical solution to the problem of transmitting data with integrity from a client, you either need to design to prevent it or make it difficult enough that most people won't bother trying; that is, security through complexity.

One "prevention through design" technique is to send regular game updates back to the server. If the server sees the score increasing from 10, to 20, to 30, to 40, to 100000, it can make a reasonable assumption that the last score has been hacked and block the player. This is a small example of a large set of integrity-based solutions, some of which was discussed in Chapter 10. If a client machine sends a message to the server saying the player has been awarded three achievements on level 17, then the server can determine if those achievements are indeed possible on level 17.

Another method is to send the same data in different ways. If you send the score, followed by the score with each bit flipped from 0 to 1, and then the score represented in hexadecimal, a hacker would have to discover, track, and modify all three versions of the data. Otherwise, the server would examine all three values and reject any case where they didn't match.

There are others techniques, for sure, but the important point is that such hacks exist and will always exist. By introducing networked features, you achieve more polish than most games that don't try. And by introducing such preventative techniques, you might persuade the zealous hackers to try and break someone else's game instead of yours!

High Scores and Achievements

An obvious inclusion. This is also the least worthwhile system to crack if you restrict the results to the player's close friends. By cheating, they are only cheating their friends, and no one wants to play with a cheat, so the system should become self-regulating.

■ **Tip** You don't always need technological solutions to fix technical problems. Sometimes simple social coercion works!

Implementing a basic high-score system can be achieved with very basic server-side components. You need a basic user management system where the player can (securely) pass their credentials to the server and receive a token. This token is then used to make remote API calls to the server. These API calls send scores and achievements for storage and recall.

■ **Caution** The user management system is bigger and more complex than you might realize. Forgotten passwords and emailing reset links, verifying the account email, salting passwords, rainbow table lookups, to name the first things that come to mind. Use an existing library or package instead of trying to build one yourself.

For small projects, you can use Google forms and spreadsheets to handle the server-side data; AJAX requests to post score data to the form; and an API like briefcase.js[17] to download it again. If you have a large user base, however, having every player download the whole spreadsheet every time is wasteful, so you need to upgrade to a better solution.

The next step up is a DBaaS (Database as a Service) or BaaS (Backend as a Service) platform. These are also known as "database in the cloud" platforms, which provide APIs through AJAX to read and write your data to their own DB. There are free versions of many of these products, like AppWarp or Photon,[18] that let you experiment on a small scale. Ultimately, they are no more complicated that the Google Forms approach, and an improvement.

To step further up, you need to prepare your own server and worry about the problems of big data, scalability, and ACID (atomicity, consistency, isolation, durability) properties for database transactions—all of which are far beyond the scope of this book.

Facebook Integration

Even if your game is not suitable for inclusion within the Facebook platform, you can still utilize its API to send messages to your user's friends or to post high scores and achievements. This isn't a heavy investment, but if it's likely to attract new users to the game, then it can be worth the integration time. The same goes for Twitter. Remember that for both Facebook and Twitter, you need to create specifically sized images to go along with the text in the post.

Obviously, games that fit directly within the Facebook platform can use all manner of tricks and posts to convince users to share things and earn rewards from each other. In this case, however, the functionality is a necessary part of the game and not considered polish.

■ **Note**   You need an SSL certificate for your game page if you wish to place it inside an iframe on Facebook. This certificate is useful to gain favor with Google search algorithms and to create secure transmissions to an API server that you're running. It is a good investment in any case.

A Website

Unless you have a website, you're a nobody. Or so it seems. Therefore, your game will probably need one too. It should contain screenshots, character profiles, and links to buy the game. Information about the developers is also worthwhile, especially if you're a small company.

Building a website is no longer difficult, but modern web design standards are quite exacting. In order for a page to be responsive and work well on the myriad desktop platforms, mobiles, and tablets takes a lot of effort. If you're an established company, then you already have a small band of web developers on hand who are able to change and update the site to include your new game. If you're small, then either hire a developer or buy a web template.

---

[17]See https://github.com/Lily2point0/briefcasejs
[18]See https://github.com/relatedcode/ParseAlternatives#backends-for-game-developers

Collateral

Collateral is a fancy word for *stuff!* The fluffy stuff that exists around the game to accompany it on its journey into the digital world. The basic collateral you need is dictated by the platform for which you're developing. A web game needs a favicon.ico,[19] for example. A game destined for the App Store has a specific set of guidelines for the size and number of icons and screenshots required for each of the various iOS platforms. It also requires the following:

- A formal app name

- Copyright notice

- Support URL, detailing your company's privacy policy and support

- Support email

- Review notes for the version

- Description of the game

- Keywords

By the time you read this, Apple may have introduced some more! Most of them are simple enough, although some will cause arguments about which part of the name should be shortened to fit the iPhone screen! In fact, this sort of issue is likely to take more time and effort than is spent setting up a separate support email account and building a webpage for the support URL and privacy policy!

In addition to the required collateral, there are the optional extras. None of which are truly optional, although some may be done by non-developers to ease the burden. They include the generation of screenshots for web and print. While this seems like an easy job, there are several complications. The first is getting a well-composed image. When the game is playing, it's very likely that the random movements of the enemies will obscure vital parts of the screen, like the score or health.

■ **Tip** You want all elements of the game UI to be in the screenshot to give the best impression possible.

Similarly, you might want to show more than one enemy type on-screen at once, even though it rarely happens in the real game. This also covers the case where special enemies and bosses appear. You don't want to have to play through 30 minutes of the game just to reach this point, only to be sucked into the game so that you can't get a decent screen grab. Consequently, many screenshots require the skills of an artist to take

---

[19]A small file that lives in the root of the file server and appears on your favorites bar, often alongside the URL in the web browser.

the basic backdrop and characters, and composite them into a new tableau. The same effect can be achieved with the programmer or scripter writing short pieces of code to position the enemies in appropriate positions. This latter method is used when there are many in-game effects that can't be easily replicated outside of the engine.

At a technical level, all screenshots for print magazines should be at least 300dpi. This means that the image from any game rendered to a small screen needs to be upscaled. The skills of an artist are necessary to take those screenshots and fix the fuzziness that often comes with automated scaling.

There is also a technical solution whereby each quadrant of a given scene is rendered separately to fill the entire screen. Each quad can then be combined in your least-unfavorite art package to make a higher resolution image than would normally be possible.

Summary

Regardless of how much work you do, there will always be something lacking. From more assets to more detailed assets, there is never a problem in finding work to do, regardless of the discipline.

What is great about this type of work, however, is that you should already have the complete game running. This means that you can work on new and improved elements of the game at your own pace and simply drop them into the game when they're ready. Or save it for version 2.

Appendix A

Space Bounce

A Breakdown

Throughout the book, I made general references to the practice of game polish. I gave specific advice on many different game styles and genres. We built a small game, called Space Bounce, to demonstrate a number of these points. Let's now break down the game to describe each element, not all of which will be obvious from a casual play through.

You can play the game at MarquisdeGeek.com/spacebounce.

The source is available at github.com/MarquisdeGeek/SpaceBounce.

Loading Page

The image contains the stylized font and imprint graphic instead of the O that features throughout the game. There is also an animating loading bar. The game isn't large enough to warrant much more, since it takes mere seconds to load.

Title Screens

These obligatory pages have a basic fade up and down feature. They can be interrupted only after the first two seconds, and automatically fade out if nothing is pressed after around five seconds. The fade out is quicker than the (anticipatory) fade in.

Each page has its own customizable time-outs and musical stings. These pieces of music have their own normalization group, so that they won't be accidentally (or purposefully) muted by the in-game user controls.

Credits

We store the job titles in a language-specific text file, but keep the names in the UI layout file since this text doesn't change.

This screen also displays the spaceman climbing up the side of the screen, so there is something animating. He doesn't appear for the first few seconds, so the player can read the credits without distraction. His appearance is timed so that just before they click away from the screen, they see the spaceman climbing up, which causes a surprise, so they stay a little longer on the screen to see if he does anything else.

© Steven Goodwin 2016
S. Goodwin, *Polished Game Development*, DOI 10.1007/978-1-4842-2122-8

Once the spaceman exits the top of the screen, he reappears at the bottom almost instantly. This is to highlight that it's now on a loop, and nothing else interesting is going to happen.

Exiting the credit screen is through the button *released* message. Otherwise, it might confuse the player using a mouse since entry to the screen is made via the credits button. If the mouse position doesn't move, the mouse button down message would return the player to the main menu, but the pointer would still be over the credits button they just pressed.

Instructions

As with credits, the text is stored in the language-specific file and a small animation (a halite crystal) on-screen. Additionally, when changing between the two pages, one screen slides off as the other one slides on. There is also the spaceman swinging from his rope between the pages as this happens.

Main Menu

A fairly traditional screen, but with music and sound effects controls at the top of the screen. The states of these options are remembered between plays via the browser's local storage functionality.

This is the first truly interactive screen shown with a prominent two-button style. The primary option is shown in black text on a white prominent background, while the other buttons are a less-imposing white text on a black background, demonstrating their lesser status. Since the font contains only uppercase characters, the text here uses slightly shorter letters in place of lowercase.

Musically, there is also a fade out effect when the player stops it from player. It loops. And there is code to ensure that it restarts when turned back on.

The Main Game

Once the game has begun, each phase shines in its own way.

Preparing the Level

The mine shaft is computed in such a way that you cannot get two obstacles so close together that it is impossible to jump between them to collect any halite placed there. Also, no obstacles are placed within the first three areas of the shaft, so the player can start their descent with ease.

Graphically, there are different tiles and obstacle images for the left- and right- hand sides of the mine shaft. Also note the flat surface is on the underside of the obstacle, lest the player think that they can safely stand on it.

Only the halite is animating. This is because the eye is drawn toward moving objects and because we want the player to be drawn toward the rewards.

As the player moves through each level, certain parameters change:

- Each level is deeper than the one that precedes it.

- There are more obstacles.

- There are more halite crystals to collect.

- More damage is taken for colliding with the obstacles.

- The speed increases.

Each change is a basic linear increment, which when combined with the other changes, causes gentle but exponentially increasing difficulty. Also note that the rescale parameters occur at different points in the game. The chance of halite increases first at level 2, whereas the chance of an obstacle increases first at level 3.

Drawing the Screen

Every image in the game conforms a single core design aesthetic: handcrafted. Each part of the graphic is based around either a paper or a cardboard texture, and colored roughly with monochromatic pencils as if the paper's prototype had come to life. These elements are drawn in several passes so that the depth is handled correctly.

First, the sky has a gradient, so it merges nicely into the ground. It also has stars and a moon. The moon is rendering dynamically (i.e., not baked into the sky background) so that it can be repositioned at will. It was placed deeper into the screen, so it's not confused with a button (buttons are rendered 20 pixels from the left edge of the screen). The phase of the moon is computed from the relative position of Earth's moon and rendered accordingly.

The shaft edges move at a different speed to the background so that a slight parallax effect occurs.

We use a viewport metaphor so that the player can appear static on-screen for the majority of the game, but fall slowly when the floor is in sight.

There are draw and postDraw methods to render all features at the right depth. From back to front they are as follows:

- Shaft background

- Shaft edges, obstacles, and halite

- The rope

- The winch

- The player

- An overlay texture to add a subtle full-screen effect

The Audio

There are six mixing channels in the game.

- Music, covering both the main menu theme and the in-game music

- Voices, for the Space Bounce shout-outs in the main menu

- Player, for the in-game voices that the character says

- TitleFX, for the three pre-game musical stings

- SFX, for the real-world game effects that aren't spoken by the player

- UI, for the click sound (and maybe others in the future)

These are completely distinct and controlled independently. Of particular note are the player voices, which have been processed to make them sound as if they're coming from within a space visor. The aural effect of those sounds required a separate sound channel for better equalization.

The handcrafted visual aesthetic is mirrored in the audio by literally having the voice actor say, "Ouch," and make the sound of the winch unraveling instead of using a real-world effect.

The Winch Sequence

Before the game properly begins, we see the spaceman hanging on to the edge of the cliff, and the winch unwinding, implying that something has gone wrong and that he's about to fall. This sets up the player's anticipation.

The Player Descends

Once the player begins the descent, the moon soon disappears off the screen, so the health can be faded in. It helps to have this at the top with the other statistics, but to prevent the screen from appearing cluttered, it is omitted at the start of the game to make way for the moon.

The hands and feet are always animating to indicate that he's scrambling at the rock face. Notice that his hands overlap the rock slightly to provide the illusion of depth.

The descent speed is controlled by the level index and incremented in a linear fashion after each level. By using only whole numbers, the difficultly increases quite quickly.

Bouncing from Left to Right

The game supports both the left and right cursor keys to bounce across the shaft (for PC-based gamers) and a one-touch interface (triggered by touching anywhere on the screen) for tablet play. The bounce motion is executed in three parts.

- The character springs away from the wall and turns.

- The character moves across the shaft.

- The character turns to grab hold of the opposite wall.

The width of the shaft changed during development. Ultimately, it was not an even number of tiles, so there is extra code to handle the overshoot.

There are 10 explicit animation frames of the rope attached to the character so that the rope could be styled visually by an artist rather than a coder. This could be improved in future versions with more frames, as it's obviously an animation. Or some genuine rope physics could be written. The rope and character are drawn separately so that move animation frames can be added without needing to rebuild the animation of the other.

The code throughout this section applies a data-driven approach using the width and height of the textures. This accommodates any late or sudden changes by the artists.

Scoring

As covered extensively in Chapter 2, whenever a score is awarded, the text and surround pulses slightly and changes color to let the player know that something has happened. This animation is visible to the player's periphery without the need to read the actual numbers, so the player can keep their eyes focused on the action.

There is also a bonus awarded if you collect all the halite on a given level. This differentiator means that each crystal is worth 30 (instead of 25) points.

Health

We store health as a basic percentage from 0 to 100, with 10% being lost each time that the player hits an obstacle. This increases as the levels progress. So that the moon can be seen, the heart icon is only shown once the player descends. To indicate that health has changed, the heart icon pulses using the same code as the score.

The In-Game Menu

The in-game menu can be triggered with the top-right button or by pressing the Escape key. In addition to an exit game feature, it provides access to the music and sound effects controls to minimize clutter on the main game screen. Notice also that the button style established in the main menu is replicated here, with the Resume option presented in black text on a white button, indicating that it's the default option.

Even when the menu is open, the game is still visible (and often animating) in the background.

Ending the Game

There is a multiphase sequence that forces the player savor the death of their character with an image that zooms in, a screen fade, and a second image. This sequence can't be skipped since it increases the frustration the player feels having failed, and therefore increases their adrenaline for the next game.[1]

We allow both keyboard and touch events to move on to the next screen.

In successful level completions, there is only a single image that zooms in, so that the player can continue as quickly as possible. Yet it appears to be slightly slower to give players more time to self-congratulate themselves. Impatient players are allowed to preempt this sequence, however.

---

[1]*Cannon Fodder* famously made you sit through the names of the dead soldiers at the end of the game, without the option of skipping it. In doing so, it created a powerful anti-war message.

Index

Get the eBook for only $5!

Why limit yourself?

Now you can take the weightless companion with you wherever you go and access your content on your PC, phone, tablet, or reader.

Since you've purchased this print book, we're happy to offer you the eBook in all 3 formats for just $5.

Convenient and fully searchable, the PDF version enables you to easily find and copy code—or perform examples by quickly toggling between instructions and applications. The MOBI format is ideal for your Kindle, while the ePUB can be utilized on a variety of mobile devices.

To learn more, go to www.apress.com/companion or contact support@apress.com.

Printed in the United States
By Bookmasters